RESISTANCE AND HOPE

South African essays in honour of Beyers Naudé

Greetings! Beyers Naudé

EDITED BY
CHARLES VILLA-VICENCIO &
JOHN W. DE GRUCHY

22 October 1985

Wm. B. Eerdmans: Grand Rapids

First published 1985 in Southern Africa by David Philip, Publisher (Pty) Ltd, 217 Werdmuller Centre, Claremont 7700, South Africa

Published 1985 in the United States of America and the rest of the world by Wm. B. Eerdmans Publishing Co., 255 Jefferson Ave. SE, Grand Rapids, Michigan 49503

ISBN 0-86486-032-3 (Southern Africa)
ISBN 0-8028-0098-X (elsewhere)

Printed and bound by The Citadel Press, Polaris Road, Lansdowne, Cape, South Africa

Contents

The authors and editors

ALLAN BOESAK
  NG Sendingkerk Chaplain, University of the Western Cape, and President of the World Alliance of Reformed Churches
DAVID BOSCH
  Dean of the Faculty of Theology, University of South Africa
FRANK CHIKANE
  Director, Institute for Contextual Theology, Johannesburg
JAMES COCHRANE
  Director, Careers Research and Information Centre, Cape Town
JOHN W. DE GRUCHY
  Associate Professor, Department of Religious Studies, University of Cape Town
STEPHEN DE GRUCHY-PATTA
  Graduate Research Student, Department of Religious Studies, University of Cape Town
JAAP DURAND
  Vice-Rector, and former Dean of the Faculty of Theology, University of the Western Cape
DENIS E. HURLEY
  Roman Catholic Archbishop of Durban
WOLFRAM KISTNER
  Director, Commission on Justice and Reconciliation, South African Council of Churches
ITUMELENG MOSALA
  Lecturer, Department of Religious Studies, University of Cape Town
MARGARET NASH
  Ecumenical Consultant
ALBERT NOLAN
  Priest, Dominican Order, Johannesburg
PETER RANDALL
  Lecturer, Faculty of Education, University of the Witwatersrand
WILLEM SAAYMAN
  Associate Professor, Faculty of Theology, University of South Africa

GABRIEL SETILOANE
  Associate Professor, Department of Religious Studies, University of Cape Town
BUTI TLHAGALE
  Priest, Regina Mundi Pro-Cathedral, Soweto
DESMOND TUTU
  Anglican Bishop of Johannesburg, formerly General Secretary of the South African Council of Churches
CHARLES VILLA–VICENCIO
  Associate Professor, Department of Religious Studies, University of Cape Town

Foreword
DENIS E. HURLEY

This collection is a salute to Dr Beyers Naudé on his seventieth birthday. It can also be considered an observance of the twenty-fifth anniversary, the silver jubilee, of his conversion; of the end of that painful period in his life which culminated in his final rejection of apartheid and his self-dedication to love and justice transcending social barriers.

During these twenty-five years Dr Naudé has been at the heart of the transforming process in South Africa, believing in it, promoting it, encouraging it, suffering for it; convinced that his faith, a Bible-nourished fervent faith in Christ, is of its very nature profoundly and inescapably political.

'Political' is a word with a variety of connotations. It can signify the quest and the exercise of political power. It can refer to political ideologies and systems. It can be applied to the political parties competing for power. It can be used in a very general way about all that concerns a political community: its organisation, its culture and education, its industry and commerce, its communications, its preservation of its identity and defence of its interests, its vision and its ethics.

In this last sense a vast proportion of vision and ethics is political. How we understand life and how we behave is concerned mainly with other people, with the society to which we belong and that society's relations with other societies. I am talking of our philosophy of life – or theology, if its principal ingredient is faith in God – and of the standards of social behaviour that it inspires.

Social vision and social ethics account for a very large share of political policy, and political policy is woven of human decisions and human actions which have all sorts of consequences for people: some painful and some pleasant, some beneficial and some detrimental, some just and some unjust. Political policy can cause immense suffering, can be tyrannical and oppressive, can stifle human rights and inhibit human freedom.

Such stifling, such inhibition is sinful. Because the decision or complex of decisions producing that result is political makes it not less sinful but rather more; for it affects many people most profoundly.

The church, made up of sinful members, constituted in fact of sinners hopefully on the mend, is of its very nature concerned about sin – about its roots and motivation, about standards of behaviour, about endeavours to correct the sinner, about repentance and reconciliation and forgiveness.

In our own day the church is beginning to see much more clearly that its duty to deal with sin applies as much to social sin as to personal and domestic sin – as much, indeed more, because social sin does the greater damage.

Sin, however, is far from being the unique ethical concern of the church. The church opposes sin, in its own members and throughout the human family, in order to cultivate goodness.

Goodness by Christian standards is loving God above all things and our neighbour as ourself for God's sake – an impossible ideal made possible to Christian faith through a conviction about the abiding presence of Christ and the gift of his Holy Spirit.

Strange as it may seem the Christian ideal of goodness, the law of love, is supposed to be applied not only to personal and domestic behaviour but to political behaviour too. It sounds incredible, but that is the teaching of Jesus. His followers, who unfortunately generally undermine the credibility of his teaching, are supposed to strive for this observance of the law of love in politics as in other aspects of life.

That is why Christian faith and practice are or should be profoundly and inescapably political. Not in the sense of seeking power or promoting secular ideologies or political parties but in the sense of fostering a Christian vision of society and Christian standards of social behaviour.

For twenty-five years that has been the burning concern of Dr Beyers Naudé. But all seventy years of his life have made their contribution, for the seed of the last twenty-five was planted and nurtured in the first forty-five.

Because he was perceptive enough and brave enough and faithful enough to let the seed grow, experiencing to the full what the Master had said about the grain of wheat dying to produce the harvest, we salute him on his seventieth birthday.

DENIS E. HURLEY O.M.I.

Preface

It is no longer a major achievement to reach the biblically allotted life-span of three score years and ten. It is, nonetheless, worthy of celebration. What is even more worthy of celebration is a life, no matter how short or long, which personifies a struggle for human dignity and political liberation from oppression. This is especially so if that struggle is on behalf of others, a costly and dangerous one. In presenting this volume to Dr Beyers Naudé on his seventieth birthday on 10 May 1985, we celebrate not only what he has accomplished, but also the person he is – husband, father, pastor and counsellor, prophet, friend, and, not least, a true South African. For us, as for many, Beyers Naudé is a symbol of resistance against all that oppresses in our society, and a symbol of hope for the future.

In planning this volume, we decided that the best way to celebrate this occasion was to provide a contribution to the present debate in South Africa – a debate of which Beyers Naudé is such a central part. This debate is wide ranging and involves different disciplines. For that reason alone it was necessary to narrow the focus and concentrate to a large degree on theological issues. This does not mean that Naudé's interests are narrowly confined; on the contrary, for him theology has to do with the whole of life and reality. The essays which follow, whether they be theological or more historical, share the same perspective.

It was an invidious task to select contributors. So many able people have known Naudé well and worked closely with him over the years that is was almost impossible to know where to draw the line. We certainly wanted contributors from different theological traditions in South Africa, but we also felt it necessary that all should have shown a commitment to the struggle for justice in South Africa which epitomises the life we are celebrating. We have also chosen contributors who, over the years or in more recent times, have known Beyers Naudé personally, and who share a common concern for our society. We regret that it was impossible to include everyone who might have met these criteria, and we also regret that time constraints prevented some who were approached from participating. We are grateful to those who have contributed as a labour of love and respect.

This volume is not intended to be one in praise of Beyers Naudé, though such could hardly be avoided given his significance for church and society in South Africa. There are essays which tell his story, and others which allude directly or indirectly to his role and importance. The book is also structured around themes and issues which are central to his life and range over a wide terrain, for Naudé was and remains an Afrikaner, a Reformed pastor, preacher and theologian, an ecumenist, a social prophet, and one whose reputation and bonds of friendship reach across the continent of Africa and the globe. But the volume is not a nostalgic journey backwards. It seeks to describe what it means to resist oppression, evil, fate and despair, and live in hope because of faith in the gospel of Jesus Christ today. It is our hope therefore that it may also make a contribution to the worldwide church, for the issues which concern us are universal, even though their contextual character is unique.

It may be of interest to mention that a Beyers Naudé and Christian Institute archive is presently being established in the Jagger Library at the University of Cape Town. In this connection we refer especially to the bibliography of Naudé's writings included in this volume and the request for help in making the archive as complete as possible.

We are grateful to David Philip for his readiness to publish the book. Together with the contributors, he expressed no hesitation in committing himself to publication, even though the deadlines have been such that others, less committed, may well have declined. We are also indebted to several other people who have helped to produce the book. In particular we wish to thank Eileen Villa-Vicencio and Arlene Stephenson who took the proofreading in their stride, and Cheryl Mann who was responsible for much of the word-processing.

We offer this volume in celebration of Beyers Naudé's seventieth birthday out of deep respect, and trust that he and his wife Ilse may yet enjoy many more years of life together.

CHARLES VILLA-VICENCIO
JOHN W. DE GRUCHY

University of Cape Town
February 1985

DR BEYERS NAUDÉ (PHOTO: *CAPE TIMES*)

Beyers Naudé: his life and work

A life of resistance and hope
CHARLES VILLA-VICENCIO

All too often Beyers Naudé has been portrayed as larger than life by those who admire him most – a kind of Promethean character, and an all-wise mythical figure who can do no wrong. The problem with such euphoric assessments is that they tend to be ahistorical. They fail to do justice to the agony and trauma of the life of a person torn between hope and fear, who dares to question the fundamental structures of the community which gave him birth. And when these structures are those of Afrikaner nationalism, the journey is painful, costly, and not without its moments of spiritual, moral and ideological compromise.

It is warm-blooded imperfections and human ambiguities as much as leadership qualities, that have made Beyers Naudé such a controversial figure among those who know him best. It is also these characteristics that have endeared him to that vast cross-section of people who are best able to discern what it means to affirm one's humanity amidst conflict in a dehumanising society – oppressed people, not only in South Africa but around the the world. These same characteristics make him a prophet without honour among his own people, and leave lesser beings and underminers of his character, on both sides of the political divide, barking and snapping at his heels.

To understand the historical events which have forged the character of this man is to pay him tribute. Yet to understand is also to affirm those values, and that Beyers Naudé would count as more important than a thousand laudatory words.

Afrikaner of the Afrikaners

Naudé is a white Afrikaner of white Afrikaners.[1] If any have reason to boast in the flesh, important as this is for *die eie Afrikaneridentiteit*, it is he: Born within a Nederduitse Gereformeerde Kerk (NGK) parsonage. Of conservative Voortrekker and Dutch stock. His father a Boer chaplain during the Anglo–Boer War, and founder member of the Afrikaner Broederbond. Baptised Christiaan Frederick Beyers, the name of a rebel Afrikaner general. A graduate of the patriotic Stellenbosch University. Member of the elitist Afrikaner Broederbond. Moderator of the NGK in the Transvaal. He was finally banned for seven years by the leaders of the same Afrikaner nationalism that gave him birth.

It is this heritage and identity that makes Beyers Naudé such an enigma to so many, as if racism and white economic privilege are the peculiar prerogative of Afrikaners alone. The South African English are in fact probably every bit as racist as their Afrikaner counterparts, as is witnessed in their confused and ambivalent response to the message of people like Naudé.[2] Naudé's challenge reaches beyond the confines of Afrikanerdom to strike also at the heart of English and indeed Western values. It is with this realisation that many nations and individuals beyond South Africa's borders need also to come to grips. Prophets require more than admiration from a distance; they demand fundamental change and renewal in the land that is the object of their prophecy, but also in other places. This is because ultimately the world is a global village, of which one part cannot be changed without affecting the equilibrium of the whole. Sometimes conservatives and reactionaries understand this better than the radicals and would-be revolutionaries. It is this that makes Naudé such a troublesome patron and irascible doyen of many, both in South Africa and abroad, who 'support liberation'. The trouble with prophets is that they have a way of challenging and disturbing the very people who would like to support them, and who like to imagine that they share their prophetic vision. But how did Naudé come from the womb of a narrow and exclusive form of Afrikanerdom to become what he is, an Afrikaner with a broad ecumenical vision and an uncompromising global perspective on life?

The contours of human identity

The complexity of the contours of human identity always eludes simple analysis, and it is a risky business to delve into the dark recesses of the human psyche or the social maze of character formation, in order to *explain* a life quite as provocative as that of Beyers Naudé. What follows must therefore be no more than an unpretentious exercise in identifying some of the events which Naudé himself points to as having been formative influences on his life. It is the qualitative consistency of his response to these events that seems to point away from any sharp conversion, which most of Naudé's biographers have identified in his career.[3] He is obviously a different person from the one who, for example, showed decidedly pro-Hitler tendencies when South Africa went to war against the Third Reich in September 1939, and who joined the Afrikaner Broederbond the following year. However it is ahistorical, even if pleasingly romantic, to talk of the Cottesloe years as a dramatic Damascene-type conversion experience. This was rather the outcome of certain entrenched values and convictions which bored away at his character, and gradually by the sheer weight of evidence convinced him that he was wrong and that he needed to change.

A dominant home

I suppose it could be argued with some psychological persuasion that Naudé's post–Cottesloe transformation was an expression of his liberation from the super-ego dominance of his father, Jozua Francois Naudé. Certainly his father was a determined man, a zealous nationalist with an uncompromising sense of divine mission, committed to instructing his eight children, and above all his two sons, in his understanding of the ways of God with the Afrikaner people. He instilled within them the stories of British military aggression and their flagrant disregard for the human rights of the Afrikaner people. Certainly, he convinced the young Beyers of the just nature of the Afrikaner struggle against an aggressor, and enshrined within his memory the stories of the conditions under which the Afrikaner forces waged their guerrilla war, the suffering of Afrikaner women and children in concentration camps, the social effects of the scorched earth policy, and the economic and imperialist motivation behind the British war effort. He was also told of the campaign of evangelism among the indigenous black tribes, conducted by General Beyers, under whose command his father served, as they camped in the Soutpansberg during the war. In this way, he was taught the role of the Christian Afrikaner, both with regard to their own people and with regard to the indigenous black population. There is today still little doubt in the mind of Naudé that the British were the aggressors, and the cause of the Afrikaners essentially a just one, although he hastens to add that those were the days when the rights of the black population were not yet seriously on the agenda. For him the Afrikaners were the oppressed, and they fought a just struggle for their liberation, with a deep religious faith in a God who is the God of the oppressed.

His mother, Adriana Johanna Zondagh van Huyssteen, was a strong but gentle person, deeply and pietistically religious, of whom Naudé today speaks less readily than he does of his father. She had strong views on the way in which her children should be raised – well-educated, religious and obedient. She showed an unbending prejudice against the British and never questioned the rightness of the Afrikaner cause or their goal of eventual political dominance. In fact, Naudé regards her as a stronger influence on his childhood than his father. Her influence took the form of unquestioned values and passive dominance, and his own perception is that it was essentially from maternal captivity that he sought to escape.

From his parents Naudé inherited a sense of religious piety, a captivity to certain imposed moral norms, a sense of social and political justice with a bias in favour of the Afrikaner, and an obligation not to deviate from the cause predetermined by this medley of influences. Yet it would be this clear synthesis of moral and theological principles with a rigid form of nationalism that would eventually cause the turmoil in Naudé's personal identity and social commitment. Ultimately he would find himself exposed to a different context, and it was ironically these same religious and moral norms that within this new context separated him from his own people, whom he would come to regard as every bit the aggressor as the British were at the turn of the century. The provocative factor in his life is that these deeply entrenched principles and norms, so important for his own personal and corporate struggle for self-dignity and liberation, could transcend that historical situation, later to impinge on both his own life and his perception of his people. Those very instruments that had been such a mighty weapon in the Afrikaners' fight for existence and liberation, ultimately became their implements for oppressing others. What makes Naudé different is that he came to affirm the same weapons of Afrikaner liberation as a basis for black liberation as well.

Academic years

The alliance of theology and nationalism, and indeed the religious fervour and social reality established in his parents' home, proved for Naudé to be uneasily aligned during his time at Stellenbosch University. His recollection of those days at a university that had come to provide the intellectual soul of Afrikaner nationalism focuses largely on three names: Johan du Plessis, who had been tried for heresy and dismissed from the NGK Seminary attached to the university, H. F. Verwoerd, who lectured Naudé in sociology and eventually became Prime Minister, and B. B. Keet, his seminary professor of ethics.

There is today still a certain animation in Naudé's voice when he speaks of what he calls the pettiness, the corruption and the closed-minded attitude of the NGK with regard to Du Plessis's heresy trial. The Supreme Court eventually ruled in Du Plessis's favour, but the church refused to allow him to lecture, although it was compelled by the court to pay him his full salary for the rest of his working years.

There is in turn a reflectiveness in his voice when he refers to Verwoerd. He speaks of a brilliant, coherent, well-prepared and disciplined lecturer. Verwoerd would enter the class precisely on time, read his lectures, close his books, and walk out. There was no discussion, no personal contact with students, and, at least in Naudé's Sociology I lectures, he was quite apolitical. It is the uncompromising logic of all that Verwoerd taught and demanded of students that Naudé recalls most vividly. Was he surprised when Verwoerd's grand scheme for apartheid later emerged? 'Yes I was,' came Naudé's immediate reply. Then, more thoughtfully, he attributed it to what he regarded as Verwoerd's 'ruthlessness of logic'. It frightened Naudé because it left out important human elements, did not allow for human aggression, irrationality, failure, admission of error, historical irony, or grace and forgiveness.

Then there was Professor B. B. Keet: 'Bennie', as Naudé remembers him; 'the only theology professor who made a real impression on me.' Keet elicited a negative response from his colleagues and found himself politically isolated, but Naudé established a firm friendship with him, which would in the post-Cottesloe period develop into a deep sense of theological and political solidarity, nurtured by Naudé's regular visits to his mentor and confidant.

Stellenbosch evoked within Naudé the beginnings of a form of religious scepticism, especially for religious institutions and ecclesiastical hierarchies, a distrust of academic logical detachment, and the first inklings of theological and political dissent. Before these seeds of nonconformity could, however, grow and bear fruit, the power of Afrikaner nationalism, the church, and personal cost factors, would demand the kind of conformity that made one commentator suggest that Naudé could have been destined for the highest office in the land. Naudé quickly identifies his hankering to remain an accepted member of the Afrikaner volk, and the personal cost he compelled his wife, Ilse, and four children to bear, as the major drag factors which both delayed his fateful break with the Afrikaner establishment, and have repeatedly caused him to ask, 'Do I continue?'

NG pastor

Naudé's ministry began as *hulpprediker* (assistant minister) in Wellington in 1939. A few years later he became predikant to the Laxton congregation in the Karoo, and then moved to Pretoria East. It was here that he read Ben Marais' *Kleur Krisis en die Weste* (The colour crisis and the West), which the latter wrote after visiting the World Council of Churches (WCC).[5] By today's standards the book is patronising and even reactionary, but at the time it was enough to create a storm within the Afrikaner community by raising questions about the biblical justification of apartheid. Shocked at the thought of an Afrikaner theologian questioning the scriptural basis of its theology, the Afrikaner community unleashed a storm of protest against Marais. A decade later he would remember those days and show initial support for Naudé and the Christian Institute, but this, like so much other early support, was soon to dissipate. In 1953 Naudé undertook his first journey abroad as a member of the NG *Kerkjeugvereniging* (NG Church Youth Association), and with this his ecumenical exposure began. He remembers being confronted with numerous questions about his Dutch Reformed theology, but his Afrikaner–theologised identity held. Throughout this period he voted for the ruling National Party, and opposed South Africa's engagement in the war, regarding Britain as fulfilling her conventionally aggressive policy in confronting Hitler, in much the same way as she had done against the Afrikaners during the Anglo–Boer War. It was also during his time in Pretoria that he met the Prime Minister, General J. C. Smuts, and earned his wrath for suggesting that he would lose the forthcoming and now infamous 1948 general election, which swept the National Party into power.

It was, however, his years spent in Potchefstroom from 1955 to 1959 that he regards as most formative. He attended the Reformed ecumenical synod which met in that town, and again his parochialism was exposed to ecumenical contact, and he soon realised that not only were the Reformed family of churches in other parts of the world at theological loggerheads with the white Dutch Reformed churches in his country, but that they actually confirmed his own innermost doubts and questions. It was in Potchefstroom that he was also visited for the first time by a group of young white ministers whom he had met as theological students in Pretoria, and who were now serving black, coloured and Indian congregations. They exposed him to the effects of Group Areas and apartheid legislation on black people, and gradually enabled him to begin to move beyond the limits of the white exclusivity within which he was ensconced. He went, he visited their congregations, he saw and he grieved. This was a totally new experience for him. A further significant event within his Potchefstroom years was his contact with the conservative Gereformeerde Kerk, the Doppers. From members of this church, and essentially lay people who attended his Bible studies and eventually his worship services, he gained a decisively new existential understanding of the Word of God, within the life of the Christian. Today when he is asked to explain theologically what the Word of God is, his response is rather precise. 'It is', he tells us, 'one's understanding of the declared will of God made known in the Scriptures.' This must be tested within a community of people of goodwill, including both Christians and those who care not to be known as such. It must be concretised in relation to ongoing political and economic analysis, and ultimately verified in a deeply personal inner conviction. He is today at once a deeply spiritual and a profoundly secular person. Potchefstroom was an important point of transition in this regard.

In November 1959 he accepted a call to the Aasvoëlkop congregation in Johannesburg. Four months later, in March 1960, the police shot and killed 69 black people who had reported to the Sharpeville police station to hand in their passbooks and invite arrest. The resultant unrest was quelled, individuals and organisations banned, and white dominance re-established. Yet it is clear – Sharpeville represented a turning point in the history of African nationalism. Protest hardened into resistance and blacks were forced to think in terms of a revolutionary strategy.[5] In December of that year a WCC delegation responded to the crisis by meeting with South African member churches at Cottesloe in Johannesburg. With this meeting the South African church entered into a new phase of its history. The name of Beyers Naudé was poised to become a household word throughout South Africa, and soon it would be known in Christian circles around the world.

Cottesloe

Sharpeville had focused the world's attention on South Africa. The South Africa member churches of the WCC, which included the Transvaal and Cape synods of the NGK and the Nederduitsch Hervormde Kerk (NHK), meeting together with the WCC representatives at Cottesloe, were to produce a document of far-reaching symbolic value, while the Gereformeerde Kerk declined to participate.[7] The NHK delegates eventually rejected the Consultation Statement out of hand, while the majority of the NGK delegates supported it. The recommendations of the consultation were certainly not of a radical kind, even by the standards of the day. They would have been accepted as self-evident by most Christians around the world at the time, and undoubtedly could have been dismissed as reactionary. But South Africa is a strange society, and a storm was unleashed. The recommendations were seen to be a signal that the church, and more significantly the NGK delegates to the consultation, were ready to reject the biblical and theological justification of apartheid. Prime Minister Verwoerd, ever the logician, perceived danger and magisterially called the NGK delegates to order. He told them that they had allowed themselves to be unduly influenced by the liberal views of the WCC, and reminded them that theologians too had to have a single mind in affirming the high purposes of apartheid. He told them they needed to recant, and recant they did. It was Beyers Naudé alone who refused to deviate. He stood alone and experienced the icy winds of alienation which he would feel again and again in later years. The night before the Transvaal synod made its final decision on the Cottesloe Statement, he wrestled with his conscience:

I had to decide. Would I because of pressure, political pressure and other pressures which were being exercised, give in and accept, or would I stand by my convictions, which over a period of years had become rooted in me as firm and holy Christian convictions? I decided on the latter course, and put it clearly to the synod that with all the respect which I have for the highest assembly of my church, in obedience to God and my conscience, I could not see my way clear to giving way on a single one of those resolutions, because I was convinced that those resolutions were in accordance with the truth of the gospel.[8]

Was he surprised that he alone would ultimately defend the carefully considered Cottesloe resolutions which his fellow NGK delegates had earlier found to be firmly grounded in the Scriptures? 'I was not only surprised, but deeply shocked,' comes the reply. He knew that some would fall, but he also names those who had played such an important and creative role in the consultation, and laments *their* capitulation. Many of them could justify their revised position – strategy, the need to work 'from within', realism, the pastoral necessity to stand with one's people, and so on. Yet as one questions Naudé on each of those who still today argue that they did not simply capitulate, there is no doubt whatsoever in his mind: 'They may not have capitulated in their minds, in their person . . . but they became silent and that is capitulation.' The NGK, like the NHK, withdrew from the WCC and at the same time set up a commission to investigate the teaching of the Bible on questions of race. The outcome was the well-known study entitled *Ras, Volk en Nasie en Volkereverhoudinge in die Lig van die Skrif*, which would contribute so largely to the Ottawa decision to declare apartheid a heresy, and the suspension of the membership of that church from the World Alliance of Reformed Churches.

The aftermath

History moved fast for Naudé after Cottesloe, but not without a moment of unexpected irony. He was elected moderator of the Transvaal synod only two years after the synod vote which rejected the Cottesloe findings and voted to withdraw from the WCC, and two months after his widely publicised and recriminatory resignation from the Broederbond. 'My election came as suddenly and unexpectedly as the lifting of my banning order. I was quite overwhelmed and stunned,' is his response to this event.

The first request the synod made of its new moderator was that he resign his position as editor of *Pro Veritate*, which he had established the previous year. For Naudé this was an intensely difficult moment. In retrospect he sees it as an attempt to establish a quid pro quo. The church would affirm his integrity and insight, and in return he would be expected to affirm the position of the NGK. Such moments are most difficult to negotiate. When colleagues and adversaries are being pleasant and conciliatory it is not easy to stand rigidly by one's principles. He asked for time to consider their request, and a week later he rejected it. This was in April 1963, and to quote Naudé, 'once the bloodhounds of ideological Afrikanerdom had obtained the scent they would never let go'. In August of that year he founded the Christian Institute. A month later he was forced to resign as moderator, and was denied clergy status by the NGK immediately after he preached his farewell sermon to his Aasvoëlkop congregation, *Obey God Rather than Man*.[9] His inaugural lecture as director of the Christian Institute was significantly entitled *Versoening* (Reconciliation), delivered at the Central Methodist Church in Johannesburg, then under the pastoral care of one of the great patriarchal figures of Methodism, the Rev. Dr J. B. Webb.[10] When Naudé talks of those who meant most to him at a personal level in those days he refers to Ds Tema, E. E. Mahabane, Seth Mokitimi, J. B. Webb and Joe Wing. At first there was also support from some colleagues in his own church, the white NGK, but the cost of alienation from the Afrikaner community is perhaps something that only the Afrikaner can understand, and once again Naudé was to know what it is to be a lonely individual before God. It was, however, also the beginning of a new solidarity with a different community – an ecumenical community, a resisting community, and eventually that would be largely a black community.

Christian Institute

From the founding of the Christian Institute until the time of its banning, when banning orders were also served on its leaders on 19

October 1977, the life and person of Naudé was inextricably bound up with the fortunes and tragedies which constituted that organisation. [11] What the story of the Institute witnesses to is Naudé's remarkable propensity for change. Many people catch glimpses of a different world 'out there', some even test the climate of that world, but most to a greater or lesser degree do not venture boldly beyond the warmth and security of home. This is what makes Naudé different. With an insatiable and at times   reckless quest for liberation from what he perceives as contextually imposed presuppositions, he relentlessly pursues the lure of the larger dimension of truth. It is this that drew him out of his captivity to a narrow nationalism, and this that would throughout the days of the Christian Institute enable him and that organisation, in spite of its many top-heavy structural restraints, to show a remarkable flexibility in responding to new insights and needs. A Christian Institute that bore the marks of Naudé's white, Reformed and scholarly theology was obliged in the beginning to undergo numerous changes and redefinitions in response to the different cross-currents of ecumenical thought and above all of black thinking and critique.

As the Institute became increasingly black, so Naudé's personal identity underwent further change. Many withdrew from the cauldron of encounter between races, ideologies and theologies during this time, and those who stayed were buffeted at times in one direction and at times in another. Theirs was undoubtedly a heroic struggle for both social relevance and Christian identity, and without wanting to distract from the enormous contributions made to this struggle by numerous people, we can say that it was fundamentally the leadership role of Naudé which facilitated the process. It was this quest for relevance and identity that probably caused Naudé and the Institute to be attacked consistently from both the left and the right during its fourteen years of existence. For some it was too radical, while others saw it as too cautious and traditional. The government ultimately decided it was too dangerous.

It was also during this period of time that Naudé gained enormous international recognition while experiencing at home persecution and rejection, especially at the hands of the white community. The events of crisis and splendour surrounding his life were extensive: harassment by the Security Police, right-wing terrorism, libel suits, the decision of the NGK to declare the Institute heretical, arrest and trial, honorary doctorates, awards and recognitions, numerous speeches and lectures, visits abroad, involvement in every major political event of the time, countless engagements with both the exalted and lowest members of society – and finally, a five-year banning order served on him in October 1977, renewed in 1982 for a further three years, and quite suddenly lifted on Wednesday 26 September 1984.

Seven lean years

The years as a banned person were lean. It was one way of silencing Naudé and ensuring that he was not able to influence society. Yet, for the authorities, he became embarrassingly visible. Church leaders, politicians, overseas visitors, concerned citizens, black and white people, the young, the old, and friends, beat a path to the door of the Naudé home. He had become a symbol of *resistance and hope*. His spirited protest and resistance has made the opposition of so many other people seem quite frail and bloodless, while his indefatigable hope has persisted when there was positively no tangible reason to do other than despair. Then came the lifting of the banning order. With this a society seething in captivity and hungering for hope began its tumultuous demands all over again.

The night was late, the day had been a long one.[12] I thanked him for his willingness to talk so patiently about his life, apologising for being one of those who were adding to the demands. He graciously thanked me for taking him through his seventy years, stressing that it was conversations such as ours which allowed him to 'discover himself again', and that it is this process of ongoing self-discovery that enables him to be 'what God requires of me as his child and minister'. That, for Naudé, is still the bottom line. Then, with a kind of facetious spontaneity, he said: 'I sometimes long for those more restful days of my banning!'

The human personality

There are the musings of the psalmist, the artistic creations of the poet, the ponderings of the philosopher, the enquiries of the psychologist, and the reflections of all who affirm their place within the human species. Yet still we stand mystified by the complexity of the human personality – and not least of all by those who come out of the same womb, but are blatantly different, and at times qualitatively superior to their siblings. Is the human being no more than a cosmic accident, a bundle of social and psychological impulses, simply what he or she eats, or the product of socio-economic forces? When one has worked through the moments of history, of adversity and healing, of protest and hope, that have formed the character of Naudé, it is difficult to conclude that there is no remainder left unaccounted for. Hegel often pondered the nature of those whom he called the 'great men [people!] of history', those who for some strange and often inexplicable reason have made a formative contribution to life. They, he thought, at once personified the spirit of the times, and articulated those values which their people held most firmly, but, he suggested, they also created the spirit of the times and anticipated the spirit which was yet in the process of birth. For Hegel both the present and the future dimension are important for a definition of greatness. The absence of the former makes one no more than a visionary, but the absence of the latter makes one no more than a popularist politician. History is plagued with the likes of these. Naudé is a symbol of the deepest aspirations of many, perhaps the majority of people in South Africa, but more than that, he has anticipated a tomorrow when we shall be compelled to live together as brothers and sisters, because there is no other alternative. He is a product of those events which gave birth to his character as we know it today; but what was it that enabled him to venture when others turned back? There is a remainder left unaccounted for. Perhaps that is what we mean by human personality. A *sui generis* quality, which is an entity in its own right, that needs to be accounted for.

It is quite wrong to suggest that Naudé has escaped what theologians like to call the double nature of humanity – what Thomas Carlyle discerned as 'the depths in man that go down to the lowest hell, and the heights that reach the highest heaven'.[13] Simply stated, contrary to the opinion of those who admire him from a distance and turn him into a mystical icon of their cult, he is a human being. He has made his mistakes. He can be a stubbornly independent person, quite reckless with passionate abandon, and over-enthusiastic about ideas that simply cannot work. He can be a terrible judge of human character, and then fiercely loyal to colleagues and friends even in the face of the most damning evidence against them. All this has at times had a way of driving his closest friends to near despair.

He is of course aware of all this, and has readily admitted as much in many an intense conversation beneath the famous peach trees in the backyard of his Greenside home during his long years as a banned person. As one reflects on his life's journey, one begins, however, to discover how many of these idiosyncrasies have been forged on the anvil of his struggle *to be*, and to share in the liberation of a land and all its people. He has been compelled to stand alone so often, as a person referred to by Kierkegaard, 'as an individual in a crowd.' He knows the imperfections of humanity, and as a deeply introspective person he has meditated on his imperfections, and held firmly to the need to forgive and overlook the failings of others. He has dreamed dreams bigger than reality, and at times they have not materialised. If, however, politics is the art of the possible, the function of religion and theology is to hope for and anticipate what is at the present time not yet possible.

Naudé is in the last analysis a minister of the gospel. He regards himself as that. He insists that he is no longer a pietist. Definitions are always ambiguous things. He prays regularly, insisting that prayer is a marvellous and necessary complement to our frail efforts, but a dangerous substitute. He reads his Bible daily, and regards authentic worship as an important, but not indispensable, part of the Christian life. It is in this realm of meditation and ritual that he finds his identity and his strength to engage the world. His is a worldly Christianity, but one deeply grounded in a very traditional understanding of theological identity.

A short history of the Christian Institute
JOHN W. DE GRUCHY

Cottesloe and the formation of the Christian Institute[1]

The tragedy of Sharpeville, late in 1960, signalled the beginning of a new era in the history of South Africa. It also marked a fresh stage in the story of the church's struggle against apartheid, initiated by the Cottesloe Consultation and, a few years later, by the formation of the Christian Institute of Southern Africa (CI).[2]

In response to Sharpeville, the South African member churches of the World Council of Churches gathered together in consultation in the Johannesburg suburb of Cottesloe from 7 to 14 December 1960. The Cape and Transvaal synods of the Nederduitse Gereformeerde Kerk (NGK) were then still members of the WCC, and were represented by leading members and theologians of the church, including the acting moderator of the Transvaal synod, the Rev. Beyers Naudé. Also represented was the Nederduitsch Hervormde Kerk (NHK), whose delegates proved to be the most conservative and reactionary.[3] The overwhelming majority of the delegates at Cottesloe, including those of the NGK but not the NHK, approved its concluding statement, a relatively moderate rejection of racism.[4] But the Cottesloe Statement, moderate as it was, did present a serious challenge to some of the corner-stones of the ideology and practice of apartheid. Hence its dramatic repudiation by Prime Minister Hendrik Verwoerd, and its subsequent rejection by all the synods of the NGK.

The rejection of Cottesloe by his church was a bitter blow to Beyers Naudé and others within the NGK, and some like Professor Albert Geyser in the NHK, who were persuaded that apartheid was morally wrong and that their churches were guilty in giving it theological justification and practical support. It was also the beginning of a process of self-created isolation for the NGK. Of the NGK delegates to Cottesloe, only Naudé stood firmly by its decisions at the Transvaal synod.

Those within the NGK who supported the decisions reached at Cottesloe were very few in number but deeply committed to changing the mind of their church. During 1962, with Beyers Naudé as editor, they launched the monthly journal *Pro Veritate*. Though ecumenical, *Pro Veritate* was initially directed at Afrikaner Reformed clergy and laity. The Reformed tradition was called into the struggle on behalf of the unity of the church, ecumenical participation, and the struggle against apartheid. The early issues also show how much its editor and authors were influenced by the Confessing Church struggle in Nazi Germany, and especially by the Barmen Declaration of May 1934.

Beyers Naudé personally felt that *Pro Veritate* was, by itself, insufficient for the task at hand. His vision, shared by some colleagues both within the NGK and other churches, was for a Confessing Church movement which would express more concretely that to which *Pro Veritate* bore witness. There was resistance to this idea on the part of NGK ministers who otherwise supported Naudé. In a letter to Robert Bilheimer of the WCC, dated 8 August 1962, Fred van Wyk, a close friend of Naudé's and a NGK elder, wrote:

Our ecumenical paper, *Pro Veritate*, is doing amazingly well with Beyers as final editor, and pressure is being exerted on Beyers by many of his DRC friends not to risk forfeiting his status as DRC minister by undertaking any other ecumenical work.

The question of ministerial status was the biggest hurdle facing Naudé and his supporters at this moment of decision. Few doubted that the proposed institute would be rejected by the NGK, and that anyone who accepted a position within it would soon lose his status as a NGK minister and therefore his influence within the church.

By October 1962, Naudé had determined to take the risks involved and move ahead with his plans for an ecumenical institute as the spearhead of a Confessing Church movement. During October two meetings were held that confirmed his decision. On 1 October, twenty Afrikaans Reformed ministers met together to debate the issues and finally agreed that a Christian Institute should be formed. Three days later a meeting of ministers from a variety of other denominations concurred, and a public meeting was called for 1 November. Chaired by Dr J. B. Webb, the leading Methodist minister in Johannesburg, the meeting was attended by almost 200 people, clergy and laity, black and white.

Contrary to the hopes of Naudé, Fred van Wyk and others, the meeting on 1 November decided not to proceed with the formation of the Christian Institute at that stage, despite a large degree of unanimity among those present that there was a real need for it. Apart from some practical difficulties which would have made it difficult to form the Institute, several NGK participants expressed fears that the time was not ripe. They recommended that the formation of the Institute be shelved at least until after the Southern and Northern Transvaal synods had met in April 1963. This would then give at least three years' breathing space before they would meet again, and therefore before they could officially take any action against the Institute and its members. As it happended, the General Synod of the NGK, meeting in 1965, resolved that all members of the church should resign forthwith from the CI.

It was not until a meeting on 13 June 1963 that agreement was reached to proceed with the formation of the Christian Institute of Southern Africa. The actual launching took place on 15 August when the Constitution was approved by 180 founding members. In a press announcement the following day extracts were published, which stated:

The aim of the Institute is *to serve the Church of Christ in every possible way*. The basis is defined as follows: *The Christian Institute is based upon the Word of God, upon belief in God the Father, in Jesus Christ the Son, Redeemer and Lord, and in the Holy Spirit, and upon the conviction that for all who share such a common loyalty it is desirable and necessary that determined effort be made to express and foster their unity in Christ.*

The announcement continued by stating that membership would be open to 'any Christian who approves of the basis and aims of the Institute' and that it would 'in no way detract from the loyalty of any member to his own church or creed'. It was stressed that membership was personal and not representative of any denomination because the 'Institute is not an *institute or council of churches* but of individual Christians'. It then indicated some of the ways in which the Institute would seek to fulfil its aims, giving priority to study and discussion groups, conferences, publications and participation in ecumenical organisations committed to the same ideals.

Although the General Secretary of the Christian Council of South Africa (the forerunner of the SACC), the Rev. Basil Brown, had strongly supported the formation of the Christian Institute at the 1 November 1962 meeting, there was some hesitation on the part of the Council about overlap. Thus in a further document published at the time, the Director Beyers Naudé commented:

If the Dutch Reformed Churches had been members of the Christian Council of South Africa, these circles [that is, NGK ecumenical study circles in support of Cottesloe] would probably have functioned under the Council, but as the Dutch Reformed Churches are, unfortunately, not in the Council, it was felt that independent study circles could offer the ecumenically minded Dutch Reformed Christians some comfort and a 'home'.[5]

Throughout the history of the Christian Institute its relation to the Christian Council and its successor, the SACC, was close and co-operative, though not without tension. The CI had a freedom to operate that the Council did not have because of its accountability to its member churches.

The relationship of the CI to the churches was also an issue from the beginning, although several prominent church leaders were on its Board of Management from the beginning. This led Beyers Naudé to prepare a public statement on the subject, in which he explained:

The Christian Institute is a voluntary association of members of different denominations of the Church of Christ in South Africa. The Institute is a witness to the unity of all believers in Christ and in this way it endeavours to promote the one-ness of the church in obedience to Christ and his word. In addition the Institute seeks to co-ordinate the witness of Christians in the present critical state of our country. The Institute wishes, in every way, to assist Christians in their witness; and especially by making believers more aware of the privilege and responsibility they have for studying the Word of God and accepting mutual responsibility for the calling of the Church in the world.[6]

Thus the Christian Institute was launched with Beyers Naudé as its Director and, shortly after, Mr Fred van Wyk as its energetic Administrator. *Pro Veritate* remained an independent journal, but was housed within the CI. The CI was controlled by a Board of Management appointed by the Annual General Meeting, and the membership of the first Board is indicative of the widespread ecumenical support which the institute had at its inception. Naudé was able to spend increasingly less time in his capacity as the final editor of *Pro Veritate*, and within a few years the position was filled by another NGK minister, Dr Ben Engelbrecht. Naudé's own energies were largely devoted to organising the CI, developing its resources, programmes and staff, and responding to the ongoing crises in the country.

From the beginning cloud storms were visible on the horizon both within the NGK and the political arena. And despite the support which Naudé had gathered from within the English-speaking churches and the Christian Council, there is no doubt that he was surprised by the suspicion and caution which he also found within these circles. Moreover, although there were black members of the CI from the beginning, and black leaders such as the Rev. E. E. Mahabane involved in its Board of Management, its orientation was towards the white membership and leadership of the churches. As Peter Walshe aptly comments:

Naudé and the Christian Institute had a long way to go before coming to the full realisation of the centrality of the black viewpoint for the future of Christianity and of justice in South Africa. Nevertheless, something new had been started in the Institute. A prophetic Christian voice was being heard and simultaneously there emerged the prospect of a prophetic ecumenical movement.[7]

A Confessing Church movement

A careful perusal of *Pro Veritate* from its inception until its banning in 1977 shows a gradual shift in theological orientation. It was always ecumenical in emphasis, but for most of the sixties its theological orientation was Reformed and its main source of inspiration was the Confessing Church struggle in Nazi Germany. Towards the end of the sixties and until its demise, its orientation was more influenced by black and liberation theology. This correlates with the development of the CI itself and with developments in the church more generally. But undoubtedly the initial vision was that of a Confessing Church movement critical of the church's failure to respond prophetically to apartheid, a movement seeking to express the unity of the church in opposition to racism and injustice.

Much of the energy of Naudé and the CI in its early years was taken up with the internal struggle within the NGK church. This struggle for the soul and integrity of the church was regarded as fundamental to the struggle against racism in South African society. It was part of the raison d'être of the CI to act as a prophetic critic of the Afrikaner Reformed churches because of their failure to respond positively to Cottesloe. Time and again in speeches, sermons and through *Pro Veritate*, Naudé and other Afrikaans Reformed ministers within the CI circle touched on the somewhat raw and sensitive nerve endings in their churches. The churches were not slow in responding. Walshe reminds us:

Tension rose dramatically as the Institute set out to extend its contacts in the Afrikaner community, circularising DRC clergy and promoting *Pro Veritate*. The result was a smear campaign launched by *Die Transvaler* (an Afrikaner Nationalist daily newspaper published in Johannesburg) in September 1965 with a series of vituperative articles. It became commonplace for leading members of the DRC to use their pulpits to condemn the Christian Institute, reserving their most bitter comments for Beyers Naudé and his Afrikaner colleagues. The *volk* were warned again and again to oppose any blurring of racial divisions and the Institute's 'liberalistic' and 'Communist' tendencies.[8]

The CI's theological response to this attack was determined by its conviction that these Afrikaans Reformed churches had departed fundamentally from their confessional basis. They had turned away from their Reformed and Calvinist heritage and sold out to a *volksteologie* in which Afrikaner cultural and political interests were prior to those of the gospel. An open letter to 1 500 NGK ministers set out this conviction, arguing that apartheid was contrary to the Word of God and the confessions of the church.

The specific articulation of the need for a Confessing Church in South Africa was made in an article by Naudé published in *Pro Veritate* in July 1965. Entitled 'Die tyd vir 'n "Belydende Kerk" is daar' ('The time for a "Confessing Church" has arrived'), it was written shortly after Naudé's home and the offices of the Christian Institute had been searched by the Security Police for documents relating to communism and the banned African National Congress. To Naudé the event smacked so strongly of Nazi-style tactics that he was convinced that the time for a Confessing Church in South Africa had arrived. What he had in mind was not identical to the German Confessing Church, but a movement within the churches which would be bound together by a common faith and concern, united in study and action in obedience to Jesus Christ as Lord within the church and society. Naudé concluded his article by stating that such a movement had already come into existence with the formation of the Christian Institute.

Though the idea of a Confessing Church movement remained the focus of Naudé's and the CI's vision, by 1965 its work had grown in a number of different directions. This is reflected in the rapid growth of staff and the development of new programmes. Initially the heart of the work of the CI was the formation and nurture of bible study groups, for which purpose study guides were prepared and several people employed as organisers. The CI also sought to influence the thinking of the churches in other ways. It devoted much time and effort, for example, in obtaining study and travel scholarships so that Christians in South Africa, and especially the younger clergy, could experience the church in other parts of the world and obtain further education. It also sponsored the visits to South Africa of eminent church leaders and theologians.

The CI increasingly felt the need to respond to particular needs in the churches and society as they arose. One such need was the desire of many leaders within the African Independent churches for theological education. Rather than approach the mainline churches for help, because of a history of suspicion and rejection, these leaders approached the CI in 1964, and by the beginning of the following year a programme had been launched to help them. The Rev. Danie van Zyl, a Presbyterian, was appointed to co-ordinate the programme and to help in the formation of AICA, the first Association of African Independent Churches. A seminary was also established at Lovedale in the Eastern Cape. The motivation for this involvement by the CI was to enable the African Independent churches to participate in the life of the wider ecumenical church and to realise their potential more fully in the life of society as a whole. In order to fulfil its commitment to AICA, the CI required considerable financial help. Massive donations were received for this purpose from church groups, especially in Holland and Germany. Despite such help, AICA drained the resources of the CI, sapped the energy of Naudé and his staff, and eventually failed to achieve its goal.

While the central office of the CI in Johannesburg was the hub of its activities under the administrative direction first of Fred van Wyk, who provided its initial drive, and then of Brian Brown, a Methodist minister who provided an administrative anchor during the turbulent years that led to the banning of the CI, regional offices, particularly in Cape Town and Natal, played a vital role in developing grassroots support. In Cape Town, Theo Kotze, also a Methodist minister, provided the CI with dynamic leadership, particularly in responding to local issues, but he also made a major contribution in shaping the CI as a whole in the seventies. For a short period, also in the early seventies, the CI in Natal was directed by Dr Manas Buthelezi, who subsequently became a bishop of the Evangelical Lutheran Church.

Quite apart from support for AICA, throughout its history the CI was heavily funded by ecumenical and church groups in Europe and Britain, and later on by some in the United States. Without their support its work would have been severely curtailed if not entirely prevented, for there was little financial backing within South Africa itself. Quite apart from external financial backing, the CI was also deeply influenced by theological and other developments which took place within the wider ecumenical movement during the sixties. Naudé and others from within the CI participated in a variety of conferences around the world, including Africa, and developed strong ties with people and groups.

Of particular importance for Naudé's own development and that of the CI was his participation in the Church and Society Conference held under the auspices of the WCC in Geneva in 1966. Naudé attended the Geneva conference together with the Rt. Rev. Bill Burnett, an Anglican bishop who had recently been appointed General Secretary of the Christian Council of South Africa. Just as the Geneva conference proved to be a watershed in the history of the WCC and the ecumenical movement as a whole, so it markedly shaped the future of both the CI and the SACC.

On their return from Geneva, Naudé and Burnett initiated a series of regional conferences, which were held during 1967 in Cape Town, Durban and Port Elizabeth culminating in a National Consultation in Johannesburg in February 1968. A significant contribution was made at these conferences by lay people whose expertise in economics and the social sciences enabled the discussion and resolutions to achieve considerable concreteness. But only a beginning had been made.

During this same period another development was initiated by Naudé and Burnett which complemented these consultations and decisively shaped the future of both the CI and the SACC. In 1966 the Christian Council (it became the SACC in 1967), at the request of Burnett as General Secretary, formed a Theological Commission to 'consider what obedience God requires of the church in her witness to her unity in Christ in South Africa'. It was this Commission, comprised of theologians involved in both the CI and SACC, which prepared *The Message to the People of South Africa*.

The Message was read to the delegates at the final session of a Conference on Pseudo-gospels held in Johannesburg at the beginning of May 1968, a follow-up to the Church and Society Consultation held earlier in the year. But *The Message* was not made public until September 1968 when Bishop Burnett, as General Secretary of the SACC, presented it at a press conference. In the final paragraph of his prepared statement, Burnett declared:

The Message asserts with the utmost clarity . . . that the apartheid ideology cannot be squared with the Gospel of Jesus Christ. The implication of the message undoubtedly involves planning for the future on the basis of responsible, orderly and increased integration. Like the Barmen declaration produced by the German Confessing Church *The Message* is a challenge to the conscience of every Christian in terms of the Gospel. This does not mean that the situation in Germany in the thirties is in all respects comparable to present-day South

Africa nor does it mean that a Confessing Church is now inaugurated here. But who can say where Christian obedience will lead the church in the months and years that lie ahead? We trust in God.

For the first time an official South African church document declared that apartheid was a false gospel, paving the way for the declaration that it was nothing but a heresy. It also paved the way for a more thorough attempt on the part of the CI and the SACC to work out the implications of the gospel for South Africa, namely, Spro-cas, the Study Project on Christianity in Apartheid Society.

The radicalisation and demise of the CI

The publication of *The Message to the People of South Africa* exacerbated the growing tension between the state and the SACC member churches in South Africa.[9] It also created additional stress within the churches themselves even though the assemblies, conferences and synods generally expressed support. But the CI and the SACC did not expect the churches to follow it up and therefore determined to press ahead in several complementary directions.

Firstly, attempts were made to obtain the support of clergy and lay people in their personal capacities. 'Obedience to God' groups were formed, especially on the Reef, to enable those who had signed *The Message* to work out its practical implications together. Secondly, the official confirmation of *The Message* by the member churches of the SACC was sought. Thirdly, the CI and SACC jointly sponsored Spro-cas, a most significant development for the future of the CI. Spro-cas was a response to the question: what does *The Message* actually mean in terms of education, law, economics, the church, politics and society as a whole. It is one thing for the church to be prophetic, it is another for it to provide concrete models and alternatives to apartheid, as well as strategies for change, which take into account the complex realities of the South African situation. Without doubt, its reports were the most comprehensive on the situation in South Africa ever produced by a church-related organisation. The fundamental question remained, however: how to translate recommendations into actions.[10]

It must be kept in mind that developments within the CI, SACC and the churches at this time were profoundly affected by the launching of the WCC Programme to Combat Racism in 1970.[11] There can be no doubt that the PCR proved to be the major catalytic event which determined the public agenda of the churches for the seventies, including their relationship to the state, bringing into prominence the debate on violence/non-violence in working for change. Thus it gave a fresh urgency to the task which Spro-cas had undertaken.

The Message and Spro-cas were white initiatives dominated by white participation. Certainly in the beginning Spro-cas operated on liberal assumptions. By the late sixties the agenda for South Africa and the churches was more and more being set by black political and theological thinking and praxis which not only rejected apartheid categorically, but also called liberal capitalism into radical question. It regarded co-operation with whites in the struggle for justice as problematic on the grounds that when the crunch really came white participation would either crumble or else compromise black demands. This conviction was especially strong within the black consciousness movement, which was rapidly gaining ground amongst students under the leadership of Steve Biko and Barney Pityana.

The black renaissance, represented by black consciousness and theology, nevertheless had a decisive impact upon the CI. Black staff members such as Oshadi Phakati challenged the CI to commit itself unequivocally to the black struggle for liberation. The challenge was accepted and every effort was made by the CI to relate to black consciousness organisations, trade unions, and black leaders. This meant the radicalisation of the CI, and it led to the formation of Spro-cas 2 (Special Programme for Christian Action in Society).

Spro-cas 2, as its name indicates, was action-oriented. In order to put words into deeds it created two separate programmes, one aimed at whites, the other at blacks. Very soon it became evident that the attempts to change whites was not likely to succeed, and the programme ground to a halt. But whereas Spro-cas failed in its mission to whites, its Black Community Programmes directed by Bennie Khoapa had much more success, and had its activities not been curtailed by state action, it had the potential for a much greater impact.[12] It also had a decisive impact upon the CI itself, which Peter Walshe sums up when he describes it as

a conduit for the flow of ideas from the black consciousness movement into the Christian Institute, a factor which, when allied to the appointment of black staff members in the Institute, helped to transform the thinking of Naudé and his colleagues.[13]

The CI was rapidly moving away from an organisation aimed primarily at changing white attitudes and the white church, to one which understood its role as that of support for the black struggle for justice and liberation.

Black participation in the CI had always been a problem. In the first instance this was because the CI's focus of attention was on the white NGK. But later, when the CI had given up trying to influence the NGK and had begun to identify more radically with black interests, the black consciousness movement had already begun to make blacks wary of participation in any multi-racial organisation. Given this background, black involvement at this time in the CI was remarkable. The reason was undoubtedly the unequivocal commitment which the CI and Naudé had made to black liberation. This was the burden of Dr Manas Buthelezi's address, 'The Significance of the Christian Institute for Black South Africa', to a Cape Town rally on 26 October 1974.

Dr Buthelezi made two major points. Firstly, he said that the CI 'tries to retrieve discarded values'.

Like a hungry tramp who retrieves crumbs of food from garbage cans, the Christian Institute is seen to be trying to retrieve certain discarded Christian values from the dirt bin of the South African way of life.

He went on to say that he thought this imagery appropriate, given,

on the one hand, the fact that the Christian Institute is an outcast in relation to the bulk of powerful white South Africa, and, on the other, that articulate blacks pitifully doubt its chances of success.

Secondly, Buthelezi declared that the CI 'witnesses and suffers'. Referring to *The Message* and Spro-cas, he said:

Since this was tantamount to stepping on the toes of political structures, the leadership of both the Christian Institute and Spro-cas was subjected to one form of suffering or another. In case anyone was in doubt it was also here that one got a glimpse of how South Africa is fundamentally an unjust society.

For Buthelezi, the CI suffered because of its prophetic witness, its witness to the redemptive power of the cross.

Redemptive life is power beyond words; it is the sum total of the impact of putting your life at stake for the welfare of others. This is what Christians from times immemorial have called the power of the cross. People have often asked, what happens after Spro-cas? My answer is, beyond the message of the theology of Spro-cas lies the theology of the power of the cross.

And so Buthelezi summed up the significance of the Christian Institute for black South Africa:

it is the power of the theology of the cross the Christian Institute is now living. Black people can understand this theology because they have always lived it, theology of power beyond words.[14]

However sceptical blacks might have been about the chances of the CI to affect change, they accepted its credentials and were prepared to work alongside, if not always within it.

Buthelezi's perception was, at a profoundly theological level, a testimony to what was the experience of the CI and its staff – suffering at the hands of the authorities and the white community in general. Of course, Naudé and others within the CI began to suffer rejection, slander and abuse from the very beginning of the CI. But this increased in tempo and character the more the CI responded to the challenge of black theology and the black struggle for justice. Many CI supporters and workers, and especially those working for the Black Community Programmes, were banned and detained at one time or another, and often their homes and families bore the brunt of callous and cruel deeds; offices were raided by the Security Police, publications were seized or banned, passports were confiscated or denied, and visas for overseas workers or visitors refused. At no time was the CI a large organisation, but it must have kept a large number of security officials busy. And it was because it was perceived as a threat to state security that finally the government initiated action which led to its eventual demise.

The Commission of Enquiry into Certain Organisations (Schlebusch/Le Grange Commission) was established by the state in 1972. Its mandate was the work of the University Christian Movement (which was already defunct), NUSAS (National Union of South African Students), the South African Institute of Race Relations, and the CI. In the course of its investigations it also examined the Wilgespruit Fellowship Centre. Beyers Naudé and other CI staff members refused to give evidence or testify to the Commission on the grounds that it was a parliamentary commission (as distinct from a judicial enquiry), therefore already biased against the CI, and because its hearings were held in camera. Such a refusal was illegal, and Naudé's stand resulted in a trial which lasted three years.[15]

In the meantime several developments took place which further alienated the CI from the authorities and pushed it deeper into radical commitment on behalf of black liberation. Amongst these were the escalating hostilities in Namibia and the growing militarisation of South Africa; the SACC resolution on conscientious objection adopted at the National Conference in 1974, a resolution seconded by Beyers Naudé; the toughening up of security legislation and the ongoing banning and detention of black consciousness leaders and Christian workers; and the emergence of illegal black trade unions as a powerful catalyst for change.

The CI's own change in character and emphasis is seen not only in the development of Spro-cas, but also very clearly in the pages of *Pro Veritate*. By 1970 the editorials no longer bore a distinct Reformed, Confessing Church stamp, but were increasingly influenced by Latin American liberation theology, black theology, and the issues raised by the Programme to Combat Racism. This led, amongst other things, to a radical questioning of capitalism as the corollary of racism. In May 1975, for example, the editor, Roelf Meyer, rejected liberal-capitalism by which blacks were reduced to poverty, and spoke of the need for black liberation from both economic and political dependency. Similarly, a joint statement by Beyers Naudé and Chief Gatsha Buthelezi published in February 1976 called for 'a radical redistribution of wealth, land and political power'. 'In South Africa', they said, 'for over a century capitalistic paternalism has produced the conclusive evidence which makes us reject government by a minority elite'.[16]

Eventually, in 1975 the Le Grange Commission reported to Parliament and recommended that the CI be declared an 'affected organisation'. This meant that it could no longer receive funds from abroad, which meant a very serious curtailment of its work. The state argued that the CI had become a political organisation and therefore should not be funded externally; the CI and its supporters argued that its political witness derived from the gospel and was thus an essential part of its Christian vocation and responsibility. The CI had now to cut back on its programmes, retrench staff, and reconsider its priorities. One of these was related to the emerging protest within the black Reformed churches represented by the *Broederkring*, the forerunner of the *Belydendekring*, led by the Rev. Sam Buti and Dr Allan Boesak. But history overtook it as it set about these tasks.

If Sharpeville was the indirect cause of the CI, the eruption of Soweto in June 1976 unintentionally led to its end. By the time Soweto made headlines, the CI, as we have seen, was deeply committed to and involved in black initiatives. It was certainly a major source of support for black community leaders within the black consciousness movement. Thus when Soweto and other townships exploded in 1976, the CI not only identified itself with the grievances of the students and their parents, but it also sided with them in condemning the violent reprisals of the police and publishing allegations of police brutality. The CI's protest intensified as violence spiralled in the townships until its tragic and fateful climax in the death of Steve Biko on 12 September 1977.

By now the state had had enough. On 19 October 1977, the CI was declared illegal, many of its black staff were detained by the police, imprisoned or, like Oshadi Phakati, fled into exile, and senior white staff, Beyers Naudé, Theo Kotze, Brian Brown, Cedric Mayson and Peter Randall, were all banned. An Anglican priest, David Russell, who worked closely with the CI in Cape Town amongst the squatter communities, was also banned. The same day many black organisations experienced the wrath of the state, and thus with a not unexpected suddenness the CI was silenced after sixteen years of witness, along with many of the black groups with which it had found common cause.

Several key figures, like Theo Kotze and Brian Brown, soon went into exile in Europe, or joined others, like Horst Kleinschmit and Oshadi Phakati who were already there. There was a shortlived attempt to create a CI in exile, based in Holland where support was particularly strong. But Beyers Naudé and others felt that this would serve little purpose. The CI might not have accomplished what it set out to do, but it had attempted to keep alive its witness to the kingdom of God as faithfully as possible. The time had come to accept the fact that the CI had done what it could and that state action had prevented it from achieving its ultimate goals. Others, such as the SACC, soon to be led by Bishop Desmond Tutu, and its member churches, now had the full responsibility for bearing that testimony.

The editofial of one of the final issues of *Pro Veritate*, published in March 1977, reflected on hope for the future in South Africa. Its words still demand attention and sum up that which motivated the CI from its inception:

Gloom and despondency dominate many white Christians. The future looms before them in dreadful greyness, unrelieved by any sparkle of hope or delight, so they seek means of sensual or spiritual escapism, and let the government be their god. Sixty-seven years of white power have failed to produce a peaceful and hopeful society, and government promises to secure the future of whites by the use of massive armed force are no comfort. The economy is breaking down under the cost of forcefully segregating and subjugating 80% of the population. Is there no shame when whites must shoot hundreds of school children to maintain their superiority? Superior in what? But Christians who prophesy only doom must realise they are not speaking with a Jesus voice. There is an alternative programme in which the positive contribution of whites is fully demanded, arising from the faith that **God is busy with his programme. The strategy of God is at work in our history and it is our task to find and follow his purposes. That is what the Christian faith is about, and the task for which we are sent to make disciples.**

Beyers Naudé: a bibliography
STEPHEN M. DE GRUCHY-PATTA

When the Christian Institute was banned by the South African government in October 1977 its library and records were also confiscated. Many of Beyers Naudé's personal papers were amongst the documents taken by the Security Police and are no longer available. A considerable number of his papers are now lodged in libraries in North America and Europe, but no catalogue of all the material has been produced. This has made it very difficult to prepare a complete bibliography of his addresses, papers and writings; what follows is an initial attempt. It is our hope that those who have additional information in this regard will communicate with the Librarian at the University of Cape Town where the Beyers Naudé Archive has been established so that a complete record of Dr Naudé's contribution to church and society may become available. We have also concluded the bibliography at the time of his banning in 1977. Since its lifting at the end of 1984 Dr Naudé has already spoken widely and delivered major addresses, some of which have been published. But it has not been possible to include them at this time. We have not included his early writing as a student.

1955. *Kerk en Jeug in die Buiteland en Suid Afrika* (Kaapstad, Kerkuitgewers vir Kerkjeugvereniging, 1955).
1960. 'Afrikaanse kerke voor gevaar van verwarring', *Dagbreek en Sondagnuus*, 18 December. 'Afrikaans churches in danger of confusion', unpublished mimeograph (English translation).
1961. Speech to NGK synod after Cottesloe. In *Die Burger*, 8 April, 'Afgevaardiges na Cottesloe antwoord ook skerp'.
1962. 'Wat ons wil', editorial, *Pro Veritate*, 15 May.
'Lack of contact', editorial, *Pro Veritate*, 15 June.
'Bybelse voorligting oor rasseverhoudinge', editorial, *Pro Veritate*, 15 June.
'Kritiek oor "Pro Veritate"', editorial, *Pro Veritate*, 15 July.
'Conflict of loyalties', editorial, *Pro Veritate*, 15 August.
'Kritiek van kerkblaaie: ons antwoord', editorial, *Pro Veritate*, 15 August.
'Die kerk: eenheid en verskeidenheid', editorial, *Pro Veritate*, 15 September.

'The voice of the younger churches', editorial, Pro Veritate, 15 September.

'Separatist churches: responsibility and opportunity', editorial, Pro Veritate, 15 October.

'Van alleenspraak tot samespraak', editorial, Pro Veritate, 15 October.

'Better understanding through honest criticism', editorial, Pro Veritate, 15 November.

'Nouerskakeling van die Afrikaanse kerke', editorial Pro Veritate, 15 November.

'The challenge to the ministry', editorial, Pro Veritate, 15 December.

'Kosbare tweelingwoord', editorial, Pro Veritate, 15 December.

1963. 'Tyd is nie ryp nie', editorial, Pro Veritate, 15 January.

'Ecumenical meetings in Africa', editorial, Pro Veritate, 15 January.

'The churches' answer to the youth's questions', editorial, Pro Veritate, 15 February.

'Sendingstrategie', editorial, Pro Veritate, 15 February.

'Aktivering van lidmate', editorial, Pro Veritate, 15 April.

'The church in times of crisis', editorial, Pro Veritate, 15 April.

Opening address to the 1963 Southern Transvaal synod of the NGK, at which Naudé was elected Moderator. In Die Kerkbode, 15 May.

'Opmerkinge oor sinodale besluit', letter written with 25 others, in Die Kerkbode, 15 May.

'Die eindredakteur besluit', editorial, Pro Veritate, 15 May.

'The church in Africa makes history', editorial, Pro Veritate, 15 May.

'Communicating the gospel', editorial, Pro Veritate, 15 June.

'Die familielewe van die Bantoe en Kleurling', editorial, Pro Veritate, 15 June.

'Beter menslike verhoudinge', editorial, Pro Veritate, 15 July.

'The church and immigrants', editorial, Pro Veritate, 15 July.

'Christian witness in African states', editorial, Pro Veritate, 15 August.

'Gesamentlike evangelisasie-aksie', editorial, Pro Veritate, 15 August.

'Dr. P. G. Geertsema', editorial, Pro Veritate, 15 August.

'Die kerk en kommunisme', editorial, Pro Veritate, 15 September.

'Development of African Christian leadership', editorial, Pro Veritate, 15 September.

'Die Christelike Instituut', editorial, Pro Veritate, 15 October.

'A crusade of prayer', editorial, Pro Veritate, 15 October.

'Repliek op korrespondensie i.s. sinodale besluit', a letter written with 25 others, in *Die Kerkbode*, 20 October.

'Die taak van die profeet', editorial, *Pro Veritate*, 15 November.

'Theologians meet in study and prayer', editorial, *Pro Veritate*, 15 November.

Statement on SABC Radio concerning the Broederbond exposé, 20 November.

'Ds. Naudé antwoord die Broederbond', *Die Transvaler*, 22 November.

My Beslissing, and *My Decision*, three sermons published by the Christian Institute in December. The sermons are entitled 'Gehoorsaam aan God' ('Obedient to God') preached on Sunday 22 September 1963 in the Aasvoëlkop NGK when Naudé announced his decision to become Director of the Christian Institute; 'Vuurvlam en voorhamer' ('Flame of fire and sledgehammer') preached on 3 November at his farewell service, Aasvoëlkop, Johannesburg; 'Versoening' ('Reconciliation'), preached at the Central Methodist Church on Sunday 15 November.

'Kom buig daar in aanbidding', editorial, *Pro Veritate*, 15 December.

'Day of the Covenant', editorial, *Pro Veritate*, 15 December.

'The Christian Institute of South Africa: reply against attacks', *South African Outlook*, December.

1964. 'Population growth and missionary development', editorial, *Pro Veritate*, 15 January.

'Kongres oor kommunisme', editorial, *Pro Veritate*, 15 January.

'Anarchy and responsibility', editorial, *Pro Veritate*, 15 February.

'Die roep van hongerlydendes', editorial, *Pro Veritate*, 15 February.

'A Statement from the CI on the Church and Communism', unpublished paper, 21 February.

'So word kommunisme bevorder', editorial, *Pro Veritate*, 15 March.

'A call to the people of South Africa', editorial, *Pro Veritate*, 15 March.

'Veni Creator Spiritus', editorial, *Pro Veritate*, 15 April.

'Jou naaste soos jouself', editorial, *Pro Veritate*, 15 May.

'Mindolo', editorial, *Pro Veritate*, 15 June.

'Theological training in Southern Africa', editorial, Pro Veritate, 15 June.

'God, die gesin en die owerheid', editorial, *Pro Veritate*, 15 July.

'Geweld: die Christen se antwoord', editorial, *Pro Veritate*, 15 August.

'Die IDAMSA Conference', editorial, *Pro Veritate*, 15 August.

'Rampokkerland?', editorial, *Pro Veritate*, 15 October.

'Church hypocrisy: the only valid reply', editorial, *Pro Veritate*, 15 October.

'What other way?', editorial, *Pro Veritate*, 15 November.

'Die CSV by die kruiswee', editorial, *Pro Veritate*, 15 November.

'As u gesin Kersdag saam is . . . ', editorial, *Pro Veritate*, 15 December.

'Friendship through service', editorial, *Pro Veritate*, 15 December.

1965. 'Die stryd om Afrika', editorial, *Pro Veritate*, 15 January.

'The British Council of Churches and the Reformed Churches', editorial, *Pro Veritate*, 15 January.

'Weighed and found wanting', editorial, *Pro Veritate*, 15 February.

'Tydige begrafnis of nuwe geboorte?', editorial, *Pro Veritate*, 15 February.

'Die regte benadering', editorial, *Pro Veritate*, 15 March.

'Multi-racial religious gatherings: clarity needed', editorial, *Pro Veritate*, 15 March.

'Verkiesing en evangeliebevordering', editorial, *Pro Veritate*, 15 April.

'His suffering and ours', editorial, *Pro Veritate*, 15 April.

'The prayer we need', editorial, *Pro Veritate*, 15 May.

'Laat God's woord die oordeel vel', editorial, *Pro Veritate*, 15 May.

'The Christian Institute', *Challenge*, June.

'Wie nie teen one is nie, is vir ons', editorial, *Pro Veritate*, 15 June.

'For the record', editorial, *Pro Veritate*, 15 June.

'The extended home', editorial, *Pro Veritate*, 15 July.

''n Lofwaardige voorbeeld', editorial, *Pro Veritate*, 15 July.

'Die tyd vir 'n Belydende Kerk is daar', *Pro Veritate*, 15 July.

'Die ASB en ons/The ASB and us', editorial, *Pro Veritate*, 15 August.

'Kerk het vernuwing dringend nodig', *Pro Veritate*, 15 August.

'Director's Report for the Period 1st August 1964 to 31st July 1965', printed address, 19 August.

'Please define!/Definisie asseblief!', editorial, *Pro Veritate*, 15 September.

'Die eer van die kerk/The church's honour', editorial, *Pro Veritate*, 15 October.

'Nogeens die "Belydende Kerk"', *Pro Veritate*, 15 November.

'Cape and Transvaal: conflicting voices?/Kaapland en Transvaal: botsende stemme?', editorial, *Pro Veritate*, 15 November.

Offer to open the CI up to an NGK investigation. In *Die Burger*, 30 November.

'Try the spirits', an open letter with three other Afrikaans theologians in the CI to 1 500 ministers of the NGK, in *South African Outlook*, November.

'Misdaad toename: die kerk se taak/Increase in crime: the church's task', editorial, *Pro Veritate*, 15 December.

'Nou juis die "Belydende Kerk"', *Pro Veritate*, 15 December.

1966. 'Must the Institute disappear from the scene?/Moet die Christelike Instituut van die toneel verdwyn?', editorial, *Pro Veritate*, 15 January.

'Kerke voor belangrike beslissings/Important decisions facing the church', editorial, *Pro Veritate*, 15 February.

'The coming election/Die komende verkiesing', editorial, *Pro Veritate*, 15 March.

'Skadu oor Distrik Ses', editorial, *Pro Veritate*, 15 March.

'Kerk en nywerheid/Church and industry', editorial, *Pro Veritate*, 15 April.

'Ut omnes unum sit', editorial, *Pro Veritate*, 15 May.

'Geweld in Afrika/Violence in Africa', editorial, *Pro Veritate*, 15 June.

'The more onerous demand/Die swaarder eis', editorial, *Pro Veritate*, 15 July.

'Apartheid as anti-evangelie/Apartheid as anti-gospel', editorial, *Pro Veritate*, 15 August.

'The Christian Council: more support from member churches imperative/Christenraad: meer steun van lidkerke onontbeerlik', editorial, *Pro Veritate*, 15 September.

'Prohibition of Improper Interference Bill', press statement, 24 September.

'Report of the Director of the CI covering the Period 1st August 1965 to 31st July 1966', printed address, 26 September.

'Some reflections on the Prohibition of Improper Interference Bill, 1966', unpublished mimeographed paper, October.

'In reply to the criticism of A. P. Treurnicht', press statement, mimeographed, 22 November.

1967. 'Freedom in our Society Today', published address, University of Cape Town, Day of Affirmation of Academic and Human Freedom, 1 June 1967.

'Die Kerkbode, die Christelike Instituut en die NGK, *Pro Veritate*, 15 August.

'CI Director's Report covering the Period 1st September 1966 to 31st August 1967', printed report, 12 September.

'Christelike Instituut en die Kerk', address at Stellenbosch on 21 September, in *Pro Veritate*, 15 December.

The Afrikaner and Race Relations, a public address in December, published by the South African Institute of Race Relations, Johannesburg.

1968. 'Our coloured community: a challenge of conscience to the church and the South African community', address to the Institute of Citizenship, 28 September, in *Pro Veritate*, 15 January.

'CI Director's Report covering the Period 1st August 1967 to 31st July 1968', printed report, 12 August.

1969. 'Our concern is for the salvation of South Africa. An open letter to the Prime Minister of the Republic of South Africa', with Bishop Bill Burnett, in *Ministry*, 9, 1.

'Endorsing out of clergymen/Uit-endossering van evangelie-dienaars', guest editorial, *Pro Veritate*, 15 January.

'Die volk/The people', guest editorial, *Pro Veritate*, 15 February.

'Bantoekerke soek dringend hulp', *Pro Veritate*, 15 April.

'What Calvin really stood for', *Sunday Times*, 2 May.

'Waaroor het dit eintlik vir Calvyn gegaan?', *Pro Veritate*, 15 May.

'CI Director's Report for the Year July 1968 to June 1969', printed report, 8 August.

1970. 'Progress towards justice and peace', *Pro Veritate*, 15 March.

'Die Afrikaanse kerke en die komende verkiesing', *Pro Veritate*, 15 April.

'CI Director's Report for the year August 1969 to July 1970', printed report, 31 August.

'Die skeiding van die weë/The WCC aid to liberation movements', *Pro Veritate*, 15 October.

'Apartheid Morally Unacceptable', unpublished address, probably given in Johannesburg, 10 November.

'Apartheid is in stryd met God', *Ster*, 13 November.

'The "Bantu Administration Act Draft Bill"', press statement, 18 December.

1971. 'Menschenrechte für Südafrika: gesprach mit C. F. Beyers Naudé', *Evangelische Kommentare*, 4, 1971.

'Wendepunkt in Südafrika', *Luther Monatshefte*, 10, 1971.

'State Action against Clergy and Church Workers', statement authorised by the Board of Management of the CI, 25 February.

'Konfrontasie tussen kerk en staat', *Pro Veritate*, 15 March.

'Black Anger and White Power in an Unreal Society', The 1971 Edgar Brookes Lecture, University of Natal, Pietermaritzburg, 19 May.

'CI Director's Report for the Period 1st August 1970 to 31st July 1971', 20 July.

'South Africa Is a Violent Society', unpublished mimeographed address, Durban, 5 August.

'Die kleurling waarheen?' address to SAAK, University of Stellenbosch, 5 May, in *Pro Veritate*, 5 August.

'Wreedsame geweld', *Pro Veritate*, 15 November.
'Geloftedag: Christusfees of Baalfees? 'n Ope vraag aan Suid
    Afrika oor Gelofte Dag', written with Roelf Meyer, in sup-
    plement to *Pro Veritate*, 15 December.
1972. 'Die toekoms en . . . kleur, kolonialisme en kommunisme', *Pro
    Veritate*, 15 January.
'Reflections on resignation from the Broederbond', *Cape Argus*,
    17 July.
'CI Director's Report for the Period 1st August 1971 to 31st July
    1972', 31 August.
'South Africa tomorrow/Suid-Afrika môre', guest editorial, *Pro
    Veritate*, 15 November.
1973. 'Blanke ootmoed oor trekarbeid', address at the Rondebosch
    Common upon the arrival of the Pilgrimage for Family Life,
    in *Pro Veritate*, 15 February.
'The need for reform', speech in Durban on 12 July given in a
    series of Spro-cas lectures on the need for reform, in *Pro
    Veritate*, 15 July.
Statement by staff members of the CI as why they would not
    testify to the Schlebusch Commission of Inquiry, in *Sunday
    Times*, 11 August.
'CI Director's Report for the Period 1st August 1972 to 31st July
    1973', 31 August.
'Beyers Naudé – the free Afrikaner: Marshall Lee talks to Naudé,
    Daily Dispatch, 11 October.
''n Teken van solidariteit', speech upon receiving honorary
    doctorate at the Free University of Amsterdam, in *Pro Veri-
    tate*, 15 December.
'Memorandum on the pass laws, influx control and migrant
    labour', *South African Outlook*, December.
1974. 'Beyers Naudé's feeling of deep sadness: Naudé talks to Lambert
    Pringle', *Star*, 12 January.
'Metropolitan Portugal', guest editorial, *Pro Veritate*, 15 May.
'"Afsonderlike ontwikkeling" op Bybelse gronde', address be-
    fore DATUM 80, an open forum on the land question in
    Pretoria, 18 April, in *Pro Veritate*, 15 June.
'White reaction evades the issue', a CI statement on the Ham-
    manskraal resolution on conscientious objection, signed by
    Naudé, Brown, and Meyer, in *Pro Veritate*, 15 August.
'CI Director's Report for the Period August 1, 1973 to July 31,
    1974', 31 August.
'Nie meer "ons mense" nie', *Pro Veritate*, 15 October.
Address at press conference in Dreibergen, Netherlands, on
    returning from receiving the Reinhold Niebuhr Award in
    Chicago, in *EcuNews*, 27 November.
1975. 'Christianity and nationalism in the light of Pentecost', in T.

Sundmeier (ed.), *Church and Nationalism in South Africa* (Johannesburg, 1975).

'Christian involvement in the struggle for human rights and justice', acceptance speech for R. Niebuhr Award for 1974 at the University of Chicago, in *Pro Veritate*, 15 January.

'Beyers Naudé responds', an address at the University of the Witwatersrand, Johannesburg, on the CI being declared an Affected Organisation, in *South African Outlook*, June.

'Statement on behalf of the Board of Management of the CI to refute allegations of the Le Grange Commission', 28 May, in *Pro Veritate*, 15 June.

'Statement with Prof. C. Gardner on behalf of the CI after reading the Le Grange Commission Report', 29 May, in *Pro Veritate*, 15 June.

'Die stem van swart Christelike besorgheid/The voice of black Christian concern', guest editorial, *Pro Veritate*, 15 August.

'A Glimpse into the Future of South Africa', address at the University of Natal, 22 August.

'CI Director's Report for the Period August 1 1974 to July 31 1975', 29 August.

'Enthusiastic response to CI's financial need', *CI News*, August.

'The Individual and the State in South Africa', address read in absentia before the Royal Institute of International Affairs, London, 16 December.

1976. 'Justice in South Africa: an interview with C. F. Beyers Naudé', *Reformed Journal*, December–January.

'Die gaping steeds groter', *Pro Veritate*, 15 February.

'Foreign Investment in South Africa', joint statement by Chief G. Buthelezi and Naudé, mimeographed, 10 March.

'A national convention on Christian concern for southern Africa. A response by white churchmen', by Naudé, Desmond Hurley and Timothy Bavin, in *Pro Veritate*, 15 March.

'On majorities and minorities', address to the Natal Indian Congress, in *Pro Veritate*, 15 April.

'Introduction' to *Detention and Détente in South Africa* (Johannesburg), 30 April.

'Responsible liberation', address in absentia to J'Accuse Club, Holland, 4 May, in *Pro Veritate*, 15 May.

'The South Africa I want', address at University of Cape Town, 3 June, in *Pro Veritate*, 15 June.

'Sequel to Soweto', *Pro Veritate*, 15 August.

'Foreign investment in South Africa', address at Rhodes University, in *Pro Veritate*, 15 August.

'Introduction' to *South Africa: A Police State* (Johannesburg), 20 September.

'The Director's Report (1975–1976)', in *Pro Veritate*, 15

October.

'Message to Christians in Europe', 31 October.

1977. 'The Afrikaner as rebel', address at the University of Cape Town, 4 February, in *Pro Veritate*, 15 March.

'Easter Message', 4 April.

'Christian ministry in a time of crisis', address to Federal Theological Seminary, 16 March, in *Pro Veritate*, 15 April.

'Press release on the banning of Mrs. Oshadi Phakathi', *Pro Veritate*, 15 April.

'Statement of the CI re the Report of the Van Rooyen Commission, May 24', *EcuNews*, 8 June.

'The strategic position of the teacher in relation to Christianity', address to the Transvaal United Teachers' Association, May, in *Pro Veritate*, 15 June.

'Beyers Naudé reports: Director's report to the AGM of the CI, 12 September', *Pro Veritate*, 15 September.

1978–1984: the years of silence. As a banned person Beyers Naudé could not publish or be quoted in South Africa.

Afrikaner and reformed

Afrikaner piety and dissent
JAAP DURAND

Since the publication of Dunbar Moodie's book on Afrikaner civil religion,[1] there has been a lot of research on this phenomenon, especially as far as the relationship between Dutch Reformed theology and civil religion is concerned. In spite of some deviations from the Moodie thought-pattern his main line of argument is substantiated by most researchers: that three major forces each in its own way played a definite role in helping to shape the Afrikaner civil religion – Scottish evangelicalism, Kuyperian so-called neo-Calvinism, and secular romantic nationalism.[2]

The different analyses of how these three spiritual forces interacted to produce the final form of Afrikaner civil religion in the late 1940s and 1950s, make almost compulsive reading. The impression that one gets is one of inevitability. Given the interplay of these forces with Afrikanerdom's political and socio-economic history, the end result seems to be an unsurprising and foregone conclusion. The only surprising thing in this development is that a few dissident voices were at all able to make themselves heard within the seemingly monolithic theological structure of the Dutch Reformed Church. It is true that dissident Afrikaner theologians were few and far between, but they were nevertheless there, long before the political and social climate encouraged dissidence of any sort.

Theological dissent and neo-Calvinism

As far as I know no serious research has been done on the phenomenon of theological dissidence within Afrikaans Reformed circles during the final phase in the development of the Afrikaner civil religion. The reason for this lack of research or interest or both can be twofold. The first and most obvious is the absence of any significant numbers of dissidents during this period. The second and less obvious reason is that on the face of it there were at that time no clear-cut divergent theological trends within Afrikanerdom; this lack makes any attempt on the researcher's part to find a theological explanation for the existence of the few dissidents a hazardous undertaking. The emphasis falls on 'on the face of it' and 'clear-cut'. Although, as I have pointed out in the beginning, two Reformed theological traditions – Scottish evangelicalism and Kuyperian neo-Calvinism – converged as it were in the final shaping of Afrikaner civil religion and its supportive theology (romanticism was strictly speaking not *theological* by nature), followers of the two traditions did not differ on those social and racial issues that formed the raison d'être of Afrikaner civil religion. This is precisely the reason why they could converge despite differences in emphasis as far as other more 'theological' questions were concerned.

Comparing the Afrikaner theological situation during those years with what happened in the theological arena during the German church struggle under the Nazi regime will perhaps convey more clearly what I am trying to explain. The theological origin of the Confessing Church could never have been in doubt. Karl Barth's Christological concentration and his emphasis on the centrality of Christ, his crusade against all forms of natural theology and his criticism of religion itself, formed the immediate springboard for the Barmen Declaration and the subsequent theological split in the German churches. In Dietrich Bonhoeffer, the most significant of the 'dissident' theologians in Nazi Germany, the same Christological concern and deep conviction that theology should be Christ-centred *and* world-centred – 'it is only in the midst of the world that Christ is Christ'[3] – gave rise to his implacable resistance to the German Christian version of civil religion based on a theology of creation orders. In South Africa, on the other hand, such a clear-cut distinction between opposing theologies was absent during the specific phase of Afrikaner theological development that we are discussing. True, in the Afrikaner version of Kuyperian theology more than one trend reminds us of the German *Ordnungstheologie,* because of the use of Kuyper's cosmological apparatus and the subsequent emphasis on the orders of creation, but it was never as crude as the German version. At the same time Kuyperian cosmology was combined with orthodox Reformed Christology in such a way that any effort to subject theology to a Christological criticism was defused right from the start. As a net result, the dormant natural theology in the Afrikaner Kuyperian version was never recognised for what it was. One of the great tragedies in the development of Afrikaner Reformed theology in the three decisive decades of its evolvement (1930–60) was that Karl Barth's criticism of religion and of natural theology was never really heard or given any opportunity to be heard in those Kuyperian circles that needed it most.

It must be clear from the above that in my opinion the Kuyperian line of tradition was not able to, and in fact did not, produce critical and dissident voices in a period when the historical circumstances and the general spiritual climate were not conducive to this kind of thinking. It was only after external circumstances had started to change that a new note could be heard in the utterances of adherents to this line of tradition.

It can of course be argued that I am begging the question by simply asserting the impotence of the Kuyperian tradition in South Africa to produce a dissident, without explaining the reasons why I make this assertion. To make the factual observation that the Kuyperian tradition did not produce a dissident voice is something completely different from stating that *it could not do so,* especially in the light of the well-known Kuyperian motto that all spheres of life, including the social and political, should be brought under the control of Christ and His Word. In the next few paragraphs I shall make a brief attempt to remedy this inadequacy in my presentation, before returning to the other possible source of dissent, the Scottish or Murray evangelical tradition.

Two main reasons can be given for the Kuyperian neo-Calvinist inability to steer clear of the dangers of a civil religion and an apartheid theology. The first is historical, while the second has more to do with the hermeneutical and structural problems of this specific theology.

Historically speaking, Kuyperian theology was introduced to the South African scene in the second and especially in the third decade of the twentieth century when Afrikanerdom was in a sense looking for a theology that was not only Reformed and orthodox but also able to accommodate a fastgrowing nationalism characterised by an aversion to English domination and a fear of eventual black domination. Kuyperian theology seemed to fit or was *made* to fit this need. An increasing number of young Dutch theologians as well as their counterparts in the Reformed Church (Gereformeerde Kerk) visited the Free University of Amsterdam, the bastion of Kuyperianism, and when the decisive time came for a theological response to the Afrikaner's self-understanding in his national, social and political circumstances, Kuyperian theology and cosmology had already deeply entrenched itself in the Reformed Church and had won a significant and influential following there. The aftermath of the heresy trial of Professor J. du Plessis of the Theological Seminary at Stellenbosch enhanced Kuyperian theology still further as the guardian of the orthodox Reformed faith in the church. It was, after all, the more Kuyperian-oriented theologians and students who in the years immediately following the trial took up the cause of the opponents of Professor Du Plessis's seemingly liberal and unorthodox theological views. Through this development it became increasingly difficult for any Afrikaner theologian openly to oppose the Kuyperian system in its South African version. Opposition to it could not only be misconstrued as treason to the Afrikaner cause, but also as an indication of theological unreliability and as a threat to the Reformed tradition as such.

By the end of the forties, at the time when the National Party took political control in South Africa, the Kuyperians had already gained the upper hand in all the theological debates that concerned the social and political structuring of South African society. The rather more pragmatic approach to these issues by the remaining non-Kuyperian theologians in the Dutch Reformed Church was officially obliterated by resolutions that opted for an approach in which 'biblical principles' were to be applied to the social spheres of the people's life *(volkslewe)* in South Africa.

The idea that the Word of God contains eternal and unchanging norms or 'principles' for the whole of life, combined with a very biblicistic approach to the Bible in which little respect for context or historical situation is shown, is the second reason why it was almost impossible for a South African Kuyperian suddenly to come out in opposition to the theological and political development of his day. Once certain principles have been established as biblical, opposition to those principles can easily be seen as opposition to the Bible itself. But, after all, why would our Kuyperian in any case oppose these principles if they seem to support the notions and aspirations of the group that he belongs to?

The ease with which Kuyper's theology was transplanted to the South African soil and was adapted to the Afrikaner's national struggle and aspirations is not surprising in view of the basic concepts of his theology and cosmology that were presented as biblical principles: the separate spheres of life (such as church, state, family) as part of the order of creation, the principle of sovereignty for each of these social spheres, and, last but not the least, the principle of diversity as a principle rooted in creation. Although Kuyper himself never mentioned the people *(volk)* as one of the social spheres with its own sovereignty, the idea itself was not alien to his cosmology, and therefore made it easy for Afrikaner academics to see the people as a separate social sphere with its own structure and purpose grounded in the ordinances of God's creations.[4] And as God willed the diversity of peoples, He preserves their identity. From here the rest follows: an apartheid theology based on the biblical principle of the diversity of peoples. Two parts of Scripture (Gen. 11 and Acts 17: 26) could be – and were – quoted to substantiate the claim that diversity is indeed an unchanging norm, and the whole fortress of apartheid theology became impregnable from outside, let alone to anybody trying to undermine it from inside. For a real Kuyperian to have challenged these concepts would have been theological suicide.

The pietist and missionary tradition

In the preceding paragraphs I have tried to explain the reason why the Kuyperian tradition was not able to produce any critical and dissident voice of consequence. The question now remains: from what background did the few come who did in fact protest against the direction in which things were going?

The obvious answer to this question is of course the Murray evangelical and pietist tradition. However, the answer is not so obvious as it seems. It has already been observed that the supporters of this evangelical tradition did not differ on those social and racial issues that lay at the heart of Afrikaner civil religion. Afrikaner national aspirations and the idea of the calling of the Afrikaner people were just as prevalent in this group as amongst the Kuyperians. In some instances they went further than the latter in the very close identification of the people and the church (the *volkskerk* concept). As far as this particular issue is concerned, the Kuyperians were very careful, in theory at least, to steer clear of the idea of a *volkskerk,* a restraint that was not so evident in the evangelical tradition. It is therefore necessary to have a closer look at this tradition, before we proceed to look at the small handful of dissident theologians.

When the Scottish ministers came to the Cape Colony they brought with them an orthodox evangelical piety that did not differ substantially from Reformed evangelicalism (a combination of pietism and Calvinist orthodoxy), which had already become a clearly distinguishable movement in the Dutch Reformed Church through the labours of ministers like Van Lier and Vos.

A marked characteristic of this 'movement' was its missionary zeal directed towards the slaves and the indigenous black population, a quality that was strengthened by the arrival of the Scottish ministers in the 1830s and the subsequent evangelistic revivals in the Cape in the 1860s. Outbreaks of communal ecstasy occurred in village after village throughout the Cape, and the church was filled with a contagious enthusiasm for Christian witness. In the course of time the revivalistic side of the church's life was somewhat tempered, and by the turn of the century three groups, broadly speaking, could be distinguished: a smaller, more pietistic and revivalistic group, a bigger group that was less revivalistic but nevertheless evangelistic in its approach, and thirdly a group that actually cut across the first two groups, comprising a substantial number of ministers and church members who took the missionary calling of the church seriously and kept the original missionary flame alive in the Dutch Reformed Church. For future clarity I shall restrict itself to a very brief discussion of those characteristics of the second and the third groups that are of significance for this essay.

As far as the second group is concerned there was in terms of theology and spirituality very little to distinguish them from the main stream of evangelicalism prevalent amongst most of the Protestant churches in the Cape Colony during the latter half of the nineteenth century. However, because of the awakening of Afrikaner nationalism, especially after the South African War (1899–1902), the idea of a *volkskerk* gradually took root among adherents of this group. Among the full-blooded pietists and revivalists this never happened, because pietism, with its emphasis on a vertical relationship with God, has no particular interest in national identity. The *volkskerk* idea was much more than a merely theoretical identification of church and people. It took concrete shape in the church's concern for the plight of the Afrikaner after the war, and its efforts to combat poverty. During the first three decades of the twentieth century the poor white problem became one of the major issues for the Dutch Reformed Church.[5] In this action the church demonstrated its conviction that the vertical relationship with God included horizontal social relationships, in other words that the gospel has definite socio-economic consequences. But, and this is important, in most instances the concern for man's social (and political) needs stopped with the Afrikaner. There is no evidence that there was within this group a clear vision of the social needs and problems of non-Afrikaners, especially the blacks who were even worse off than the poor whites.

The only possible place where this restricted view could be overcome was amongst the members of our third group, who kept the missionary spirit of Van Lier and De Vos alive in the Dutch Reformed Church. After all, it was impossible to concern oneself with the spiritual needs of the black people without coming across and doing something about their very real earthly needs. Or was it perhaps possible? On the available evidence no clear-cut answer can be given. On the one hand there are strong indications that members of this third group were not blind to the plight of the blacks or to injustices done to them. As early as 1860 the Rev. D. P. M. Huet, who described himself as a zealous adherent of the missionary cause and a defender of those who were hated because of their missionary work, denounced blatant discrimination against blacks in church and society.[6] At a later stage articles and letters in *De Volksbode,* a publication in which most of the missionary-minded ministers in the Dutch Reformed Church voiced their ideas and concerns, leave no doubt that the authors were not guilty of an exclusive vertical spirituality. One remarkable example is found in a letter from 'Kolonist' in *De Volksbode* under the heading 'Ons volk'(Our people).[7] In this letter the writer reacted against an editorial in *De Zuid Afrikaan* which made no bones about the fact that the white colonists should have every piece of land, including the 'native areas' where anything could be gained for the general interest of the European race. 'Kolonist' responded as follows:

Does the white man have the right, merely because he is white and more civilised and stronger, summarily to remove a Kaffir tribe if he needs their land, or if the barbarian acts like a barbarian or gives any the least provocation? The majority of the English nation considers itself to be just as much superior to the Afrikaners as we consider ourselves to be above the Kaffirs. What would one say if they were now to declare: the higher race is entitled and is called, also in the interest of the lower race and of civilization in general, to clear up the Afrikaner and expropriate what belongs to them?

And then follows significantly:

I am first a Christian and then an Afrikaner. In other words, I hope that I belong to the true Afrikaners who place Christianity first and those who, even if at a certain stage they should be in danger of acting in conflict with their Christianity, will, once better informed, cease to do so. I only want us to treat the barbarians as people, which is how Christians would act, because injustice committed against them will be repaid even more certainly than when committed against those better able to look after themselves.

While on the one hand evidence like this can be found, on the other there were those who clearly tried to fulfil the Lord's commission in Matthew 28 in a more spiritual sense, not indicating (at least not openly) that the social and political implications of the gospel for the blacks were fully understood. It is significant in this regard that during the 1920s missionary-minded ministers tried to keep the interest in missions alive in the face of an encroaching concern in the church for poor whites, by pointing out that missionary work amongst the blacks would in the long run materially benefit the Afrikaner and its poor. Hardly any mention was made about the material needs of the blacks. A sort of schizophrenic attitude developed, in which the *volkskerk* idea created a formidable social consciousness as far as the own Afrikaner group was concerned, but as far as the blacks were concerned the church's calling was seen as spiritual with very little emphasis on the social side. What emphasis there was was confined mostly to the educational field. In this respect the Dutch Reformed Church truly excelled.

At face value we have little promise here for an eventual world-shattering protest against the course of Afrikaner theology and history – and of course the results *were* meagre. But still they were there, as I shall try to point out in a brief discussion of the few theologians who battled against the overwhelming tide of Afrikaner civil religion. There must therefore have been some hidden forces in this tradition that made dissent possible. In my opinion we have to look for these forces in this theologically much maligned pietism and the equally maligned idea of the Afrikaner's missionary calling.

Rebel theologians

During the 1940s and 1950s, when virtually all Afrikaner theologians and intellectuals subscribed to apartheid as an ideology, only Professor B. B. Keet and Professor Ben Marais rejected the idea that apartheid was theologically justifiable, although they conceded that there could be some practical reasons for racial segregation. In the late 1950s a few other tentative voices were also heard,[8] but the one person I should like to include in my discussion is Dr Beyers Naudé. Although it was only in the beginning of the 1960s that he emerged as the most significant Afrikaner opponent to apartheid, together with a new breed of young theologians in the Dutch Reformed Church, he was in fact a contemporary of Dr Ben Marais, while his spiritual struggle with these issues started in the latter half of the 1950s.[9]

Professor Keet came to the Theological Seminary of Stellenbosch, having received a doctorate at the Kuyperian stronghold, the Free University of Amsterdam. At the seminary, however, it soon became clear that he was no Kuyperian. In his theology the dogmatics of

Herman Bavinck set the tone, and in the heresy trial of Professor Du Plessis, Keet made it clear that he did not wish to side with the opponents of Du Plessis, although he did not support Du Plessis, at least not openly, in all aspects of his theology.

In 1939 Keet sounded his first warning about the growing enmity between white and black because of the resentment caused amongst 'non-whites' by the white agitation for racial segregation.[10] But it was only in 1949 that he joined battle in the *Kerkbode* with those theologians who tried to justify apartheid on biblical grounds. He criticised their way of using Scripture as a handbook containing direct instructions for national, economic, cultural and other issues, ignoring the fact that the Bible is a history of salvation.[11] Apartheid, he continued, could only be justified on practical grounds, taking in consideration the effects of sin in man's life. He realised that such a point of view could be considered weak, but he preferred it to a standpoint that made use of principles and then bent Scripture to accommodate them. Keet was no stranger to the idea of the calling of the Afrikaner people, but in this calling as the ultimate goal, he emphasised, apartheid could only be tolerated as a 'temporary measure, only adopted as the lesser of two evils' (referring to the sinful situation in which man lives and the animosity between people that results from it).[12] In 1955 Keet published his *Whither South Africa?*,[13] in which he more or less reiterated his *Kerkbode* views. This little booklet became a milestone in the short and almost insignificant history of Afrikaner theological dissidence in the face of a rampant ideology.

Professor Ben Marais joined Keet during the 1940s in his criticism of the Dutch Reformed Church's attempt to justify apartheid in the light of 'biblical principles'. As a matter of fact his first public statements in this regard were made before Keet's memorable *Kerkbode* articles. As a student of Keet in the beginning of the 1930s, Marais took an even more clearly anti-Kuyperian stance than his teacher, and became in the aftermath of the Du Plessis struggle the leader of the students who opted for a broader evangelical approach, reflecting as they saw it the true spirit of Du Plessis and the Dutch Reformed Church. Du Plessis's intense missionary involvement and ecumenical spirit enhanced his image amongst this group of students. No wonder that Marais's first disillusionment with Dutch Reformed racial policy happened at the world missionary conference of the International Missionary Council at Tambaram, Madras, in 1938, where the Dutch Reformed delegation stood alone in its defence of racial segregation against the rest of the Christian world.[14]

Upon his return to South Africa his appearance at so many different church meetings was characterised by his consistent opposition to a scriptural justification of apartheid. Like Keet, his own approach to the racial issue was strictly pragmatic: wherever Scripture does not give direct instructions for or against something, the Christian must act in the light of his understanding of his own specific situation. This meant, in fact, that the notion of apartheid based on the idea of the diversity of peoples could be tolerated under certain circumstances, but not as a permanent and static order of creation.

If we look back today at Keet and Marais, it seems as if there is nothing to get excited about, theologically speaking, until we realise the full import of any effort to dismantle the edifice of biblical apartheid in the South Africa of that period. These two men prepared the way for Marais's contemporary, Beyers Naudé, to rid himself of the shackles of a deadly and dangerous ideology, enabling him to go much further than they had ever dreamt of doing.

Beyers Naudé's background reflected clearly the evangelical Dutch Reformed tradition. His father, the Rev. J. Naudé, was a true-blooded evangelical of the old stock, and Beyers himself underwent a profound experience of spiritual conversion as a result of a series of Pentecostal sermons given by his father.[15] But at the same time Beyers's father was a man of very strong and firm nationalistic convictions, one of the few Boers who refused to lay down arms after the South African War. According to Beyers Naudé himself, his father never saw or experienced a conflict between the evangelical and nationalistic traditions.[16] As we have seen, the close identification of Afrikaner people and church was to a greater or lesser degree prevalent in evangelical circles. In this Beyers's father was no exception. At the same time he was very much involved in missionary work. In a certain sense he embodied the stereotype which I have sketched of an Afrikaner churchman who combined concern for the welfare of his own people with a very real commitment to the church's missionary work.

Coming from this background Beyers began his studies at Stellenbosch in 1932. He did not distinguish himself as a theological student, and today he does not hesitate to single out Keet as the one theological professor who had considerable influence on him, although – and this is significant – he also mentions G. B. A. Gerdener, his professor in church history and the history of missions.[17] His attitude towards the conservative professors who were all opponents of Du Plessis, namely Van Rooyen, Lategan and Malan, was decidedly negative.

The significance of Gerdener's name in this regard does not relate to his (Gerdener's) political or racial attitudes – Gerdener never became an open critic, like Keet, of the apartheid ideology – but to his missionary orientation, in which he reflected the spirit of Du Plessis and the evangelicals. The dividing line in those days was, according to Beyers Naudé, between the politically and nationally motivated Kuyperians on the one hand and the missionary-oriented followers of the evangelical tradition on the other, and he has no hesitation in positioning himself in the latter group.[18] The subsequent personal history of Beyers bears this out. His conflict with the South African political system originated in an intensive missionary involvement during the critical pre-Cottesloe years. His rebellion did not come from a clear and well-defined Reformed theological system, but from a deep Christian commitment to the missionary calling of the church, a commitment nurtured by the pietist and evangelical impetus of the Van Lier, Vos and Huet tradition in the Dutch Reformed Church.

The foregoing account of Keet, Marais and Naudé places them clearly within the broad and rather amorphous evangelical Dutch Reformed tradition. I deliberately use the term 'amorphous' to emphasise the fact that this tradition did not have a clear and well-defined theological system as had the later Kuyperians in their approach to social, cultural and political issues. This fact has been a source of much criticism against the Dutch Reformed Church, especially from the side of the Kuyperian-oriented Reformed Church (Gereformeerde Kerk), as well as of course from within its own ranks. In this criticism the pietist part of the tradition is singled out as the real culprit that kept the church 'other-worldly' and away from the social issues of the day. This criticism is a gross oversimplification, which is unfair to the tradition of Reformed pietism. The mere fact that resistance against the *way in which* the Afrikaner churches involved themselves socially and politically came, however belatedly, from an evangelical–pietist background should be a warning against too readily making pietism the scape-goat of all that went wrong in South Africa.

In his article on Afrikaner civil religion David Bosch says of pietism:

In a sense, then, pietism became a *negative* preparation for Afrikaner civil religion. It operated on a dualistic understanding of reality. The activities and forces at work in one part of reality could remain almost completely untouched by those which gave life to the other part. Pietism emphasised personal faith, and in doing so willy-nilly gave *carte blanche* to other forces to take over the nation's public life. [19]

This quotation reflects a theoretical as well as an historical evaluation of pietism in the development of Afrikaner civil religion. As far as the theoretical side is concerned, Bosch is correct, strictly speaking, but it must be emphasised that historically a pure theoretical pietism is nowhere to be found, least of all within the Reformed tradition in South Africa. Even pietists had to grapple with social issues, especially in a missionary situation where problems of a social, cultural and educational nature brought themselves ineluctably to the attention of the missionary church. The pietist's response to these problems was usually a *practical* one, because his type of 'vertical' spirituality kept him from going to Scripture too readily to find a normative answer to problems outside of the religious sphere. This attitude of course allows for factors other than those determined by the Christian faith to become operative in 'horizontal' relationships, something that indeed happened as we have already seen. But, and this is the point that I would like to make, the weakness of pietism can also be its greatest strength in a situation of social development and change. The pietist will be less likely to justify his social actions by an appeal to unchanging biblical principles or to use the historical situation in which he finds himself as a grid for biblical interpretation. The resistance of a Keet and Marais against the scriptural justification of apartheid bears this out. Although they were not pietists in the strict sense of the word, their evangelical–pietist background rebelled against identifying a social and political policy with biblical principles. They recognised the grid of interpretation. Ultimately they had a greater sense of the ongoing processes of history than their Kuyperian counterparts, who tried to mould history according to a set of fixed principles, supposedly derived from God's creation.

To this must be added the even more important fact that the missionary orientation in the evangelical–pietist tradition by its very nature gave rise to a deep commitment to the welfare of other people. Even though the original pietist concern was for the *spiritual* welfare of other peoples, it could not forever remain exclusively spiritual, as I have endeavoured to point out. It is not insignificant that when Beyers Naudé, introduced by his missionary interest to the appalling suffering of the blacks under the apartheid system, came forward with his controversial witness, he was joined in the early sixties by young white missionaries (as they were called then) from the Dutch Reformed Church and one or two others who had the same missionary interests as Beyers himself.

DRC schizophrenia

Earlier I referred to the Dutch Reformed Church's schizophrenia with regard to its concern for the social and political welfare of the Afrikaner people, on the one hand, and its apparent lack of concern for the same problems amongst blacks who were brought into the fold of the church through its missionary work, on the other hand. In a certain sense this schizophrenia was vicariously resolved in the person of Beyers Naudé. Two parallel lines merged in the realisation that the social and political implications of the gospel transcend the narrow confines of self-interest, and embrace all people.

It has always been a source of great wonder to many people outside the Dutch Reformed Church how it is possible that a church so committed to the missionary task can also be supportive of such an inhuman social and political system. The answer to this riddle is usually found in the fact that the missionary vision of the Dutch Reformed Church was so closely linked to the notion of the calling of the Afrikaner amongst the peoples of South Africa that the two things (mission and apartheid) became compatible. However, the recognition that they were indeed incompatible came from the very ranks of those who had originally talked about the calling of the Afrikaner but did not use the idea merely as a slogan for the theoretical safeguarding of Afrikaner identity. A truly missionary spirit had in the long run to break the fetters of an ideology.

After what has been said, one should be careful not to be too enthusiastic about the evangelical–pietist role in the theological resistance that emerged in the ranks of Afrikaner theologians in the 1960s. Its role was very modest, sometimes in a more negative than positive sense. Theologically it was too weak to resist the Kuyperian apartheid theology effectively. In that sense it did indeed give *carte blanche* to other forces to shape South African society. At a crucial stage of its development Afrikaner theology missed the corrective of a theology which was theoretically stronger than Reformed evangelical pietism and had less obvious weaknesses. In the beginning of this essay I identified Barthian Reformed theology as a theology that could have been such a corrective influence, in spite of many reservations that one could have about certain of its aspects. But this correction did not take place during the 1940s and 1950s. Awareness of a new theological paradigm with a definitely Barthian flavour only started to show itself amongst the young theologians of the sixties who to a greater or lesser degree joined forces with Beyers Naudé. In some instances a clear break occurred with the Kuyperian theological paradigm – the influence of the Dutch theologian, Berkouwer, played a big role in this process – while in others there was a more gradual development away from the orthodox evangelical tradition.

In an interesting and provocative article[20] Willem Vorster makes the statement that the shift from an apartheid theology to an anti-apartheid theology amongst Dutch Reformed theologians was not so much a shift in paradigm as in values. Vorster clearly refers to theological changes that started to come about during the latter half of the 1970s and the beginning of the 1980s, and it is his contention that general trends in political, economical, educational and other areas of society brought about a gradual shift in the value-system of a significant group of theologians and ministers of the Dutch Reformed Church.

Vorster's notion, justifiably emphasising the ever-present inclination to employ an interpretation grid in the use of Scripture, is certainly applicable as far as the still-present Kuyperian tradition in Afrikaner theology is concerned. Especially in the academic and theological circles of Potchefstroom and the Reformed Church (Gereformeerde Kerk) the shift from an apartheid theology to a less apartheid-oriented and more critical theology is evident. Here indeed one finds more a shift in values than in paradigm. However, Vorster overstates his case when he refers to apartheid theologians who have undergone a conversion to anti-apartheid theology because of a change in the value-system. The fact of the matter is that there is to my knowledge no apartheid theologian of significance who has undergone a clear conversion to an anti-apartheid theology.

Today's anti-apartheid Afrikaner theologians are the same small band of men who in the sixties and early seventies started to make use of a new paradigm in their quest for a new theological approach to South

Africa's problems, long before a shift in the value-system became evident. It is an everlasting tribute to the role of Beyers Naudé in South African church history that some of them, through his courageous example, chose to be branded dissidents at a time when it was decidedly unpopular to do so.

Rebels and prophets: Afrikaners against the system
WILLEM SAAYMAN

South Africa is making history anew. I do not mean our participation in the European War [World War 2]. That war is far away and foreign, and is waged for the sake of other interests, not ours. . . . But out of that declaration of war was born, as an act of God, something of lasting value. That is the bringing together of all nationalistically inclined elements, or, to put it differently, the political unification of Afrikanerdom.[1]

Thus did Dr D. F. Malan, leader of the National Party, describe Afrikaner unity on the eve of the 1948 apartheid victory. In this description we find reflected two presuppositions, widely held by Afrikaners, of the political system that has governed South Africa since 1948, namely that this system is the explicit will of God for South Africa, and that it is basically (almost exclusively) an Afrikaner system. The duty of all Afrikaners to this system was therefore also quite clear according to Dr Malan: they were soldiers in an army whose highest duty was to defend and protect the *volk*.[2]

Why was (and is) the political unity of Afrikanerdom (as a precondition for Afrikaner political victory) so important for Afrikaners? Mainly because this was seen as the only way in which the Afrikaner *volk* could survive amid the black multitudes of Africa. This survival of the Afrikaner *volk* was a divine imperative: the continued existence of the 'light of the gospel' in (southern) Africa depended on the survival of the Afrikaners as *volk*.[3] What is at stake, however, when the ideological rationalisation has been stripped away, is Afrikaner power – as was already made clear in a Broederbond circular in 1934: South Africa under exclusive Afrikaner rule.[4] This goal had to be (and was) pursued with single-minded devotion – indeed, as W. A. de Klerk pointed out, we are dealing here with a form of political messianism, an obsession with a 'holy vision, carried forward by a terrible urge to save mankind. . . . The inhuman death-dealing things which duty necessitates are only temporary. The end will justify all. The ultimate happiness, which is also served by extreme measures, will sanctify everything. Faith in the cause calls for unquestioning loyalty, whatever the present cost.'[5] This initial characterisation of Afrikaner Christian-Nationalism (though all too brief and too general in nature) is necessary if we want to evaluate Afrikaner opposition to a system created by Afrikaners.

Outsiders have often viewed Afrikanerdom as monolithic and uniform. This was so possibly because the leading Afrikaner politicians themselves set such a high store on unity and on presenting a united front against all opposition. In this regard, one can refer for example to Dr Malan, who entitled his memoirs, *Afrikaner Volkseenheid en My Ervarings op die Pad Daarheen* (The unity of the Afrikaner people and my experiences along the way). He also stated explicitly that the establishment of this unity (political and cultural) of the Afrikaner people, following on the divisions caused among other things by the Anglo-Boer War of 1889–1912 and the Rebellion of 1914, was *the* goal of his public labour of 40 years as a (Dutch Reformed) clergyman, newspaper editor, and politician.[6] Another reason for this prevalent view may have been the united front Afrikaners succeeded in maintaining in cultural affairs through the FAK (Federation of Afrikaans Cultural Organisations) and (at least since World War 2) in political affairs through the National Party. Finally, opponents from within Afrikaner ranks during these years were few and far between – perhaps mainly because the system demanded total submission, and dealt harshly with dissidents like B. B. Keet, Ben Marais, and later Albert Geyser and Beyers Naudé.

The late sixties saw the rise of the *verlig/verkramp* (enlightened/conservative) debate in Afrikaner ranks, producing the first signs that Afrikaner political unity (Malan's 'act of God') might be breaking up. Since the secession of the Herstigte Nasionale Party (HNP) in 1969, but especially since that of the Conservative Party (CP) in 1982 and the formation of the Afrikaner Volkswag (AV – Afrikaner Peoples' Guard – a 'cultural' organisation) in 1984, that unity has indeed been publicly shattered. Whereas during the seventies the National Party still drew between 83 per cent and 85 per cent of the Afrikaner vote in general elections, in the 1981 election the National Party drew only 63 per cent of the Afrikaner vote, with 33 per cent going to the right-wing parties (basically the HNP) and 4 per cent to the official opposition, the Progressive Federal Party (PFP).[7] This public demonstration confirmed what political leaders (such as Dr Malan) and cultural and church leaders have known all along: Afrikaner unity has always been threatened by divisions from within. (In Afrikaner mythology this inherently rebellious and individualistic streak is embodied in the crusty Thirstland Trekker who sits on his veranda somewhere in the African bushveld, sees the smoke rising from the chimney of a new neighbour's house far on the horizon, and orders his wife, '*Vrou*, pack up, let's move – the place is getting crowded!') It was because of the threatening divisions that Dr Malan had to work so hard for unity, and that dissenters were treated so harshly. As other writers deal more specifically with the subject of division in Afrikaner ranks, I am not going to explore it any further here. Suffice it to say that Afrikaner unity has been publicly shaken by opposition from within the ranks.

The question that concerns us here is: how significant is this division in Afrikanerdom? Does this opposition signify the beginning of the end of Afrikaner supremacy and the policy of apartheid?

In a paper entitled 'Die Afrikaner as rebel' (The Afrikaner as a rebel) which Beyers Naudé read in 1977, he was still quite hopeful that Afrikaner opposition could bring about decisive change in South Africa.[8] Indicating clearly the crisis situation brought about by the racial policies of the Afrikaner, Naudé argued that true liberation of the Afrikaner *volk* would come about only if sufficient numbers of Afrikaners themselves were willing openly to oppose the suffocating policies and to expose the false ideology of racial supremacy. He realised how difficult it would be for Afrikaners to oppose the political status quo, but did not consider it an 'idle dream' only. Have the changes which have taken place, the divisions which have come about, brought Beyers Naudé's hope any closer to realisation? In order to attempt an answer to this question, it is necessary to distinguish various schools of thought among Afrikaners more clearly.

Perhaps the easiest to identify are the various right-wing groups. They are still imbued with the pure apartheid vision as propounded especially by Strydom and Verwoerd, in which separation between the races is carried to its absolute logical conclusion – all blacks, coloureds and Indians having their own 'spheres of geographical sovereignty' (homelands), and South Africa becoming in truth a white man's country. They are of the opinion that the present regime, especially since P. W. Botha took over the leadership, has become unfaithful to this ideal, among other reasons by including coloured(s) and Indian(s) in the white cabinet and accepting the permanence of (at least some) urban blacks in white South Africa. It is this view which has led to the formation of the HNP, the CP, the AV and the AWB (Afrikaner Resistance Movement). We have here no rejection of the ultimate goal of Afrikaner political hegemony; on the contrary, we have a massive and open confirmation of that goal.

A second group, at this stage still the largest, is comprised of *verligte* (enlightened) Afrikaners. One will find quite a variety of emphases among them, but there are, in my opinion, two common features in particular which characterise them as *verligtes*. In the first place there is a realisation that white Afrikaners will not be able to maintain political power on their own according to the exclusive apartheid blueprint. Various other groups, including even coloureds, Indians and some middle-class blacks, therefore have to be co-opted on a limited scale and with great care so as not to let political power slip from Afrikaner hands. The second feature is this. As we have already been pointed out, the Afrikaner system is an inclusive whole (it includes political, cultural and religious dimensions), which has to be pursued with total devotion. As the Afrikaner middle-class (*burgerstand*) grew in conjunction with increasing urbanisation and growing Afrikaner political and economic power during the mid-century,[9] the system came to be characterised more and more by middle-class puritan morality. (Examples include stricter legislation against sports and recreation on Sundays, and stricter censorship of books and films.) *Verligte* Afrikaners find this enforcement of middle-class morality suffocating and unsophisticated, and therefore rebel against it. There is, however, no fundamental rejection of the ultimate goal of the maintenance of Afrikaner political hegemony. The furthest some of them would be prepared to go, in accordance with the strategy of co-option, would be (sometimes vociferous) protest against the constraints on free social and cultural intercourse with upper-class blacks and black intellectuals (for example, campaigns to open theatres and restaurants for all races). Although it can be said therefore that *verligtes* oppose some aspects of the Afrikaner system as envisaged by Malan, Strydom and Verwoerd, in another sense they are the true heirs of the system, as they are the present-day custodians of Afrikaner political supremacy.

There is a third group that can be identified. The distinguishing characteristic of their opposition to the system is the fact that it is aimed at the central pillar of that system: the goal of the maintenance (for pseudo-theological or economic reasons) of Afrikaner political power. They do not oppose some aspects of the apartheid policy only; in other words, they do not call for some minor or major *amendments* to be made. Rather, they realise that apartheid itself (or any policy based on racial separation and dominance, by whatever name it may be called to disguise this fact) has to be eliminated. This kind of opponent of the Afrikaner system has been few and far between – not least because Afrikaners deal harshly with Afrikaner dissidents to the 'left' of the National Party; and also because the Nationalists have been very successful in portraying such opponents as opponents of God and of the Bible – and few Afrikaners are willing to run *that* gauntlet. Because of the radical nature of their opposition to the system, these opponents perhaps merit to be called prophets. As has already been said, they have been few; yet, prophets there were: some who can perhaps better be called precursors of the prophets (for reasons which are explained in Jaap Durand's essay), like Professors B. B. Keet and Ben Marais; to be followed by the prophets themselves, minor and major ones, with the main prophetic inspiration emanating from Beyers Naudé.

Before attempting to evaluate this Afrikaner opposition to the apartheid system we should deal with an intriguing question, one that has not been studied adequately yet: what is it that distinguishes these Afrikaner prophets from *verligte* and right-wing Afrikaners? What is it that brought them to such open opposition against their own system? It is not idle curiosity that prompts this question. If real change is to come about in South Africa, and an increasingly bloody confrontation between the races is to be averted, we need a better understanding of the processes and dynamics of fundamental change in the Afrikaner psyche. What follows here is admittedly subjective, based on impressions and personal experience, and therefore no more than a preliminary exploration. At the same time I am convinced that it is not invalid either; indeed, part of it is borne out by Durand's thoroughgoing analysis. In answering the question then, the following considerations can be pointed out:

(1) There is in Afrikaner, specifically Dutch Reformed, piety a strain deeply influenced by the Moravian pietist tradition (Count von Zinzendorf) and Scottish evangelicalism (Dr Andrew Murray),[10] in which the traditional pietistic withdrawal from the world is strongly accentuated. In other words, the 'Christian' component of Afrikaner Christian-Nationalism tends to be emphasised more strongly than the 'nationalistic' component. Generally this evangelical pietism leads to non-involvement in all 'worldly' matters such as politics, but (as Durand also points out) circumstances may sometimes decree differently. Nearly all the Afrikaner prophets thus far have come from this evangelistic – pietistic background or had a 'missionary' involvement or both.

(2) The evangelistic– pietistic background, it seems to me, has to be complemented by a *real* encounter with the black world. Apartheid has been devilishly successful in establishing two different worlds in South Africa, a white world and a black world. The separation is so complete that these two worlds might as well have been continents apart. (In a discussion between black and white church councils in Pretoria recently, a 70-year-old Afrikaner elder of the DRC confessed that he knew his way around many of the big cities of the Western world, but if asked to drive to Mamelodi, a well-known black township outside Pretoria, he would not even know in which direction to start looking.) As a result, most South African whites deal with blacks only in the white environment, on white terms, and in a master–servant relationship. The opportunity of encountering articulate blacks as equals and in a normal human situation is virtually non-existent. Yet an encounter with the very human aspirations of black South Africans, and a discovery of the fact that the most radical resistance to apartheid is often fired by an idealism based on the central tenets of the Christian tradition, seems to be an essential prerequisite for an Afrikaner to break decisively with his or her ideologically inspired Christian-Nationalist way of life. This essential prerequisite is often absent in the make-up of *verligte* rebels, who often 'dialogue' with selected blacks (mostly homeland leaders, Inkatha members, and the like) in a 'dialogue insured against risk' because the ultimate article of Afrikaner belief, the maintenance of Afrikaner political hegemony, is withheld from fundamental questioning.[11]

(3) A very important change which has taken place in the lives of these Afrikaner prophets is a growth in *humanisation*, understood as the process of attaining that genuine humanity which became real in and through the life, death and resurrection of the new man, Jesus Christ. In Him, God reveals and restores to us our true humanity, our identity as

men and women created in His image, as people committed to human-kind's struggle for liberation and the fullness of life.[12] Because of the system of racial separation, South Africans tend to depersonalise (and dehumanise) people of race groups other than their own, to see them mainly as impersonal 'blocs' – 'coloureds', 'whites', 'Africans', and so on. One often hears white South Africans complain, for example, how difficult they find it to match names to individual black faces ('all these blacks look alike, you know'). And because of the racial superiority inculcated in white South Africans as a result of apartheid, they tend somehow to deny blacks their full humanity. So whites in general, and Afrikaners in particular, have to *learn* to regard and experience black people as fully human, in the process discovering how our own (white) humanity has become warped because of our basically racist society and way of life. If this does not happen, we cannot have genuine human community, liberation, and fullness of life in South Africa. It can be argued that there are especially two important stimuli for this growth in humanisation: the encounter with the black world (discussed in the previous paragraph), and a rediscovery of the *oikoumene*, the riches of the whole people of God in all the earth.

(4) Afrikaans Christians have been isolated from the ecumenical movement, both inside and outside South Africa, since 1961, when the Hervormde church (NHK) and the Cape and Transvaal synods of the DRC withdrew from the WCC in the wake of the Cottesloe Consulta-tion. This isolation, in the course of time, lapsed into confrontation, as more and more the (irrational) conviction grew in Afrikaans churches that the ecumenical movement in general and the WCC in particular were tools employed by Soviet Russia to engineer eventual Communist domination of the world. The result is that the theological climate in Afrikaner churches is extremely isolationist and introverted, based on the conviction that they do not really need Christians in other countries; they (Afrikaans Christians) know what the Bible teaches. In any case, liberal Christians in the ecumenical movement are only out to destroy real 'biblical faith'. It is noteworthy that all the Afrikaner prophets are people with an ecumenical consciousness and experience of ecumenical contact both inside and outside South Africa (especially with black Christians). This is very necessary in order to have the warped ideologi-cal component of the peculiar 'theological' basis of apartheid exposed. As this serves as a corrective to the generally held Dutch Reformed anthropology, it also makes an essential contribution to the growth in humanisation.

(5) Finally, nearly all the prophets share an encounter with the repressive might of Afrikanerdom, especially as it is often mobilised by the secret Afrikaner Broederbond (AB). A number of authoritative analyses of the sinister role played by the AB have been published in the past few years.[13] It is unnecessary, therefore, in this essay to deal extensively with the organisation and the role it plays in mobilising

Afrikaner power to punish or reward. What must be pointed out, though, is the fact that an *open* confrontation with the Afrikaner political establishment seems to be one of the facts separating the prophets from other Afrikaner rebels and dissidents. Such a confrontation is not a prerequisite for *becoming* an opponent and critic of the system; it does seem, though, as if it has been a final confirmation of the fundamental alienation from Christian–National Afrikanerdom which had already taken place. This trend manifested itself in the history of one of the precursors, Professor B. Marais,[14] and probably reached its nadir (or culmination, depending on one's point of view) in the history of Beyers Naudé. *Verligte* rebels, on the other hand, either remain respected members of the AB, so that their (superficial) criticism is benignly tolerated (as one of the signs of the openness and tolerance of the system), or else are protected from the full wrath of Afrikanerdom (and the AB) exactly because they do not threaten Afrikanerdom's most fundamental goal: the maintenance of Afrikaner political hegemony.

In conclusion: What can be said in 1985 about Beyers Naudé's hopes, expressed in 1977, that Afrikaner rebels themselves would confront and decisively change the apartheid system? Is the new constitution, and the sight of coloureds and Indians taking their seats in the historic bastion of white political power, the Houses of Parliament, not a clear indication that we are witnessing the end of institutional racism in South Africa, and by implication therefore the end of ideologically determined Afrikaner supremacy? Afrikaner society certainly does not reveal as monolithic a character as some years ago. That we are witnessing the end of Afrikaner political hegemony is, however, in my opinion extremely doubtful. There still exists, among verligte Nationalists, as well as among right-wing conservatives, unity of purpose on one subject: the maintenance of Afrikaner political supremacy. To quote but two examples: Dr G. Viljoen, powerful Cabinet Minister and representative of the mainstream National Party, openly states that any dispensation in which white political supremacy is undermined is unacceptable. Giliomee is correct, therefore, in pointing out that the 'Afrikaner identity' which has to be protected, as defined by leading Afrikaner ideologues such as Viljoen, is nothing but a code-word for political hegemony.[15] Wimpie de Klerk, editor of *Rapport* and Potchefstroom-trained theologian, widely regarded as a leading *verligte*, declares that the 'ethnic basis' (read, racial separation) of schools, residential areas, political and other matters, is a non-negotiable, which will have to remain legally entrenched.[16] What *has* changed is the way in which white Afrikaner supremacy is publicly justified. Afrikaner spokesmen now argue that the entrenched privileged position of whites is the precondition for the economic and political welfare of *all* in South Africa; without this, political chaos will reign and the economy of the entire subcontinent will collapse. White Afrikaners can therefore continue to claim the exclusive right to lay down the terms for change in South Africa and, what is more, can do so in a much more acceptable idiom (one that white English-speaking business leaders can easily identify with). What we are witnessing in the 'new constitutional dispensation', therefore, is not the radical revision of Afrikaner racial politics Beyers Naudé so fervently hoped for in 1977. Rather we seem to be witnessing the birth of a new alliance, brought about by Afrikaner initiative and carefully controlled by Afrikaner political power, of *verligte* Afrikaners, English business people, and a minority of coloureds, Indians and black home-land leaders. This alliance is more palatable especially to liberal English-speaking South Africans (as was confirmed by their massive support for the National Party during the 1984 referendum), but the end result is still that Afrikaner hands firmly control the levers of political power. As for the black majority, they are still out in the cold, as is evidenced by the harassment of the UDF and the refusal of the South African government to negotiate with the ANC.

All this does not necessarily imply that Afrikaners are quite unrepentant and that prophetic calls like that of Beyers Naudé in 1977 are in vain. What it does show clearly, in my opinion, is the need to be realistic when thinking about political change in South Africa. For decades now, Afrikaners have been told by their political and spiritual leaders that apartheid can be justified from Scripture, indeed that racial separation and white (Afrikaner) supremacy are clearly God's will for South Africa. This conviction does not belong to the past yet and is still widespread among Afrikaners, who have not been secularised to the same extent as their cousins in Western Europe and North America; they remain more susceptible to a pseudo-theological ideology such as this.

Whoever wants to bring about real change in the social, economic and political structures of South Africa will have to deal with racism at this fundamental, ideological level. One important element of the Afrikaner ideology of racial separation is (Dutch) Kuyperian neo-Calvinism. Indeed, Afrikaners for a long time prided themselves on their Calvinist heritage, stretching in an unbroken line via the truly Reformed and Calvinist Voortrekkers, right back to Jan van Riebeeck. The falseness of this image has been clearly exposed in the past few years.[17] Yet Kuyperian neo-Calvinism *did* play an important role at a much later stage (from the end of the nineteenth century onwards) in the growth of Afrikaner nationalism, which eventually culminated in the 1948 apartheid victory of the National Party. However, Bosch clearly points out the distortion that Calvin and Kuyper underwent in the process. The essential Kuyperian Christian-Nationalism in South Africa 'came to mean *Afrikaner* nationalism. It was not understood as the embryo of an all-inclusive *South African* nationalism but as the nationalism of an exclusive group' which could be, and had to be, maintained through separation. 'Though the hopes of some were that the National Party would be a Christian political party strictly according to the Kuyperian model, the truly constituent element, as time went by, was not loyalty to the Calvinist cause but to the cause of the Afrikaner.'[18] The prophetic call to Afrikaners to oppose a system which is inhuman and which is heading inevitably towards disaster thus cannot be a simple call of conversion to Christ and his gospel, or a call to return to true Reformed principles. Most Afrikaners believe that their policy of racial separation is *already* firmly grounded in the word of Christ, and that their version of the Reformed faith is the only true remnant of Reformed Calvinism in an evil world. This conviction has to be confronted seriously and exposed relentlessly. Whether there is still any chance of success amid growing fear and unrest and increasing bloodshed is in my opinion a moot point. Yet success has never been the essential test for prophetic authenticity. That is why an Afrikaner prophet like Beyers Naudé, although mostly as 'the voice of one crying in the wilderness', could and can continue to call his people, the Afrikaners, to an alternative, more hopeful way. They did not heed his call in 1977; pray God they do in 1985.

The fragmentation of Afrikanerdom and the Afrikaner churches
DAVID BOSCH

In a recent article on 'The roots and fruits of Afrikaner civil religion'[1] I argued that three different but sometimes interrelated worldviews had influenced and shaped Afrikaner religious and political thinking. In sequence of time these were: (1) Reformed evangelicalism, epitomised in the person and ministry of Andrew Murray, Jr (since the eighteenth century); (2) Kuyperian neo-Calvinism (since the second half of the nineteenth century and particularly during the twentieth); and (3) neo-Fichtean romantic nationalism (particularly since the 1930s). The present article is intended as a supplement to the earlier one. It will at least in part look at the same phenomena, but from a different angle: it will attempt to investigate briefly the processes of fragmentation which have, since an early period, plagued Afrikanerdom and the Afrikaner churches. I shall concentrate on events and patterns of thinking in the Nederduitse Gereformeerde Kerk (Dutch Reformed Church) although I shall, at times, also refer to the other two, much smaller, Afrikaans churches, the Nederduitsch Hervormde Kerk and the Gereformeerde Kerk.

During its 333-year-old history in South Africa the Dutch Reformed Church has been, at times, the church of the establishment, and, at other times, the church of the people in opposition to the political establishment. And frequently this circumstance (that is, whether at a particular moment in history the church was church of the establishment or not), rather than doctrinal or other ecclesiastical considerations, determined the church's attitude on a particular issue. This I hope to illustrate in the following pages.

First, however, a few additional introductory remarks, to help us see the issue under discussion in its proper perspective.

Religion and the nation-state

Since the French Revolution one increasingly encounters the phenomenon of the nation-state, which for the first time truly opened the possibility for large-scale patriotism, the psychological and ideological identification of the populace with their country and what it stands for.

Prior to the French Revolution it was kings and feudal lords who symbolically represented the state. In the area of religious allegiance, the *cuius regio eius religio* principle[2] obtained almost universally. The

Revolution, however, substituted for the king and the feudal lords the notion of the people as the ultimate source of authority. This, in turn, paved the way for an intimate relationship between the *people* (not just the rulers) and a specific religious tradition, a process that accelerated in the post-Enlightenment period as nationalism spread by contagion.

It was almost inevitable that the intimate relationship between a specific people's nationalism and their inherited religious tradition would deepen during the period, particularly if we keep in mind, as Ninian Smart has recently argued, that religion typically has six dimensions – doctrine, myth, ethics, ritual, experience, and institutions – and that the national idea is usually also incarnated in the same six dimensions.[3]

In such a context religion tends to have one of two divergent functions.

Where the religious community has a privileged position in society – whether it is *de jure* a state church or simply *de facto* a church of the establishment, enjoying all the privileges that go with this – it will tend to accept the essential validity of the political order. Belief in such a common legitimacy 'is an important cohesive element with a political order, for both the leaders and the led then accept the same norms as obligatory and mutually binding.'[4] Here religion functions as a mechanism which renders stability to the wider social structure, and in turn provides a firm point of orientation for individuals. The religious community tends to emphasise its descent and its tradition; in other words, it looks towards the past rather than the future.

Where, on the other hand, the religious community does not have a position of privilege in society at large, the opposite obtains. The community rejects the accepted patterns of behaviour. The relevance and legitimacy of religion is continuously tested (whether consciously or unconsciously) in respect of the contribution it can make to help its members attain the ideal of an increasingly human society. Its orientation is therefore to the future rather than the past. It supplies the basis for social change.

It is widely accepted that South African society today harbours (at least) two very different communities, in which religion tends to play two diametrically opposing roles. In the case of white South Africa, particularly the Dutch Reformed churches, religion is often used to undergird the status quo; in the case of black South Africa, which interprets its context as one of injustice and oppression, religion is used to challenge the status quo. What is not often sufficiently realised, however, is that in the course of their history the white Afrikaner community and its churches have often also found themselves in a situation where they challenged the status quo. Sometimes they were part and parcel of the establishment, sometimes they were in opposition to it. Both traditions are deeply embedded in Afrikaner history.

Church of the establishment

When the Dutch came to the Cape in 1652 they brought with them the Reformed faith as the established religion. This went unchallenged for a considerable period. In a completely unproblematic way it was accepted that the values of the white settlers were all that counted. Society was experienced as homogeneous since it was an unquestioned premise that the values and interests of the different black groups or the slave population need not be taken into account.

In 1806 the Cape passed into British hands, that is, into the hands of another power which had its own set of values and legitimations and, in fact, its own established faith, the Anglican Church. What amazes the student of history, however, is the extent to which the Dutch Reformed Church in the Cape Colony almost immediately accepted the legitimacy of the new authority and continued to co-operate with the regime almost as if there had been no break. This must have been due, at least in part, to the philosophy (by this time deeply inculcated in the Dutch Reformed Church) that the major religious community in any given situation would, simply in the nature of the case, support the powers that be. The relations with the Anglican Church were, on the whole, quite amicable. As a matter of fact, in 1870-1 there was even an attempt to unite the Anglican Church and the Dutch Reformed Church in the Cape Colony – an attempt that failed because the Reformed church would not accept the episcopacy, and not for cultural, political or doctrinal reasons. The attempt as such is important for our purposes here, since it, too, illustrates the importance of the philosophy of a religion of the establishment for the Cape Dutch Reformed Church.

More than three decades before this attempt, however, the first important signs of a challenge to the political status quo and its religion became evident. I am referring to the Great Trek of the late 1830s which was to provide the first major challenge to the symbiotic relationship between church and government, and the first clear sign that a process of fragmentation had begun in Afrikanerdom.

During the years 1836 and 1837, in particular, wave after wave of Voortrekkers left the Cape Colony in search of a new future north of the Orange River since, for a host of reasons, they were no longer prepared to tolerate British colonial rule. The important point for our present argument is that the Dutch Reformed Church, in its official capacity, censured the Trek. The Pastoral Letter of the 1837 synod expressed synod's grief over 'the current condition of so many members of the Reformed Church, who have left hearth and home as well as their altars [an allusion to the church], moving into the desert without a Moses or an Aaron. . . . ' Synod reminded them, *inter alia*, of their duty 'to be subject to those whom God has appointed as rulers over them' (cf. article 36 of the Belgic Confession). Three years later the Presbytery of Graaff-Reinet grudgingly permitted the Rev. Taylor of Cradock to visit the emigrants beyond the Colony's borders, but only on the condition that he would neither administer the sacraments to them nor confirm any new members. It was clear that the Presbytery was, at least to some extent, anxious not to do anything that would antagonise the British colonial authorities, for when, at the same occasion, the Rev. Reid of Colesberg asked permission to visit the emigrants beyond the Orange River, 'only to proclaim the Gospel to them', the Presbytery granted him leave to do that, 'provided it can be done without transgressing the laws of the Cape Colony.'

In view of this treatment of the Voortrekkers by the official church in the colony, it should not surprise us that, when the Transvaal Republic received its first full-time pastor in the person of the Rev. Dirk van der Hoff in 1853, it was soon decided to sever all relations with the Cape church. The Transvaal Constitution of 1858 declared the Nederduitsch Hervormde Kerk to be the state church; only members of this church were eligible to be members of parliament. Thus, after having been 'disestablished' for a number of years, the Reformed church once again became the church of the establishment.

The process of fragmentation could, however, no longer be stopped. Some congregations in the Transvaal, as well as the churches in the Orange Free State and Natal, decided to retain their formal links with the Cape church – a decision which, at least in some circles in the Transvaal, evoked the suspicion that these congregations were, in fact, hand in glove with the British colonial authorities in the Cape.

This was the one side of the logic, pursued in the Transvaal: the Nederduitsch Hervormde Kerk was the state church and there were to be no links with the Cape church. The other side of the logic was pursued by H. H. Loedolff, elder of the Malmesbury congregation in the Cape and a delegate to various synods in the 1850s and 1860s. Loedolff argued that pastors of congregations outside the geographical boundaries of the Cape Colony (in Natal, Orange Free State and Transvaal) could not be members of the Cape synod. His argument was that church and political authority had to be geographically co-extensive – an argument which clearly reflected the philosophy of the established church. Synod dismissed Loedolff's objections. However, in 1862 he took the matter to court and was vindicated: delegates from outside the Cape Colony had to leave. Due to an irrational fear of a repeat of the 1862 court decision, the congregations in the north decided to organise themselves into three separate churches: for the Transvaal, Orange Free State and Natal respectively. Moreover, even before all this happened, another split had occurred in the Afrikaner churches: a theologically conservative sub-group which had its strongholds in the north-eastern Cape and parts of the Transvaal had founded the Gereformeerde Kerk in 1859. Indeed, the numerically small Afrikaner community had never been more fragmented than in the few decades following 1860.

Immediately after the First War of Independence (1880–81) – a period during which the Transvalers stood united against Britain – negotiations for the reunification of the three Reformed churches began. What was striking was that the first initiative towards reunification after the war came from the political leadership: the triumvirate of Kruger, Pretorius and Joubert advocated church union at a public meeting in Pretoria in August 1881.[5] More than any other event in the past this demonstrated the symbiotic relationship between the Afrikaner people and their ecclesiastical heritage – even if, in the end, the Gereformeerde Kerk and a few congregations of the Nederduitsch Hervormde Kerk stayed out of the union which came into effect in 1885.

Church of the people

Looking back on the nineteenth century we can say with accuracy that on the whole the Reformed church in its different manifestations was regarded as the church of the establishment. A fundamental shift in this philosophy would, however, come at the turn of the century. The catalyst for this was the Second War of Independence or the Anglo-Boer War (1899-1902). Instead of crushing the Afrikaner's spirit and making him an easy object of Anglicisation as Lord Milner and his Director of Education, E. B. Sargent, had hoped,[6] exactly the opposite happened. In fact, when Milner left South Africa in 1905 he himself admitted, with remarkable perceptiveness, 'So far from dooming the national idea, the strain of war and the shock of defeat has made the Afrikaners a people. These things were for them a greater spiritual experience even than the Great Trek.'[7] And in the darkest hour of Afrikanerdom, it was the Afrikaners' church that rallied to their cause and identified with their struggle. The church was no longer church of the establishment; it was church of the people, if needs be against the establishment.

This was the case not only in the two former Boer republics but also in the Cape Colony where, particularly since the 1870s, the Dutch Reformed Church increasingly adopted an attitude critical of the British colonial authorities and in sympathy with their kith and kin beyond the Orange River. In other words the Cape church, too, was gradually becoming a church of the people. Pastors were increasingly linked directly to their congregations, also financially, a fact which made them more and more independent of the government. And during the Anglo-Boer War the Cape Afrikaners' sympathy was, by and large, with the two republics.

Even so, the war did render a contribution of its own to the fragmentation of the Afrikaner and his church, particularly in the Transvaal. During the war, some burghers defected to the enemy, and were armed and used against their compatriots. The first synod after the war (1903) expected some form of repentance from the so-called National Scouts before they could be fully restored to the bosom of the church. However, the new British rulers – including Lieutenant-Governor Lawley and none less than British Colonial Secretary Joseph Chamberlain – sided with the Scouts and even paid the salaries of two pastors to minister to them. So a new church, dubbed the 'Scout Church', was born. It was short-lived, however, and collapsed soon after the government terminated its financial subsidy in 1905.[8]

Only twelve years after the Peace of Vereeniging (1902) the newly formed Union of South Africa sided with Britain in her war against Germany. On 9 October 1914 Lieutenant Colonel Maritz and many of his soldiers rebelled, soon to be followed by Generals De Wet and Beyers (whose name Beyers Naudé bears). Many Afrikaners, including some pastors, made common cause with the rebels. On 14 October eleven Cape pastors of the Dutch Reformed Church condemned the armed rebellion in an open letter, but as some pointed out they all lived and ministered south of the Hex River mountains, in the section of the Cape church which traditionally had been more pro-English than any other part of the church.

In January 1915 the Federal Council of Dutch Reformed churches met in Bloemfontein to discuss the political situation. Whereas the 1903 Transvaal synod censured those who had taken up arms against their lawful government (the National Scouts), the Federal Council of 1915 was, on the whole, in sympathy with the rebels of 1914, although they had to formulate this very carefully. It was clear that the Dutch Reformed Church was increasingly identifying with the Afrikaner and his cause. The Federal Council for instance unanimously adopted a motion submitted by Dr D. F. Malan (the later Prime Minister) that 'our church has received from God a special calling in respect of the Afrikaner people, with which it is so intimately related. It should therefore also be regarded as [the church's] duty to be national itself, to watch over our peculiar national interests and to teach our people to detect the hand of God in its history and genesis; it should also keep alive in the Afrikaner people the awareness of its national calling and destiny . . . .'[9]

From now on the Dutch Reformed Church would ever more clearly become a *volkskerk*, a church of the people, a notion to which both the older evangelical tradition and the more recent Kuyperian tradition contributed. General J. B. M. Hertzog, founder of the National Party and Prime Minister from 1924 to 1939, maintained an unashamedly secular view of history and differed fundamentally from those (mainly Kuyperians) who saw God's hand in every event and particularly in the history of the Afrikaner people.[10] In the long run, however, Hertzog was no match for the religiously undergirded ethnic chauvinism of the Afrikaner.

On 5 June 1918 the Afrikaner Broederbond was founded. The Rev. J. F. Naudé, father of Beyers Naudé and one of the six Boer representatives who had refused to sign the peace treaty in 1902, was hailed by the chairman, H. J. Klopper, as the 'true leader' of the new movement.[11]

The Broederbond institutionalised Afrikaner Christian-Nationalism. Through a variety of cultural organisations the Afrikaner leadership pushed for Afrikaner ethnic history, art, education and economy. It is true that, in the early thirties, the majority of Afrikaners followed Hertzog into fusion with Jan Smuts's South African Party. The Broederbond, however, with a few exceptions, stood solidly behind Malan, whose small band of 'purified' Nationalists soon became the authentic bearers of Afrikaner Christian-Nationalist sentiments and ideas. In the course of time Malan succeeded in winning over many *Smelters* (Fusionists); in 1948 this would give him election victory over Smuts.

The sympathies of the Afrikaans churches were, on the whole, with Malan rather than Hertzog, not to mention Smuts. During the 1930s and 1940s tensions between church and state increased. The church opposed rather than co-operated with the authorities. It expressed itself in solidarity with the Afrikaner community and championed its cause. Most Afrikaners of this period were poor and many, particularly those in the cities, were discriminated against; these 'poor whites' increasingly regarded both the Afrikaans churches and the National Party as symbols of hope. The 'liberation theology' language of a commission that investigated the position of the urban Afrikaner in the 1940s gives evidence of this:

City life is conditioned by capitalist exploitation. The powerful press, current public opinion, even social legislation, mostly side with capital; the labourer constantly has the worst of it. He needs a champion, a patron, the Afrikaner labourer in particular. The church should be his father, his advocate; it should stand up for the rights of the oppressed; it should proclaim social justice; it must champion social security, better housing, better labour conditions. The pulpit cannot promulgate laws but it can disseminate ideals. . . .[12]

For the capitalist profit-seeking is paramount; he pursues maximum profit at minimum cost. . . . He demands the best service from the labourer but pays as little as possible for it. It is one of the characteristics of capitalism that the labourer is being exploited. . . . In his relentless struggle for justice, for subsistence wages, . . . the labourer is painfully aware of the obstacles put in his way by the establishment. He is no longer a human being; he is a digit, a cog in the big machine; his life, his views, his interests count for nothing; all that counts are his labour and his sweat. And then it appears to him as if law and order are always on the side of the propertied classes; he seeks in vain for justice and protection.[13]

It is indeed true that labour unions sometimes act in foolish, obstinate and lawless ways; yet if cognisance is taken of the conditions under which they often have to live and work and the injustice they sometimes have to suffer, their fulminations are understandable even if not always pardonable.[14]

Once again church of the establishment

The close identification of church and party with the felt needs of Afrikanerdom paid off: only a year after the words quoted above were published, Malan's Nationalists defeated Smuts's pro-English United Party at the polls. For many in the Afrikaans churches this event spelled the dawn of the millenium. The Dutch Reformed Church once again became church of the establishment, without, however, ceasing to be church of the (Afrikaner) people. The church was still, in keeping with its evangelical roots, a missionary church, but in some circles its mission work among blacks was implicitly or explicitly regarded as serving the interests of the Afrikaner. In 1958, in an address to a Dutch Reformed mission group, M. D. C. de Wet Nel, Minister of Native Affairs, said:

An aspect which . . . is one of the main reasons why many people are still cold and indifferent to mission work, is its political significance. . . . If the Afrikaans churches succeed in bringing the blacks over into a Protestant-Christian context, South Africa will have a hope for the future. If this does not happen, our policy, our programme of legislation and all our plans will be doomed to failure. . . . Our sons and daughters should realise that mission work offers the most wonderful opportunity to serve God, but also the most glorious opportunity to serve the Fatherland.[15]

The archetypal protagonist of the identification of Afrikaner people and people of God, of National Party and Dutch Reformed Church, was the Rev. G. J. J. Boshoff, pastor of the Linden congregation in Johannesburg from 1950 to 1961. It could hardly have been accidental that he was given the opportunity to preach during services broadcast country-wide on the eve of both the 1953 and the 1958 elections. On the first occasion his text was Nehemiah 4:14; the entire sermon proceeded from the assumption that the Afrikaner people were, like Israel, the people of God. This identification, as a matter of fact, characterises his entire volume of sermons published under the title *U Volk Is My Volk*.[16]

Voices of dissent

In spite of the euphoria in Afrikaner circles during the 1950s there were, however, a few Afrikaner voices – also in the Dutch Reformed Church – that challenged the Afrikaner Nationalist–Reformed church paradigm. Those were, particularly, the voices of B. B. Keet and Ben Marais. Moreover, during the early fifties a new breed of young Afrikaner theologians, who were beginning to develop a profound mistrust of the dominant paradigm, were coming out of the Dutch Reformed Church seminaries. Some of these young pastors and theologians would in the late fifties and early sixties rally around Beyers Naudé. All these younger theologians came out of the evangelical tradition[17] and most of them had intimate contact with the black Dutch Reformed churches.

Naudé only very gradually emerged as the major challenger of the system from within the Afrikaner churches. I still remember how he first shared some of his concerns with me early in 1950, when the Rev. (later Professor) Nico Smith and I were assisting him during a 'missions week' in his Potchefstroom congregation. Soon after that he moved to the Aasvoëlkop congregation in the northern suburbs of Johannesburg where he, in the course of time, became the centre of a movement for change. By that time the marriage between Dutch Reformed churches and National Party was beginning to show strain. Doubts were expressed – even at the level of synod – about several of the implications of the apartheid policy. Blacks were becoming increasingly restive. By 1960 the general atmosphere in the country was electric.

On 21 March 1960 police fired into a black crowd at Sharpeville near Vereeniging, killing 69 people according to official sources. Some of those killed were women and children, and most were shot in the back. There was world-wide outrage, to which the South African government responded by declaring a state of emergency and banning the African National Congress as well as the Pan-Africanist Congress.

Clearly the die was cast. What would the response of the Dutch Reformed Church be to the crisis? The Cape and Transvaal churches as well as the Nederduitsch Hervormde Kerk were members of the World Council of Churches. Dr Robert S. Bilheimer of the WCC Geneva office was sent to South Africa and arrived here less than a month after Sharpeville. His visit eventually led to the Cottesloe Consultation of 7-14 December 1960, where 80 delegates of the eight South African member churches of the WCC and six WCC representatives deliberated on the crisis in the nation.[18]

The memorandum of the Cape Dutch Reformed Church was adopted as a basis for the deliberations. The final declaration reflected more than anything else the contents of this memorandum. The Cape delegates were supported in their views by those from the Transvaal church. There could be little doubt that the resolutions in essence meant a break with the Nationalist paradigm. This is also how the delegates of the Nederduitsch Hervormde Kerk interpreted them. They alone voted against several of the key resolutions. On the final day, an hour before the adjournment of the consultation, the whole Hervormde Kerk delegation distanced itself from the consultation and its findings, and left the meeting.

Some observers were amazed at the fact that the representatives of the Dutch Reformed Church (Cape Province and Transvaal), on the whole, went along with the other member churches and, unlike the Hervormde Kerk delegates, voted in favour of all the resolutions. This should, however, not come as too much of a surprise. The majority of the Dutch Reformed delegates came out of the evangelical and missionary tradition. Racial segregation was, for them, a matter of expediency rather than principle. During the late fifties some of them became increasingly disillusioned by the doctrinaire apartheid of J. G. Strijdom and, particularly, H. F. Verwoerd.

The question now was whether the Afrikaner churches and people were going to side with the Cottesloe delegates or with the National Party.

It very soon became clear that the Cottesloe delegates stood no chance of being truly heard, let alone supported. The Johannesburg daily, *Die Transvaler*, mouthpiece of the National Party, immediately attacked the consultation. The Dutch Reformed weekly, *Die Kerkbode*, with its editor Dr A. P. Treurnicht, was even more condemnatory. The fate of Cottesloe, as far as the Afrikaans churches were concerned, was however only sealed on 31 December 1960 when Prime Minister Verwoerd, in his New Year's radio message to the nation, made reference to the 'personal declarations' on colour policy of 'individual churchmen'. The churches themselves, he added, had not yet spoken; this would only happen when the synods met. 'I sincerely hope that people will now desist from implicating the names of our churches unwarrantably in a debate which at the moment is being conducted by individuals only in their own name.'[19]

Most Cottesloe delegates had put up a gallant last-ditch stand in a declaration published on 27 December 1960, but they were no match against the combined attack of the political and ecclesiastical machinery. The synodical meetings of 1962 condemned Cottesloe and the Afrikaner Reformed churches resigned from the World Council of Churches. The Transvaal synod in addition summoned every pastor to obey synodical decisions.

On the surface it appeared as though a crisis was averted and all the Afrikaans churches were back in line. Beyers Naudé, a Cottesloe delegate, could, however, not acquiesce. He was, in fact, approaching his Rubicon. Already before Sharpeville he and others were instrumental in forming 'ecumenical study circles' on the Reef and in the Western Cape. After a visit to him in Johannesburg in December 1961, I convened a meeting for white Dutch Reformed Church pastors of the Transkei and far Eastern Cape. The meeting took place in the Transkei village of Idutywa on 23 January 1962 and was attended by some twenty pastors. Beyers Naudé outlined the post-Cottesloe situation; he challenged and urged us to organise ecumenical contact in our region. This was soon put into practice and in a few years led, *inter alia*, to the formation of the Transkei Council of Churches.

When Beyers Naudé launched *Pro Veritate* and became its first editor (April 1962), resigned from the Broederbond (March 1963) and finally founded the Christian Institute (August 1963), the fury of the Afrikaner political and ecclesiastical establishment was unleashed against him. The situation was aggravated when it became known that it was he who had handed secret Broederbond documents to Albert Geyser, who in turn had handed them over to the *Sunday Times* where they were published in the course of 1963. Naudé reminisced twenty-one years after the event: 'You may resign from the Dutch Reformed Church; you may even resign from the National Party, but don't touch the Broederbond. For if you touch it, you touch the heart of Afrikanerdom, of everything the *volk* stands for. And the one who does that, commits treason.'[20]

The ranks closed against Naudé and other dissidents. It was clear that they were not to be permitted to fragment the Afrikaner people and churches. Naudé lost his status as minister. When, soon after this, he was elected elder in the Parkhurst congregation, the Presbytery of Johannesburg delared the election null and void, arguing that Naudé, in accepting the directorship of the Christian Institute, had 'disobeyed the guidance of the *Breë Moderatuur*' (Moderamen of the General Synod). Six pastors in the Presbytery appealed against the ruling but were unsuccessful. The 1966 General Synod, with one dissenting voice, condemned the Christian Institute as representing false doctrine and ordered all Dutch Reformed Church members and officials to resign from it. Only official Nationalist policy and official church views would henceforth be tolerated.

The current scene
The process of fermentation and fragmentation in Afrikaner ranks was, however, far from being arrested. On the one hand, an ever-increasing number of Afrikaners were defecting to the Progressive Federal Party, on the other hand the Herstigte Nasionale Party was founded in 1970 and the Conservative Party in 1982. In 1970 the Broederbond could still rule that no member of the HNP could remain in the Broederbond. In 1982 it was unable to demand the same of members of the Conservative Party: too many Broederbond members had joined the Conservative Party! So, today, Afrikanerdom is hope-lessly divided and fragmented politically.

On the ecclesiastical front the situation is more complex and con-fused. The 'major split' in the Dutch Reformed Church, so often predicted by the English-language press as 'imminent', has not yet materialised. Many Dutch Reformed Church members have defected to a variety of pentecostal and charismatic churches. At the other end of the spectrum some have joined one of the black Dutch Reformed churches or English-language churches, which have a clear anti-apart-heid stance. Still others have simply, for all practical purposes, ceased to be members of the church. In spite of these defections, however, the Dutch Reformed Church still expands, numerically and otherwise, and its church buildings are full on Sundays.

This tenacity of the Dutch Reformed Church puzzles many outside observers. I should like to submit that there are at least two reasons for the Dutch Reformed Church's resilience. The first and more obvious reason is that the church has adapted to the needs of its members; it provides them with an interpretative framework for their collective experiences and aspirations; its preaching readily parallels the race and class interests and prejudices of its members.

The second reason is less obvious and can only be illustrated by contrasting the Dutch Reformed Church with American denomina-tions. There churches have to compete with one another for members. The religious institutions are, sociologically speaking, agencies which market their religious traditions as consumer commodities. New arriv-als in a city tend to 'shop around' for a while among neighbourhood churches before they settle for a specific one. In the Afrikaner Reformed churches this marketing situation does not really obtain. People moving from one locality to another in 99 per cent of cases join congregations of the denomination to which they belong. This is so, at least to a considerable extent, since the Afrikaner Reformed churches offer their members more than just a religious home: they offer them a total world view and culture as well.

Precisely for this reason, opposition from within the Reformed churches is, at the same time, more difficult and more significant than it would be in other churches. More difficult, for the forces within the church demand uncritical loyalty whereas outsiders tend to dismiss the dissidents as people who are not prepared to draw the consequences of their own logic. More significant, because the protests keep alive in the bosom of the church the message of the unity of Christ's church and the prophetic challenge to the status quo. It is in these terms that one should look upon and evaluate recent voices of protest from within the Dutch Reformed Church such as the 'Reformation Day Witness' of eight theologians in 1980, the publication of *Stormkompas* in 1981, and the 'Open letter', signed by 123 white pastors in 1982, as well as the launching of *Reforum* on 25 January 1985.

On the surface it appears as if these voices of protest have little effect on the Dutch Reformed Church. The present official mood in the Dutch Reformed Church is not one that welcomes dialogue and contact with people who differ from it. In 1979, just before 5 000 Christians from all churches and races met in the South African Christian Leadership Assembly in Pretoria, with a view to 'examining together what it means to be faithful witnesses of Christ as Lord in South Africa today', the Northern Transvaal Moderamen of the Dutch Reformed Church issued a directive to all local church councils advising them to refrain from participating in SACLA. The directive stated, 'We, as Church, need not discover what it means to be faithful and effective witnesses of Jesus in South Africa. We daily study God's Word and know what it is.'

This statement suggests that the Dutch Reformed Church can go it alone and does not need the wider Christian community. When the General Synod of the Dutch Reformed Church met in October 1982, two months after the World Alliance of Reformed churches had suspended its membership because of its support of an unjust system of racial discrimination, there were, on the whole, two views among delegates. One group wanted to give the WARC another four years to repent of the injustice it had done to the Dutch Reformed Church. In both cases the message was the same: only we are in step; the rest of the Reformed world is out of step. It is true that some delegates did attempt to suggest, in carefully couched words, that the WARC might perhaps have been justified in the steps it had taken, but the synod was in no mood to listen to those voices. The overall impression was therefore, once again, that 'we can go it alone'. There seemed to be little concern over the fact that in that very year several church bodies inside and outside South Africa had decided to sever relations with the Dutch Reformed Church. There was little concern – only indignation – over the Dutch Reformed Mission Church's decision, a month earlier, to brand support for apartheid idolatry and a heresy.

Since the General Synod of October 1902 the isolation of the Dutch Reformed Church has steadily increased. The Reformed Ecumenical Synod, meeting in Chicago in August 1984, also censured the Dutch Reformed Church for its support of apartheid, though in much milder terms than did the WARC. The response of the *Breë Moderatuur* to this, in January 1985, was to provisionally suspend the Dutch Reformed Church's membership in the RES and to ask the next General Synod (1986) to ratify its decision.

From the outside it thus appears that *Afrikanerdom* is, at the moment, fragmented and in disarray, but that the *Dutch Reformed Church* is still solidly united and impregnable, except for a few dissenting voices. Appearances are, however, deceptive. First there are, apart from a number of pastors, many thousands of ordinary church members who long for change and a new direction. And secondly, even if signs of ferment and renewal may be hardly detectable, they are there. Those who are part of this process are appealing to the evangelical and Reformed orgins of the Dutch Reformed Church. As Willem Nicol put it at the launching of *Reforum* in January 1985: 'The Dutch Reformed Churches are not by nature churches of compromise. They are in conflict with themselves if they elevate ethnic and other selfish human interests above the gospel. The current aberration *[dwaling]* does not belong to our nature.'

The key thus seems to lie in the Dutch Reformed Church returning to its Calvinistic and evangelical roots, and relating these to the present context. Can the Dutch Reformed Church do this? Well, its official delegation did this 25 years ago, at Cottesloe. Moreover, the early history of ecumenism in this country is unthinkable without the initiative, role and contribution of the Dutch Reformed Church. Could history not repeat itself?

Proclamation and protest:
The lost sons
ALLAN BOESAK
Outside the gate
WOLFRAM KISTNER

Central to the witness of the church in this country, as elsewhere in the world, is the place of the Bible. In the Reformed tradition this has been so in an uncompromising manner. The life and ministry of Beyers Naudé has epitomised this. His is a biblical faith. His preaching is exegetical, and his witness is grounded in a study of the Bible.

For this reason we include in this *festschrift* two biblical reflections, by two expository preachers, who are part of the contemporary church in this land – Allan Boesak and Wolfram Kistner.

'The Lost Sons', is a Bible study on Luke 15: 11–32 delivered by Allan Boesak at the Kirchentag, in Hanover, Germany, last year and chosen by him for inclusion in this volume. 'Outside the Gate' is a biblical reflection given by Wolfram Kistner as part of his 1983 report for the SACC's Commission of Justice and Reconciliation.

THE LOST SONS: Luke 15: 11–32
We must not allow familiarity with this story to blunt our sensitivity to its possibilities for understanding our own situation. The story is not so much an illustration of something that may have happened long ago, bound to a certain time and culture. Rather, it is a reflection on the human situation as it is still today; and the two sons are two persons depicting a paradigm of what we are, still today.

The younger son demands his share of the inheritance. In so doing he takes as his that which would only have become his possession on the death of his father. His desire is to have nothing more to do with his family. He denies his relationship to his father and his brother. He turns his share into cash, indicating that he was feeling a growing hostility to the community because of his deed. He leaves for a distant country, and squanders his money. As famine strikes, he is left without money or friends, and eventually he becomes a herder of pigs, an acute humiliation for a young Jewish nobleman, and an eloquent description of the utter destitution in which he found himself.

Realising what he had done, he decides to return to his father, repent and hope for reconciliation.

What about the older son? All too often we have read the story as if the older son, at least initially, was better than his younger and more irresponsible brother. In the first half of the story he displays nothing of the greed or the rebelliousness of his younger brother. He seems the stable, obedient and more dependable son. His anger seems justified after all that has happened. But is that so? Careful reading of the parable suggests a different understanding.

First of all, as older brother, he had a special responsibility in the household. As his younger brother proceeds with his outrageous deed, the older son does not protest, nor does he seek to be a reconciler between his father and his brother. The older son maintains his silence, instead of protesting and calling his brother to order. The father divides his estate between them, while the older son accepts the arrangement and benefits from it. This raises the fundamental question of his relationship to his family.

At the end of the parable his relationship is clear. He refuses to share the joy of his father at his brother's return, he is unable to repent and he uses his obedience to his father to restrain his father's love. He does not understand the things that make for peace.

We have two lost sons. The one realises it, repents of his misdeeds and seeks reconciliation. The other stays with his father but closes his heart to him and his brother.

There are three important elements in this Parable for our situation:

The despised are affirmed by God

The first is found in the first three verses of Luke 15, providing the clue to understanding the parable. The Pharisees and scribes reproach Jesus, saying: 'This man welcomes sinners and eats with them.'

This makes clear that what follows is a defence of the gospel. It makes clear how seriously Jesus himself was pursuing the meaning of his own words when he talked about the gospel in Luke 4: 18–21. The essence of the story is table fellowship, and eating together plays an important role in the parable, symbolising not only the destitution of the younger son when lost, but the expression of the father's joy at his being found. It represents the painful moment of estrangement, the brokenness of relationships, when the older son hurts the father in the most effective way he can: by refusing to be part of the family celebration.

Jesus chose to share bread with what the Pharisees called 'the sinners'. For the Pharisees, a 'sinner' was either an immoral person who did not keep the law, or a person who was socially unacceptable. Such persons were despised and rejected by the respected members of Jewish society. To share the company of such people was not considered proper. To eat with them was unthinkable.

The offence lay in the meaning of the act. To eat with someone was an honour, an offer of peace, trust, brotherhood and forgiveness. It is to share an intimate moment, sharing not only the *means* of life, but sharing of life *together*. In this act lies openness and vulnerability, a willingness to accept the other completely. It is not the sitting down with them that really matters. It is the affirmation of a relationship, a recognition of a relationship, a recognition of the humanity of the other.

It might even be that Jesus had invited the guests, that he was the host, which makes the situation even worse as far as the Pharisees were concerned. For then it is Jesus' intention to illustrate that it is not so much he (the host) who brings honour to the guests, but that it is he and his house that are being honoured by the presence of the guests – the very ones whom the Pharisees regarded as neither accepted nor acceptable.

Following closely as it does on Luke 14 and the parable of the great feast, there is a further implication: Jesus is illustrating in a practical fashion what He has already proclaimed. The feast of the Messiah in the kingdom of God shall be shared, not by those who are 'children of Abraham', or 'keepers of the law', but precisely by those who in the eyes of the 'righteous' stand no chance at all: the poor, the blind, the weak, the despised and the rejected. This illustrates vividly what Luke so persistently proclaims throughout his version of the gospel.

Whatever the expectations of the listeners to this parable, it is the younger son who in the end wins the favour of his father. It is the despised sinner for whom the feast is held. The older son can only join the feast if he is also willing to accept fully his younger brother. This too is consistent with the biblical story. For some strange reason the God of the Bible works that way. He chooses Abel before Cain; Jacob before Esau; the young David before his older more suitable brothers; and Samuel the son of the despised Hannah instead of one of the sons of Pennina. Mary's Magnificat proclaims it and the life of Jesus illustrates it. The first shall be last and the last shall be first.

In South Africa it is clear who is considered truly human. Racism is an ideology that makes skin colour the highest achievement. When you are white you are considered to possess all that is necessary to be a true and worthy human being. That is why laws exist which apply to black people but which white people would regard as inhuman and cruel if applied to them. For years now apartheid has undermined black personhood and destroyed human dignity. In a country which is among the wealthiest on the continent, black children still die of hunger, malnutrition and inadequate medical care. Millions have lost their South African citizenship and millions more are being forcibly moved into resettlement camps. The desperate poverty of the vast majority of blacks is not an accident, but by design, the result of deliberate economic injustice and exploitation.

Behind the ideology of apartheid is the theology of apartheid. A theology has led Afrikaners to believe that they are the chosen people of God, that whites in some special way have a divine right to rule, and that their overprivileged position is somehow God's will.

The truth of the gospel cuts through this propaganda. It is liberating for black South Africans to discover that the message of the Bible is that God is the God of the poor, that He is on the side of the oppressed. He is not on the side of the poor because they are black, but because they are poor and oppressed. His reign as king of kings means that this order of things shall be overturned. In the eyes of whites, black lives may count for nothing – as seen so vividly in the murder of Biko – but in His eyes the lives of the despised are precious.

Costly repentance and reconciliation
The behaviour of the two sons is essentially the same. The difference in status and attitude is imaginary. They are both members of the same family. They are both lost, both in need of repentance, conversion and reconciliation. And they both discover that the road of life goes through the agony of repentance, forgiveness and reconciliation. They must both learn that reconciliation. They must both learn that reconciliation is not cheap.

The younger son is willing to go back to his father as a 'hired servant'. As such he seeks a measure of freedom, living independently in the village. He would be able to pay back what he had taken. He would be able to make up for what he had lost. He would save himself. He would work, pay his father back, and keep his pride. He would not eat his brother's bread. Living at home would entail reconciliation with his brother, and this he apparently did not want. Being a hired servant is an alternative that makes reconciliation with his brother unnecessary. Reconciliation with his father, his brother and the village requires a price that he is not yet ready to pay. As it happens, the act of reconciliation was initiated by the love and compassion of the father who takes the first step. To his surprise, he needs only to respond to the love of the father. It is this selfless love of the father that makes it possible for him to reconcile himself to others.

The story of the older brother is different. He comes home from the field and enquires as to the reason for the celebration. His anger is immediate. As he had done with the younger son, the father goes out to him. He refuses to listen, he rejects the younger son, refuses to participate in the feast, and demonstrates that his spirit is that of a slave, not a son: 'I have slaved for you. . . .' He does not understand that the feast is not a sign of what his brother was worth, but of the father's joy: 'You have not given me so much as a kid for a feast with my friends.' He turns his conversation with his father into a dispute about wages. He proudly states that he never disobeyed his father, yet he also shows that he has never had a real relationship with his father, nor did he understand his father's love. A party with his friends is much more important to him than a celebration with his father. He refuses to share his joy, and he refuses the offer of reconciliation.

Oppression leads to death and destruction. It takes away meaningful life for both the oppressed and the oppressor. There is no meaningful sharing of life, there is no understanding of the needs and humanity of the other. It can only continue because greed, exploitation, and systemic violence are needed to maintain the system. It creates a cycle of violence that leads to ever-deepening despair and ever more deeds of desperation. Apartheid is a perfect example of this. In order to return to life, repentance and reconciliation are needed.

It is here that the difficulty arises. Churches and Christians have used reconciliation as an 'easy way out', to escape the pressing issues in our South African situation. Too many have been unwilling to understand that reconciliation is costly. It presupposes alienation from others, from God, from ourselves even. We must not only face the fact of that alienation, we must also address the reasons for it. Reconciliation shall not become a reality until Christians are ready to face this evil, and their part in creating and maintaining it. As long as white Christians say that blacks want to create a 'false sense of guilt in whites', reconciliation will never become a reality.

Forgiveness does not mean that sins are simply covered over, and reconciliation is never the pious concealment of guilt. Reconciliation is exposure, the unmasking of sin, and a process of restitution. Too long have Christians tried to achieve reconciliation by proclaiming a unity that rests on the cloaking of evil and a pious silence about the guilt they cannot face. Reconciliation is not holding hands and singing, 'black and white together – we shall overcome'. Reconciliation means sharing pain and suffering, accepting the other so that joy can be a joy together. It means the willingness to pay the price.

Reconciliation does not occur between the oppressor and the oppressed. Reconciliation occurs between people, people who face each other authentically, vulnerably, and yet with hope. The oppressor must cease to be oppressor and become a brother and sister. Whites must cease to make of whiteness an idolatry and become human beings who need others. Blacks must cease to hate themselves and others, and become human beings, reflecting the image of God. Then reconciliation will take place. When it does, it will have political, social and economic consequences. Then there shall be restitution, there shall be sharing of life, there shall be peace.

Incomplete joy

The stories in the first half of chapter 15, the parables of the lost sheep and the lost coin, speak of completed joy. Here that joy is missing. The joy of the celebration remains incomplete because the older son refuses to share in it. The story ends with the father's plea for him to understand what it means when a brother was lost and is found, was dead and is alive again. The son makes no response. His refusal, his stubborn silence has the last word.

In South Africa it seems as if the powers of evil continue to have the last word. Apartheid in its revised and euphemistic forms continues to exist. In the new constitution racism, white minority rule and the further erosion of democracy are entrenched. Detention without trial continues. Resettlement schemes continue and violence is escalating. Violence leads to counter-violence, because people are desperate.

In Cape Town the black families at the KTC Camp in Nyanga are rounded up by the police, their pitiful shacks are broken down and they are imprisoned by the hundreds, because the government says they do not belong in Cape Town. They are being harassed, teargassed, beaten and treated like animals because they want to live together as families. For them, that is a crime. There is a continued unwillingness from the side of the government to bring about changes that are meaningful. There is a constant refusal to bring about justice, to seek the things that make for peace, to seek genuine reconciliation.

The joy is incomplete. And it shall not be complete until all South Africa's children experience human dignity. The parable is a call to return to life, away from death and destruction. It is a call to reconciliation and repentance. It is possible because the father has already taken the first step, Jesus Christ has already overcome the powers of evil, and the Spirit of the Lord empowers us to do what is right. The father has already gone down the road. The rest is up to us.

OUTSIDE THE GATE: *Hebrews 13: 13*

'Therefore let us go to him outside the camp and bear the abuse he endured', is part of a pericope in which the author of the Letter to the Hebrews reminds us that 'Jesus also suffered outside the gate in order to sanctify the people through his own blood.' The author's reference is to the hill on which Jesus was crucified, situated outside the gates of Jerusalem. It was the place where people who had been excluded from the community of the people of God, were put to death. The author points out that Christ suffered and was crucified among people who have nothing to rely on except the fact that he became one with them, was crucified and was raised from the dead by God on their behalf. The author's message is a straightforward one. Whoever wants to live in community with Christ, sustained by his power in this world, can do so only by going outside the gate and by becoming one of those people who have nothing to rely on but God's unmerited love and forgiveness.

We do not know much about the people to whom the Letter to the Hebrews was addressed, except what can be inferred from the letter. They were probably Christians of gentile background. In their group were people who were disappointed that the Lord did not return in his glory as they had expected. There was the danger that some of them would become weary and lose faith. Moreover these Christians were threatened with persecution, and asked whether it was worthwhile to rely on a Lord whose presence and power was not being experienced. In this situation the author points out where the presence and the power of Christ is to be found: outside the gate, at the place of suffering, where people have nothing to rely on but God's love and forgiveness, and where in their forsakenness they discover their power – together as Christ's brothers and sisters, as children of God.

A gospel for marginalised people

'Outside the gate', 'outside the camp', are not merely geographical terms. They describe the context to which our Lord invites us in order to experience his presence and power. This context may differ. Moreover, the details of the context within which the letter was written are not clear. The context of Jesus' own suffering outside the gate is a lot clearer, and we can draw information from historical and sociological research about people who lived at the time of Jesus. Galilee was the area where our Lord called his first disciples. It was a 'marginal area'. Many people, especially small farmers, were impoverished. They were pushed off the land by the great landowners. Many of them became indebted and lost their independence. Poverty in many cases implied cultural and religious impurity. Many of them could not observe the rituals that were expected of a Jew. The people with whom Jesus associated were described as sinners, as the poor people – primarily the 'marginalised' people.

A gospel for South Africa's discarded people

In South Africa we need to discern what the term 'outside the gate' means for us. In whose company do we encounter Christ in South Africa today? Which areas of the country are his preference areas? These areas, according to our text, are the relocation areas, the areas of the marginalised and discarded people. Possibly the prison cells of the section 22 and section 6 detainees are his headquarters for many a night and many a day. Looking for him outside the gate we find him in resettlement camps and homelands where people are crowded together and economically deprived, abandoned to starvation, unemployment and the arbitrary rule of a political oligarchy supported by the South African government. They are abandoned in a process which is ironically described as the attainment of their political independence and fulfilment of their national aspirations. It is significant that the Letter to the Hebrews describes the pilgrimage of the people of God as a pilgrimage that will reach its fulfilment only with the coming of the Son of God in his glory. Nevertheless this does not make the church indifferent towards life and conditions in the present day. It rather enhances the responsibility of Christians for what happens in their time and at the place where they live. The appeal, 'Let us go out to him outside the camp', is made with the aim that Christians should be equipped for worship that is pleasing to God (Heb. 13: 16).

Such considerations, drawn from Holy Scripture and the history of the church, have far-reaching implications for our understanding of the 'pilgrimage of pain'. We are asked to leave behind us everything that gives us false security. We are asked to leave behind us certain criteria which may be accepted in society, where status, merit, achievement and educational qualifications play a role. In the Christian community Christians in their mutual relationships have nothing to rely on except the realisation that Christ has died for them and has been raised from the dead by God, as their brother. We are accepted by God irrespective of our social standing, our wealth and any merits we may have. We are accepted only because God forgives our sins through Christ. Wherever God's forgiveness in Christ is apparent, the marginalisation of people must come to an end, and whenever marginalisation continues, the church is bound to take a stand – against any policy which discards people and makes them homeless, even if this happens under euphoric terms such as the 'homelands' policy.

Against the background of our text we have to understand the pilgrimage of pain as a continuous pilgrimage. This pilgrimage opens up the meaning of the gospel. It makes it possible for us to share with one another the experience of those who have nothing to rely on except the forgiveness of God. The gospel is best understood in the fellowship with people who have gone through such experiences, and who have no material wealth or social standing to rely on. Two such examples, one pertaining to a relocation community in the Ciskei, the other to a relocation community near Ladysmith in Natal, come to mind. Recently an Anglican minister led a group of ministers from East London to the relocation community in Kammaskraal near Peddie, in the Ciskei, where he is serving as a parish priest. The minister showed the group the small corrugated iron shack where worship services take place, and spoke about the special significance of Holy Communion in this situation. The presence of the Lord in Holy Communion, celebrated in this inconspicuous place of worship, helps to wield together dislocated and discarded people into a fellowship which is thereby equipped for common action, for mutual assistance and for sharing the suffering and the joys of the individual families and family members. In many cases this experience is the starting-point and motivating force for community initiatives in the area.

The second illustration concerns a group of twenty to twenty-five women gathered at Ekuvukeni near Ladysmith in the home of the recently deceased catechist, for a discussion of joint action which could strengthen and give new hope to the community. They were especially concerned about the children growing up in this deprived setting. At the end of the meeting they bade farewell to the visitors by singing the Magnificat. It was sung by a group of women who had suffered severely during the forced removal, who had lost most of their belongings and who were now living in an area of economic decay. The Magnificat tells of God's care for the lonely, the humble people, those who are otherwise discarded by society. He sees them and gives them a dignity and a potential of which nobody can deprive them, however deprived and despised they otherwise may be. Martin Luther once wrote an interpretation of the Magnificat as a guideline to a young prince. He recommended that the prince prayed the Magnificat every day. This biblical hymn would remind him, as the future ruler of his territory, that he had to deal with subjects who were not simply objects of his rule, but who were seen and accepted by God. In this interpretation Luther showed that the deeper people are in distress, the more specifically are they cared for by God.

Jürgen Moltmann reflects on this reality, in observing:

The path of Jesus has a distinct downward trend. The proclamation and the deeds of Jesus pertained to all people exactly because he took sides with the weak, the sick, the poor people, and the outcasts – those people in whom the brutality of human beings and their society was manifested. Jesus is a friend of the poor and, strangely enough, lays hold on human society at its bottom end.

The law according to which human societies function is based on the homogeneousness of its members. The law according to which the Christian community functions, however, is in no way based on the homogeneousness of its members and the sympathy between people of equal mind. It has to do with the acceptance of those who are different, and the creative love which unites people who are different: Jews and pagans, Greeks and barbarians, masters and servants. The walls and fences of the ghettoes, which people erect against one another in order to remain on their own and to justify themselves and humiliate the others, are demolished in the Christian community. Churches which are constituted merely by people who are equal, are heretical in their social structure. They are not more than religious societies with a slight Christian veneer. Only if the Christian community is rooted in the acceptance of those who are different and in the social embodiment of justification by faith, only in such a case can this community be a sign which points towards the human kingdom of the Son of Man.[1]

Theology in the South African context

Theologies in conflict:
the South African debate
JOHN W. DE GRUCHY

For at least three reasons theology in South Africa is not a matter of indifference but of social consequence: the all-pervasive role which the Christian church has played and continues to fulfil within society; the fact that since European colonisation commenced in the seventeenth century conflicting socio-political and economic interests have been sanctioned by religious conviction; and the significant though ambivalent role which Christians and churches play in the struggle both for and against apartheid today.

The fact that the overwhelming majority in South Africa claim Christian allegiance does not imply that they all have a common understanding of what Christianity means. This is partly because Christian faith is invariably bound up with different social interests. Christians are in conflict with one another, and each of the confronting parties legitimates its respective position by interpreting social reality and the Christian tradition in ways which are often radically different. Indeed, the conflict between races and classes within contemporary South Africa has a decidedly religious character.

Theologies have clashed with each other since the beginning of the Christian era, each claiming to be the most faithful interpretation of the Christian faith. While there is a recognition on the part of many theologians today that no one theology contains all the truth,[1] situations continue to arise when theological tolerance implies a denial of the Christian faith. Such a *status confessionis* presently exists in South Africa,[2] and the declaration that apartheid is a heresy symbolises the conflict of which we speak.[3]

Theology, social context and human interest
In the concluding chapter of his book *A Matter of Hope*, Nicholas Lash asks whether the notion of a common Christian tradition is any longer meaningful. This is a particularly serious question for Christians in contemporary South Africa because we have always believed that despite our differences of race, culture and class, the vast majority of us are bound together by the same religion. The fact that this commonalty may be in jeopardy or has already crumbled is sobering, to say the least. Lash does not answer his question but he does make three helpful observations:

Firstly, it is increasingly evident that there are, and have long been, within Christianity, fundamental differences *in ways of believing*, of perceiving the connections between human experience and Christian belief, and that these differences cut deeper than, and cut across, historically inherited denominational divisions. Secondly, that the most serious and intractable divisions within Christianity are increasingly perceived to be social, cultural and even political in character. Thirdly, that in circumstances in which disagreement and conflict have hardened to the point at which Christians find it necessary to acknowledge that the notion of a 'common tradition' has become, in practice, meaningless, simply to *accept* this fact would be to have surrendered hope.[4]

Christians in South Africa are certainly divided by denominational confessions, traditions and structures whose importance cannot be minimised. But the theological conflict is not being waged primarily at this level. The dividing lines have more to do with the varying ways in which Christians, broadly but not exclusively separated by race and class, perceive social reality, and the different ways in which they relate these perceptions to the Christian tradition and their own particular needs or interests. This is nothing new in the history of Christianity, for every denominational tradition is the product of earlier interactions between social forces, human interests, and theological convictions in some historical context.

Theology is not revelation; it is a human activity subject to human limitations and sin. A pure theology unaffected by human and social filters, a theology without any historical and therefore contextual mediation, is not a possibility. This means that even with the best of intentions and the most rigorous attempt to be faithful to the gospel alone, theology is invariably bound up to some degree with the service of particular interests, whether private, social or ecclesial.[5] The proponents of a particular theology may deny this, but that is only a sign of their lack of critical self-awareness. Theologians are part of their context; their understanding is shaped by their culture and position within both church and society. Thus theology invariably means the knowledge of God in relation to a particular tradition within a given historical context, and is always both a way of relating Christian faith to social reality and a product of that relationship.

But a genuinely Christian theology should struggle to transcend selfish interest and ideological captivity, in the service of those interests consonant with and demanded by the kingdom of God. For this reason the fundamental task of theology is to reflect on how God's self-disclosure has been discerned in those situations to which Scripture bears witness in relation to the issues facing us in our present context and our response to them. While it is beyond the scope of this essay to enter the discussion on the normative claims of Scripture or its relationship to theology, we affirm that it does make such claims upon us. Moreover, God's reign over all reality in the life, death and resurrection of Jesus Christ, to which Scripture bears witness, is the constitutive event for Christian faith, and for the life, mission and identity of the church. It also provides theology with the basis for its critical function.

The critical task of theology is to evaluate all truth and interest claims, including its own, whether in word or deed, in the light of the gospel of the reign of God in Jesus Christ. In this way theology should act as a hermeneutics of suspicion, testing all theologies and ideologies to see whether or not they are really in the service of the truth or in the service of some other interest which contradicts the gospel. If we remain aware that there is no pure theology unaffected by the pre-understanding of theologians and their place and role within their historical and social environment, we may be able to resist the temptation to absolutise uncritically any particular theology, and to welcome the enriching possibilities of theological plurality. At the same time, if we acknowledge the normative witness to Jesus Christ in Scripture in the struggle to discern the truth and expose falsehood in our historical situation, then we have a common basis, upon which we can deal with the issues. The different ways in which theology sets about these tasks (that is, theological method and hermeneutics) is one reason for the plurality of theologies. At a more fundamental level it is part of the theological conflict with which we are concerned.

The hermeneutical issues related to the theological conflict in South Africa are complex. Those familiar with both the role of historical experience in the development of Afrikaner *volksteologie* and the discussion on revelation and history associated a decade ago with the Pannenberg-circle will immediately recognise this.[6] Certainly the debate cannot be reduced to the worn-out clichés of the fundamentalist–liberal conflict. Neither can it simply be said that it is a difference in hermeneutics which separates those who affirm and those who deny that apartheid is a heresy. There is often a basic hermeneutical agreement between the opposing parties,[7] just as there is disagreement on both sides.[8]

Furthermore, the emergence of black theology in South Africa and the impact of Latin American liberation theological method upon it, have introduced a whole new methodology into the debate, including that derived from a materialist exegesis of Scripture. Whatever its merits, such a hermeneutic calls radically into question the methodology hitherto adopted by both the defenders and opponents of apartheid whether their theology was shaped by a particular confessional tradition (Catholic, Reformed, etc.) or theological school (liberal, evangelical, neo-Orthodox, etc.). These issues continually surface in one form or another in this essay and beg for further investigation.

In situations of ideological conflict where peoples and groups are struggling with each other for power, for their interests and therefore for their future, theology can become a consuming passion. For it is in such situations that penultimate concerns, demands, fears and expectations, are directly related to ultimate claims, norms and values. Theological conflict is nothing other than the clash between worldviews or ideologies and their related interests, but with reference to the transcendent or the knowledge of God's purpose. Theological conflict is, in fact, inevitable in those societies where the struggle for justice, power and reconciliation not only requires transcendent legitimation, but where the will of God also remains a matter of conviction, of life, death and hope. Hence the inevitable and inseparable relationship between faith, theology and politics.

The conflict in historical perspective

The present theological conflict is in continuity with that which began when African indigenous cultures were first confronted by colonial power and the worldview of European Christendom.[9] Though we cannot enter fully into the current debate on the nineteenth-century missionary movement,[10] it is where we have to begin.

While the *theologies* of both the Europeans, and in particular, the missionaries and that of the Africans were compatible in certain respects,[11] there were important differences with far-reaching consequences for the shaping of South African society. Central to these, as Richard Elphick points out, was the radical distinction which the Protestant missionaries made between God's actions in nature and history.

By severing history from nature, the missionaries, in part unwittingly, unleashed powerful forces in Africa. On the one hand, they closed nature down; they silenced and deadened it by eliminating personalist and magical strategies of explanation and offering instead the simplifications of mathematics which make possible the technology of industrialism. On the other hand, they blew history wide open with visions of a global brotherhood and endless improvement, all to be accomplished by free men working out the purposes of God. They stamped science on nature; and on history, revolution.[12]

Although the impact of the missionaries upon society was ambiguous, nevertheless the revolutionary potential of their message was introduced. The present debate concerns the realisation of that potential in our time.

European missionary activity produced several reactions. The missionary enterprise was regarded by the settlers as undermining colonial society. It was seen as a threat to their material and social interests. The fact that both parties gave theological justification to their respective positions is indicative of the problem we are examining.[13] In fact, we see here the beginnings of the conflict between a *volksteologie* which serves the interests of Europeans and their descendants, whether in power or in the struggle for power,[14] and those theologies which have purported to serve the interests of blacks, even though often in a spirit of paternalism or even in alliance with forces that have later proved unhelpful to black interests.

The African response to the missionary proclamation and campaign was varied. Some regarded the missionary enterprise as an integral part of European colonisation and thus a means of enforcing cultural and political domination. Others saw it more positively. But either way it posed a threat to African culture and its religious worldview: a threat not successfully countered until the late nineteenth century with the emergence of the African Independent, or, more correctly, indigenous church movement.[15] This movement, which began within the fold of the mission churches, represented the first attempt by black Christians to break free from European ideological dominance in the church and society. Its theology, fashioned out of the interaction of African traditional religion and European Christianity, was the first contextual theology in South Africa. The continued rapid growth of the movement testifies to its abiding significance.

Unless the theological conflict in South Africa today is seen primarily in terms of this broader historical, cultural and socio-political conflict between blacks and whites, with the missionaries and their successors standing uneasily and ambivalently in the middle, its true character cannot be appreciated. At the same time the internal conflictual character of European theology itself also needs to be considered, because it has not only dominated the churches of the descendants of the settlers but also shaped the Christian faith and worldview of those blacks who have been evangelised by European missionaries and who have remained within the churches of historic Christendom. In the process, it has introduced into the South African context controversies which make the resolution of our own problems more difficult.

But, almost in spite of themselves, the European theology which the missionaries brought to South Africa, as Elphick intimated, fostered the development of contextual theologies. This in turn has led in our day to the more radical exploration of the implications of the Christian faith for the issues facing the church in South Africa. Most notable amongst these has been black theology, the third significant contextual development since the African Independent church movement was born and Dutch Reformed theology gave its support to the struggles of the Afrikaner.

European theology came to South Africa as part of colonial expansion, arriving in different Western European denominational and confessional containers. The various forms of this theology were themselves contextual, though designed for a very different historical situation. As long as colonial society mirrored Europe such theologies were not regarded as requiring any modification for they served the needs and the interests of the settlers. Moreover, as long as the missionaries failed to distinguish between the Christian message and its European formulation and cultural containers, they too did not see any need to rethink their theology in the light of a new context.

Nevertheless, some tentative steps towards the contextualisation of European theology were taken during the nineteenth century largely because the missionary movement could not avoid the challenge. Consider the work of John Colenso, Anglican bishop of Natal, whose efforts at developing an indigenous theology contributed to his eventual excommunication. Colenso, for all his faults, was the first South African theologian of note who tried to relate the European theological debate of his day to African culture in such a way that they creatively interacted with each other.[16] But conflict within European theology, particularly the nineteenth-century battle for the Bible against the inroads of higher criticism, and conflict about the development of an indigenous theology, combined with ecclesiastical politics to prevent this from taking place.

The development of a contextual theology within the Dutch Reformed Church (NGK) during the second half of the nineteenth century and the opening decades of the twentieth occurred in response to three factors. In the first place, there was the struggle against theological liberalism symbolised by the heresy trial of J. J. Kotze in 1862–3 and, much later in 1928, that of J. du Plessis. Just as the Anglicans were torn apart by the Colenso controversy, so the NGK was divided between those who had imbibed liberal theological tendencies emanating at the time from Europe, and those who, like Andrew Murray, Jr., represented a more conservative evangelical Calvinism. Murray's theology itself came under suspicion and attack at the turn of the century by the advocates of Kuyperian neo-Calvinism who regarded his pietism as Arminian. These two forms of Calvinism have uneasily coexisted within the NGK ever since, though the focus has shifted to socio-political issues.

In the second place, there was the development of a missionary strategy, influenced by German missiology, which led to theological compromise and a policy of segregation within the NGK. As a result the Dutch Reformed Mission Church (NG Sendingkerk) was founded in 1881 and theological justification was thereby provided for the evolvement of political separate development. This development lies behind the intense contemporary debate within the Dutch Reformed family of churches. It also led directly to the Ottawa decision of the World Alliance of Reformed Churches to suspend the membership of the white church in 1982, and to the adoption of the Belhar Draft Confession of Faith by the Mission Church that same year.[17]

In the third place, there was a struggle for Afrikaner cultural identity, political rights and power. Out of this struggle NGK theology, protest notwithstanding, took the final decisive step towards a *volksteologie* in the service of Afrikaner interests.[18] Together, then, these three factors prepared the way for the support which the NGK gave to the rise of Afrikaner Christian–Nationalism, to the moral justification of the ideology of apartheid, and to the contemporary *status confessionis* and theological conflict. It is a tragedy for all, not least the NGK, that the most powerful contextual theology which developed within its ranks and in South Africa at large, gave its support to apartheid, and that this ideology was equated with Calvinism.

There are other interpretations of the Reformed tradition within the South African churches that have been critical of its identification with apartheid and its conflation with Afrikaner interests. Representative of this more critical position within the NGK itself was B. B. Keet, whose teaching had such a profound influence upon Beyers Naudé. This conflict continues today within the white NGK, and is one of the elements in the overall theological struggle we are describing.[19] But even more, the emergence of a black Reformed theology especially from within the very Mission Church created in response to white interest, has begun to harness Calvinism in the interests of black liberation. This has not only provided a radical new dimension to the internal Reformed theological debate, but has proved to be a major catalyst in the theological struggle as a whole.[20]

Yet long before Keet, Naudé or the advent of black Reformed theology there were non-Dutch Reformed missionaries who, Calvinist by persuasion, sought within the limitations of their time to champion the cause of the slaves and the indigenous peoples. The much vilified missionaries of the London Missionary Society were as much Calvinist as were their contemporary settler opponents. Unfortunately, the settlers, as Gideon Thom reminds us, 'did not appreciate the fact that it was Philip's Calvinism that stimulated his interest in social and political matters.'[21] This is indicative of how closely theology is bound up with social perception, and that the real conflict is often not between confessions but between group interests.

It must not be assumed, however, that the descendants of the missionaries and the English-speaking settlers, whether Methodist, Anglican, Presbyterian, Catholic, Baptist or Congregational, who now comprise the so-called English-speaking churches, have been guiltless when it comes to mixing their religion with their social, political and especially economic interests.[22] For all its strengths, the politically liberal tradition affirmed by these churches has often been paternalistic at best and self-serving at worst. Despite their sometimes courageous critique of apartheid they have been too beholden to the structures of society to break free from them in the interests of a fully just society.[23]

The only socially and historically significant *inter-confessional* theological conflict along traditional European lines has been between Protestantism, and especially NGK theology, and Catholicism, both Roman and Anglican. Some observers in the past have not only regarded the two creeds as incompatible, but have seen their conflict as central to the debate.[24] Certainly between 1930 and 1960 many Afrikaner Calvinists regarded Catholic and Anglican missions and especially mission schools as a danger to white society because they inculcated liberal social values. So *die Roomsegevaar* was as much political as theological. For ecumenical and socio-political reasons this sense of a

Catholic threat has subsided in recent years so that today Calvinists and Catholics on the left of the political spectrum find themselves arrayed against Calvinists and Catholics in alliance on the right – an irony which reveals again that the real conflict has little to do with the traditional theological controversies of the past or of European Christendom.

The major theological conflicts within the churches of the settlers during the nineteenth century were thus the result of a combination of factors. Some of these, the liberal–conservative, pietist–Kuyperian, and Protestant–Catholic conflicts, were inherited from the theological battlegrounds of Europe. In the process they not only were allowed to bedevil the life of the white church in South Africa but also created false divisions within the emerging black church. Other conflicts related to missionary endeavour and policy, the awakening consciousness of African Christians, the Afrikaner struggle for identity and then power, and the English capitalist–liberal tradition. Together these have led to the development of theological polarities and distinctives within South African theology determined by contextual concerns, and have shaped the present theological conflict in South Africa.

The contemporary debate

We shall not explore all the theological tensions in contemporary South Africa, important as each may be, especially to those involved, but rather concentrate on the central conflict we have identified because of its significance for the church and society as a whole. Epitomised historically by the clash between European and African theologies and interests, this conflict is integrally related to the wider theological debate within the universal church. The theological conflict in South Africa today can be separated neither from its history nor from the issues, debates and confrontations that concern the whole ecumene.

Before discussing this conflict, however, one other debate merits comment, namely that between ecumenical and conservative evangelical theology. This worldwide debate is a particular source of tension in most mainline denominations in South Africa, especially amongst their white constituencies. This alone suggests the need to take it seriously in considering the theological conflicts of contemporary South Africa. It is also germane to our discussion of the more fundamental conflict which is our primary concern.[25] At the same time, the debate between ecumenicals and evangelicals needs critical evaluation in relation to the more fundamental South African conflict. It may simply be a red-herring which obfuscates the real issues.

First of all, there is considerable debate today on what it means to be an evangelical.[26] Even conservative evangelicals disagree amongst themselves. Secondly, many ecumenicals, particularly within the Third World, are evangelical and many evangelicals are ecumenical.[27] Thirdly, the popular way of distinguishing the two by identifying 'ecumenism' with the 'social gospel' and 'evangelicalism' with white reactionary politics may contain some truth, but it really does not stand up to rigorous examination.

The issues raised by this debate are undoubtedly important not only for white Christians but also for the black church. Of particular importance is that of the authority of Scripture and its relationship to social witness in the South African context. But too often the debate between evangelicals and ecumenicals becomes embroiled in ecclesiastical politics, or else it replays the North American conflict between liberals and fundamentalists. In neither case does it really struggle with the more urgent issues facing us in our context. For this reason we need to be wary of uncritically accepting sterile Western debates that may only be tangential to our situation.[28]

The declaration that apartheid is a heresy and the recognition that a *status confessionis* exists in South Africa really transcend the distinctions between evangelicals and ecumenicals. Indeed, it is precisely at this point that the evangelical witness to the truth of the gospel (contrary to the apartheid heresy) and ecumenical concern for the unity of the church (contrary to the division of the church along racial lines) come together. With this in mind we turn to consider a further global debate, that between liberation and more traditional forms of theology, which in the South African context has been brought powerfully into the centre of theological discussion by the advent of black theology.

Black theology emerged in the late sixties as a response to the rise of black consciousness amongst radical black students. It was intended as a theology that would enable blacks not only to retain their Christian faith, but also to discover resources in the gospel for their struggle against apartheid. To begin with, it was a theology of protest against a dehumanising system which had reached its nadir in apartheid. But during the seventies it began to develop its potential for revitalising the black church encapsulated within the white-dominated mainline churches. For the first time since the emergence of the African Independent movement and its withdrawal from the mission churches, an alternative theology rooted in African culture and black experience was born, but this time within the historic mainline churches. This theology, varied as it may be within itself, has proved to be the catalyst which has redefined the theological map of South Africa in a dramatic way within less than two decades.[29]

Black theology has developed three distinctives within the South African context as it has moved beyond protest alone to the development of a constructive theology. Firstly, it has acknowledged that the polarity between it and African theology, in which the focus is upon integrating Christian faith and African traditional culture, is false. Though still critical of some forms of African theology it has begun to transcend the dichotomy so that the wholeness of black experience, both past and present, is served.[30]

Secondly, black theology has learnt, partly in dialogue with Latin

American theologies of liberation, that doing theology cannot be separated from social analysis and praxis. In the process it has become a methodological partner of liberation theology. The issues are no longer defined only in terms of race but increasingly in terms of class; the struggle is not just between whites and blacks, but between the rich and the poor, the oppressors and the oppressed. Lebamang Sebidi expresses the widespread conviction amongst black theologians that racism and economic exploitation cannot be separated in the black struggle and therefore in social analysis and the development of black theology:

As long as the black people in this country suffer a double bondage, racial oppression and economic exploitation, the task of Black Theology will always be double-pronged. Racial capitalism is the name of the game. That is the sin that Black Theology wants to uncover and eradicate in God's own name.[31]

More recently, black theologians have also been challenged to include in their analysis the oppression of women. This marks the beginnings of a feminist theology related to the social struggle in South Africa.[32]

A significant third development within black theology has been the attempt to relate it more directly to the major Christian confessional traditions. Black theologians cannot avoid asking what it means to be a black Methodist (Anglican, Catholic, Lutheran, etc.) today in South Africa.[33] Of particular note in this regard is the work of Allan Boesak whose latest volume of essays expresses this in its title, *Black and Reformed: Apartheid, Liberation and the Calvinist Tradition.* But the same is true of Lutheran theologians such as Manas Buthelezi and Simon Maimela; Anglicans like Desmond Tutu; Catholics like Buti Tlhagale; and the black theologians involved in the Black Methodist Caucus, the Alliance of Black Reformed Christians in Southern Africa (ABRECSA), and the Dutch Reformed *Belydendekring.* Indeed, black theology in South Africa reflects different traditional and confessional nuances even though it is basically united in method and content. Consider for example Manas Buthelezi's Lutheran emphasis upon the theology of the cross and Desmond Tutu's Anglo–Catholic theology of the incarnation.

Of course, there are dangers in this development because a new confessionalism will exacerbate an already strong sense of denominationalism within the black community, inherited from the missionary movement, and so fragment the unity discovered in a common black experience and struggle. If this danger can be avoided, however, there are considerable theological resources available which, through the appropriation of diverse elements within the traditions, could help in the struggle for justice and in the search for Christian unity and the renewal of the church.

The emergence of black theology has brought the inherent theological conflict in South Africa to a head. Whether one agrees or disagrees with it, it is impossible to ignore its challenge. In spite of the official preoccupation with ethnicity and the need to keep white and black in separate compartments, black theology has been perceived by those in power as a threat to their interests. Their perception is correct, at least in so far as white interests are best served by apartheid. Within the main-line churches, where black theology has had its most articulate expo-nents, some whites have criticised it as an ideological distortion of the gospel, the legitimation of racism in reverse. Others have criticised it for perpetuating the same way of doing theology as that embodied within Afrikaner theology in its struggle for Afrikaner identity and power.[34]

Black theology like any other is not beyond criticism, for it too is a human construction that needs constant evaluation in the light of Scripture. Certainly white theologians do black theologians no favours when they paternalistically applaud their efforts instead of treating them with the critical rigour they deserve. Black theologians them-selves are aware of problem areas and are particularly conscious of the danger that their project may be elitist and remote from the grassroots church. But critical engagement does not mean that whites should be hasty in their judgment, or too concerned 'to cast out the mote in their brother's eye'. After all, European theology gave rise to the heresy of apartheid! As indicated, this does not imply a paternalistic, uncritical acceptance of black theology. It means that critique must not become a white way of escape from the radical challenge which black theology presents.

The fact that black theology is undeniably bound up with black interests is neither surprising nor a matter for criticism even though it may become so later. Indeed, *at this point in history* the interests of black theology are those of the poor, the powerless and the oppressed, and these interests are consonant in large measure with the gospel of the kingdom of God.

For this reason there are white theologians who have begun to discern in black theology not only a legitimate expression of the Chris-tian gospel within our context, but also a theology which challenges and judges our own, and a catalyst which is forcing us to rework our theologies in ways which are more biblically faithful and more contex-tually relevant to the struggle for justice and peace. It is within this debate that we return to the question of the *status confessionis*, for it symbolises the centre of the theological conflict in which Christians of the same denomination and confession are to be found on both sides of the divide.

Several factors are involved in determining this divide. Firstly, for many Christians the gospel has nothing to do with socio-political issues, it is acontextual, 'spiritual' and a private matter. This unbiblical understanding of Christian faith derives in large measure from the eighteenth-century Enlightenment with its strong individualism and its separation of reality into the material and spiritual spheres in the interests of scientific progress. This reduces Christianity to a ghetto religion in which pseudo-piety flourishes and responsibility for the world is forsaken. Such pseudo-piety abounds within the white South African community. It is certainly encouraged by those in power, stimulated by tendencies within such movements as the charismatic renewal, and reinforced by the processes of secularisation. Thus, even before considering the divide created by the *status confessionis* we have to acknowledge the division between those Christians who so spiritualise the gospel that it is regarded as without socio-political significance, and those who believe that the Christian faith is concerned with the whole of reality.

Secondly, there is the cleavage among those who affirm the socio-political significance of the gospel, but who differ, often radically, in their analysis of socio-political reality. The conflict between Calvinists in South Africa is a very pertinent example. All who remain true to the Reformed tradition affirm the socio-political relevance of the Christian faith. Where they differ is in their interpretation of what this means in a given context. Compare, for example, the white NGK's report *Ras, Volk en Nasie* (Human relations and the South African scene in the light of Scripture) adopted by the General Synod in 1974, with the Belhar Draft Confession adopted by the NG Mission Church in 1982. For the former, the government's policy of separate development is supported on the basis of Scripture; for the latter, such support is rejected along with the separation of people on the ground of race, and the *status confessionis* is affirmed. Yet both agree on the need for the church to take a stand on socio-political issues in terms of the kingdom of God and justice.

Thirdly, there is disagreement among those who agree that apartheid is a heresy but who differ in their understanding of what this implies in practice. In some measure this disagreement stems from a different emphasis in social analysis, for the divide here is usually between those who analyse apartheid solely in racial terms and those who define the struggle as one between the oppressed poor (who are almost invariably black) and the affluent oppressors, whether white or black. This analysis contributes to a different strategy for social change hinging on whether or not the system can be changed from within or only by confrontation. It also points to a different social goal – social democracy. At this point the debate about the Christian response to the new constitution, economic sanctions, civil disobedience, non-violent and violent strategies, and socialism becomes pertinent. It is this debate which is forcing us to intense theological reflection upon our common Christian heritage, and to the discovery that it is this heritage, liberated from selfish interests, which provides the church in South Africa with the theological resources needed for its task.

Theological consensus beyond the apartheid heresy

At the end of the day some of us happen to be white, and, if honest with ourselves, we cannot avoid being concerned about our interests. Yet those interests are inescapably bound up with black interests, for without an end to racism, oppression and poverty, and without the development of a just society in which all have their rightful place as human beings, white interests as understood hitherto have no future. They are best served by 'seeking first God's kingdom and justice'.

Yet, it is only now at the end of the colonial period, under the impact of the dynamics of a changing social, political and ecclesiastical environment, that we have begun to perceive how much of our theology is wedded to particular interests that are contrary to the gospel. Moreover, European theology and church life has been shaped by its cultural heritage and the scientific worldview of the West. So while it might accuse African theology of syncretism, or black theology of ideological captivity, much European theology is guilty of both. If the present theological conflict has done nothing else it has forced upon us the need to face these issues and the need to question the usefulness and validity of imported, undigested and regurgitated theologies, and to work more consciously towards a genuine contextual theology for South Africa.

In such an endeavour the theological heritage of Europe, liberated from a colonial mentality, racism, and its captivity to a secularised Western worldview, and the theological heritage of Africa will no longer simply confront each other, but interact in the service of the gospel of the reign of God in Jesus Christ, in our context. Hopefully out of this critical interaction may come the rediscovery of a Christian commonalty that will provide the basis for and a means to enable the church and Christians to participate in the creation of a just society. But it will have to be a common, biblical tradition beyond the divide of the apartheid heresy, a truly non-racial South African theology. When and if this happens, the message of the kingdom of God proclaimed by the early missionaries, which, in Elphick's works, threatened to 'blow history wide open', will fulfil its promise.

Doing theology in a situation of conflict
FRANK CHIKANE

About three years ago the Institute for Contextual Theology (ICT) brought together concerned and committed Christians from different parts of southern Africa to grapple with the question of 'doing theology' in our situation of conflict in South Africa.

This programme resulted in small group discussions, workshops, seminars, conferences, short-term research programmes and involvement in particular social and political struggles.

Several questions have arisen from this exercise. What is the difference between 'doing' theology and 'learning' or 'studying' theology? What is the theological position of the church in relation to this conflict? This essay focuses on the theological methodology that has emerged. An attempt is made to identify a contrast between the traditional method of theology and a newly emerging methodology.

'Doing' theology and 'learning' or 'studying' theology

The expression 'doing theology' is concerned with a particular methodology or type of theology. Lebameng J. Sebidi, in a paper delivered at an Ecumenical Association of African Theology of Southern Africa (EAATSA) Conference, noted that the old, traditional method of theologising was characterised by a hefty dose of deductive reasoning. In this process, he said, 'it is therefore not really surprising that in this theological methodology the sciences that played a major supportive role were those of philosophy and rational psychology.'[1] He presented a cartoon-like picture of this traditional theological methodology:

The deductive method of reasoning can be likened to a man going about frantically with a bag full of answers (solutions) looking for questions (problems). In this paradigm it is the answers that determine the problems; the latter must adapt and accommodate themselves to the answers. Needless to say, this method is ahistorical and therefore bears characteristics of being essentialist, and unrealistic in its approach to human problems.[2]

On the other hand there is the new methodology, expressed in the phrase 'doing theology', which is emerging as a dominant methodology in the Third World. Southern African theologians who are also part of the Third World and who are committed to the *mission Dei* of saving, redeeming and liberating the world are beginning to reinterpret the tradition of the Bible and that of Israel in a more progressive way. They are reminding the church that theology is and can only be a reflection on the continuing activity of God in the world. Gabriel M. Setiloane, for example, observes that 'theology is a verbalization of the experiences of the divinity at work'.[3] Theology seeks to interpret and understand God in action with His people, in a particular situation. This methodology affirms that the Bible is a record of God's action with the Jews, a record of the struggle, involving the Israelites with their God, for justice and peace. It is the story of a God who revealed Himself in history, a history of activity directed towards a more humane and just society, which is called the kingdom of God.

José Miguez Bonino for instance says that Latin American theology of liberation is beginning to emerge *post facto*, 'as the reflection about facts and experiences which have already evoked a response from Christians'.[4] Whereas traditional theological methodology assumes that knowledge precedes action the new methodology argues that action precedes knowledge.

Miguez Bonino says that 'there is no knowledge except in action itself, in the process of transforming the world through participation in history'. Similarly, Hugo Assmann talks about the rejection of 'any logos which is not the logos of a praxis'.[5] This is to say that there is no truth outside or beyond the concrete historical events in which human beings are involved as agents. The sociology of knowledge confirms this view, showing that people think within a definite context, within a given praxis.

Black theologians, for instance, read the Bible in and from the life experiences and situations of blacks. They read it as a book of liberation. As Bonganjolo Goba observes, the prime concern in reading the Bible is 'to lift up forcefully certain biblical motives as paradigms of the liberation process'. [6] He proceeds to show that black theology is involved with a hermeneutical approach that emerges from and speaks to our experience as a black Christian community. Hermeneutical praxis of the biblical faith is not simply confined to interpreting text and experience, but concerns itself with engaging in the transformation of society. Allan Boesak concurs: 'Theology is not detached, cool, objective and neutral' but rather 'passionately involved'. Theology 'begins with the experiences of actual struggles, suffering and joys of particular communities.'[7]

Theology must be investigated in relation to the praxis out of which it emerges. This is why the imperialistic claim made by Western theology of universality must be rejected. Miguez Bonino argues that 'at this point the instruments created by the two modern masters in the art of "suspecting", namely Freud and Marx, are of great significance'.[8] We cannot receive a 'universal' theological interpretation from the rich oppressors, colonisers or racists without suspicion. We must always ask what kind of praxis a particular interpretation supports, rejects or legitimises.

Miguez Bonino raises an interesting question in elucidating this point:

Why is it, for instance, that the obvious political motives and undertones in the life of Jesus have remained so hidden to liberal interpreters until very recently? Is this merely a regrettable oversight on the part of these scholars, or is it mostly unconscious, to be sure, the expression of a liberal ideological distinction of levels or spheres which relegates religion to the area of subjectivity and individual privacy?[9]

Perhaps Leys can shed light on this issue in suggesting that when Africans read the Bible for themselves, it 'meant that the taught could discover for themselves what the teachers had failed to find.'[10] Beidelman, in turn, says that 'the missionaries were startled when natives took up modern nationalism – even though themes of nationalism and anti-imperialism fill the Old Testament, and the New preaches egalitarianism at odds with colonialism and racism.'[11]

'Doing theology' therefore means action and reflection on one's activity and involvement with the people, and participation in their struggles. The theologian must be involved with the people in the activity of God, and 'do theology' in action. No Christian can afford to be left out of the action of God with His people. If the theologian is not part of that action of God, then we must be suspicious of the side on which he or she belongs in this struggle with God to establish a just society. Theology not grounded in liberating praxis is not liberating theology.

Implications of this type of methodology

The new methodology means becoming involved in the struggle for a full humanity – in squatter camps, in makeshift shacks, in the ghettoes of South Africa, and in the barren and arid lands of the Bantustans where people are dying of hunger and diseases. It involves being in detention with the victims of the system where one will be forced to ask realistic and concrete theological questions about God. When one starts asking seemingly heretical questions, about the role of God in all this, one starts to 'do theology'. This all demands cost. It is demanding because it means theologians must relinquish their position of privilege and choose rather to suffer with the people of God: from this experience a people's theology can be born. It means priests should leave their mansions, and live with the poor, weak and downtrodden to share in their struggles. It is costly because one might be caught in the crossfire whilst ministering to victims of the system. One might become a victim of detention in solitary confinement without trial. It could mean being banned, restricted or banished. It could mean death in detention or even assassination.

In counting the costs of 'doing theology', one can almost be certain that those who are part of the status quo, those who benefit from the apartheid system and capitalist exploitation cannot use this methodology. They are not going to take the risk or pay the cost. In a recent editorial in the *ICT News* a similar analysis is identified: 'This henceforth shall be our way, and the costs to us for doing theology in our Southern African context – a context of escalating violence'.[12] To do theology in a situation of conflict demands carrying the cross. This is a methodology which exists in contradistinction to 'learning' or 'studying' theology.

Preferential option for the poor and oppressed
In the conflict-ridden situation in southern Africa, filled with racial conflict, class conflict, ideological conflict and divisions between women and men, the involvement methodology cannot, however, mean blind forms of involvement. A 1983 dialogue between Third and First World theologians, emphasised: 'Doing theology begins with involvement in the struggles and hopes of oppressed peoples.' Elsewhere it was said: 'Christians are called to practise a spirituality rooted in an option for oppressed peoples'.[13]

It is clear from this methodology of involvement that it entails opting for the victims of society. MUCCOR (Ministers United for Christian Co-responsibility), dealing with the subject of ministry in a conflict situation, expressed this same conviction:

The word of God, the humble ministers of which we are, is one and the same, a word of *judgement* and salvation, and judgement is an essential *decision* for and against issues. *Judgement is option-taking*.

The statement continues:

It is, therefore, on the basis of this intrinsically judgemental nature of God's word, that we humbly wish to make it known that, as servants of the living God, we take an option in favour of the *victims* of the conflict in our society, and unequivocally commit ourselves to justice. Our option and commitment shall be active as opposed to being merely moral.[14]

What Third World theologians have been able to expose is that there is no such thing as 'theological neutrality'. Using the instruments created by Freud and Marx in the art of 'suspecting', they have demonstrated that Western theology is not as neutral as it claims to be. Southern African theologians of liberation have similarly exposed Western theology as a theology of the status quo, which has taken sides with the racial-capitalist apartheid state against the dispossessed and disenfranchised black majority. There is no neutral theology and no neutral biblical interpretation.[15]

The Hammanskraal EAATSA Declaration reads as follows:

We believe that as much as the God of Israel was committed to the history of the people of Israel, and to their struggles for liberation, our God must be committed to the struggles of our people even today. That as much as Jesus Christ took sides with the downtrodden of his day, even today he is on the side of the poor and oppressed. We believe that God's taking sides with the poor and oppressed is not because they are better than the victimizer, but because they are victims of injustice.

We believe that option taking means a critical theological involvement on the side of good against evil and not merely for the sake of one's own group or nationalistic aspirations, lest we be like the Afrikaans ecclesiastical establishment which has contributed in producing the heretical apartheid theology.

We further note that there is not only the possibility of conformity of theologians who are part of the oppressive systems, but that there are also temptations of co-option of theologians who are part of the oppressed majority to the side of the rich and oppressors.[15]

Conclusion

There is a difference between the traditional method of theologising and the emerging new involvement-based methodology of 'doing theology'.

(1) The involvement methodology uses *inductive reasoning*, with the context usurping the 'place that used to be occupied by the a priori, major premise in traditional "academic" theology'.[17]

(2) The involvement methodology places emphasis on *orthopraxis* (the right practice) rather than orthodoxy (the right doctrine or teaching), which is the emphasis of the Western church. This implies involvement in the struggles of the people for a just society here on earth, in preparation for the kingdom of God.

(3) The involvement methodology means *taking sides* with the victims of society against the victimisers. In South Africa, this involves taking sides with the oppressed and exploited black majority because they are victims of apartheid and not simply because they are black. Taking sides must ultimately be to the benefit of both victim and victimiser, by liberating both from the sinful structures of oppression. There is no question of neutrality. Being neutral in a conflict situation means taking sides with the victimiser.

(4) The motive of this new method is that of liberation. It is committed to social change, and to approximating on earth the kingdom of God. This methodology is subversive by nature.

(5) Whereas the traditional method relied on philosophy (especially metaphysics), the new methodology demands the use of social analytical tools such as those developed by Marx and other social scientists.

This is the method and motive of liberation theology in Latin America and other Third World situations where people are subjected to economic exploitation and domination. This is the method of feminist theology in the face of sexist oppression and exploitation. This is the method of black theology both in North America and South Africa where racial oppression and exploitation is the order of the day. This is also the method of the Bible and the early tradition of the church.

African Independent churches:
a study in socio-theological protest
ITUMELENG MOSALA

South Africa is by definition a conflict-ridden society, although the exact nature of the conflict is often assumed rather than precisely articulated. It is nevertheless clear that central to this conflict are racial and economic divisions inherent in the contemporary South African scene. The pertinent task of the theologian in this situation is not merely to identify the task of theology but, more precisely, to perceive the nature and identity of conflict which is inherent in theological discourse. Theology is too often seen as 'neutral' in such conflict. Theologians do not readily understand that they are part of the conflict. They create the impression that theology is able to stand outside the world of social conflict, and from this elevation pontificate on the activities of the day. This essay attempts to correct that perception by demonstrating that theology arises out of and bears the indelible marks of racial and social conflict in South Africa, as elsewhere.

It is argued here that what is commonly referred to as 'contextual' theology must be subjected to a thorough sociological and cultural analysis. For the purpose of this task the African Independent churches are identified as a point of reference.

Obscurantism and contextual theology

'Contextual theology' has entered our vocabulary unresisted during the past fifteen years, and like many instruments of ideological manipulation, it has been accepted uncritically. There are at least three grounds on which 'contextuality' in theology ought to be criticised. Firstly, the notion implies a 'theological harmlessness'. This is not borne out by historical facts, and cannot stand up to rigorous socio-political scrutiny. The implication is that there is nothing wrong with 'theology' as such, and that it is by definition a legitimate and even a liberating activity. In contradiction, it is argued here that Western Christian theology has been and is a most pernicious religious version of capitalist ruling-class ideology.

E. P. Thompson, the British historian, has shown how in the nineteenth century Christian theology functioned as a cultural tool of the then developing industrial capitalist society. The new social discipline required by the industrialisation process demanded the legitimation of a cultural value-system. For this to be achieved, the worldly happiness of the workers had to be sacrificed in favour of a future happiness in a future state. Thompson argues, rightly, that with the material alterations introduced by capitalist industrialisation in the nineteenth century, there had to come corresponding alterations in the beliefs and consciousness of people:

It is evident that there was, in 1800, casuistry enough in the theology of all available English Churches to reinforce the manufacturer's own sense of moral esteem. Whether he held an hierarchic faith, or felt himself to be elected, or saw in his success the evidence of grace or godliness, he felt few promptings to exchange his residence beside the mill at Bradford for a monastic cell on Bardley Island. But Methodist theology, by virtue of its promiscuous opportunism, was better suited than any other to serve as the religion of a proletariat whose members had not the least reason, in social experience, to feel themselves to be 'elected'. In his theology, Wesley appears to have dispensed with the best and selected unhesitatingly the worse elements of Puritanism: if in social class terms Methodism was hermaphroditic, in doctrinal terms it was a mule.[1]

Thompson helps to explode the myth of a politically neutral theology at any stage in history. For Methodists this is especially important for showing that the theology of their founder was, whether he was conscious or unconscious of it, an instrument for the ideological manipulation of the poor classes in the interests of the wealthy classes of society. The implication of 'contextual theology'is that there can be a non-political theology, which must be made 'political' by applying it to a certain context. This is false.

The second reason why this rubric must be rejected has to do with the social class origins of the term itself. Whose idea is it that a theology concerned with the issues of oppression, exploitation, racism and sexism should be articulated in terms of contextual theology? While it is difficult to say precisely who was the first to come up with this notion, it is not difficult to identify the social groups that prefer the concept of contextualisation to liberation, feminist and black theologies. In South Africa this concept appeals more to white and privileged theologians than to black and oppressed theologians. Further, it is not certain that the political concerns of the oppressed people are part of the agenda of contextual theologians. In fact, the irony of contextual theology is that in its execution, oppressor and oppressed, rich and poor, are comrades in arms.

Thirdly, contextual theology as an attempt to do theology differently is simply tautological and theoretically bankrupt. This is because all theology is contextual theology. To claim to do theology contextually is therefore not to claim to do anything new. The real question is not whether theology is contextual, but what is the socio-political context out of which a particular theology emerges and which it serves. Is it a theology of the *context of the oppressors* or is it a theology of the *context of the oppressed?* It is one or the other, and its agenda is determined by this context. Black theology of liberation, in solidarity with other liberation theologies, declares itself to be irrevocably on the side of the oppressed.

Ambiguity and analysis

This analysis warrants a comment on the dominant theological status quo. Since the time of the German philosopher Hegel, and probably before, Christian theology has been saddled with an idealist methodology. Simply put, idealism is that intellectual framework which separates ideas, beliefs, ideologies from the concrete historical society. It fails to see causal connections between consciousness and material reality. A further, and more objectionable, aspect of idealism is the belief in the rule of ideas, and of universal principles existing in the world. Because ideas are believed to be primary, social and material reality is deduced from them without any critical attempt being made to inquire into the connection they have with social reality. It is this framework which has formed the basis of the dominant form of Christian theology for generations. Ideas about God, humanity, salvation and history are posited as independent from society, impinging on society and capable of producing a particular kind of society. That these ideas may be *causally* related to a particular kind of society, at a particular time in history, with a particular cultural bias, and in the interests of particular social class interests, is simply not addressed at all critically.

The 1960s gave rise to fundamental questions about such presuppositions, and for various reasons placed under the spotlight the social conditions of crucial parts of the world. 'The fundamental contradictions inherent in American society revealed themselves in the rise of Black insurgency, the anti-war movement, the student movement, etc. The cold war myth of America as the defender of liberty and justice against the evil tide of "communist aggression" was finally smashed as the truth of American aggression, subversion and brutality was revealed by the genocidal war in Vietnam'.[2] The eruptions of the poor and exploited in Latin America, Africa and Asia necessitated a radical debunking of the dogmas and myths that the West had perpetrated through educational institutions, church and missionary organisations, and political programmes of so-called development. Theologically, the outcome was Latin American theology of liberation, African theology, Asian theology, feminist theology, and black theology. The blatant contradictions between ideas and reality were identified for all to see.

Refusing to accept theological ideas as given, and society derivable from them, as idealism requires:

black theologians have, for the most part, been compelled to adopt a dialectical methodology. They have refused to accept what has been given to them by white theologians: they have claimed that all reflection about God by whites must be digested, decoded and deciphered. The first theological formulations by Afro–Americans based on biblical texts tried to come to terms with their white owners' view and their own servitude. Since its inception, black theology has been forced to reduce white self-deception and distortion of the gospel and make the Christian story meaningful in light of their oppressive conditions.[3]

In this way it had become clear to black people that non-sociological and non-cultural Christianity has never existed, and never will exist. Christianity, the gospel and theology, is a sociological and cultural product. It derives its texture from the conflicts and struggles of social classes in particular historical epochs and geographical places.

The question stands whether cultural and sociological analyses can form the basis for a black theology of liberation. Inherent in this question is the ambiguity of analysis. There are in fact at least three different sociological traditions which form the basis of a sociological analysis. A brief typological comment on each must suffice.

Emile Durkheim: collective representations

In his study of religion, the French sociologist Emile Durkheim proposed the notion of 'collective representations' as an interpretative category. For Durkheim 'the idea of society is the soul of religion'. The solidarity that exists among people in society generates 'collective representations' in religious form. Through this 'collective representation' human beings project the facts of their social life onto the realm of religion. In this sense, 'religious symbols have social facts as their true referents'.[4]

The difficulty with Durkheim's understanding of religion is that it does not explain why particular kinds of religion, or in our case, why particular kinds of theology, emerge. He does not address himself in any detail to the conflict between different 'collective representations'. This notion allows for no cultural historical distinctions, so that while there may be something appealing in this concept, it remains 'a vast abstraction subsuming all particular societies'.[5] Gottwald's conclusion is apposite:

When pressed to its foundations, Durkheim's conception is one more version of idealism. Society emerges out of the group mind and objectifies itself symbolically in religion. There will always be intimate connections between religion and society, but the particular concretions and combinations of society and religion, their phenomenal origins and sequences, are neither of much interest nor capable of explanation in strict Durkheimian terms.[6]

A black theology of liberation cannot derive its theology of struggle from Durkheim's uncritical understanding of the relationship between religion and society.

Max Weber: religious creativity

Max Weber, the German sociologist, was interested in understanding the *selective* force of religious ideas in the *mutual* relationships between society and religion. He argued that religious phenomena exercise a powerful and creative influence on social life. In his well-known study, *The Protestant Ethic and the Spirit of Capitalism*, Weber claimed that Calvinism gave birth to the development of the capitalist economic system by its emphasis on the ethics of hard work, thrift, punctuality, honesty and discipline. According to Weber, ideas can make history; they can create societies. In this sense he argued that the sixteenth-century Protestants laid the foundations for the emergence of capitalist society. Unlike Durkheim, he contended that religious ideas are not merely projections from below, and recognised that there is a partial reciprocal relation between society and ideas. The major thrust of his theorising is, however, that there can be a one-directional influence of ideas on material reality.

Again, Gottwald's summary of Weber's position is pertinent:

When it came to giving more precision to this general approach to social causation, Weber offered the notion of certain classes or groups within society as the bearers or carriers of certain religious ideas. At this point, two of Weber's most important ideal-typical categories served to demarcate the process of convergence by which specific social groups and specific religious phenomena were drawn together. The two categories were 'charisma and routinization'. Out of any number of religious formations which have their roots in the minds and experiences of unusual personalities, only those will become socially concretized or routinized which attract social groups strong enough to determine the future development of society.[7]

It is in this notion of charisma and routinisation (or institutionalisation) that Weber exposed the idealist roots of his sociology, 'for what the charismatic origin of religion does is to remove the question of the causes of religion from the social equation'.[8] The strategy of Durkheim and Weber in their sociological analyses is to move a step forward from idealism only to plunge back into it. Consequently Weber's approach to social change is ambiguous and in effect politically reactionary, which explains the reason why liberals round the world draw such immense inspiration from the Weberian tradition. As one writer puts it:

while we can easily identify the hard-liners, the conservatives and their allies, it is the liberals who best serve the real powers and whose very function is to mystify: to sound progressive with the left hand while the right hand engages in actions designed to 'contain, repress and pacify'.[9]

A black theology of liberation will be best served by keeping clear of such liberal sociological traditions.

Historical sociology

Aware of the limitations of the Western, liberal sociological tradition, a historical-materialist sociological approach has become the basis for a black theology of liberation. The premises of this approach as articulated by Marx and Engels 'are not arbitrary ones, not dogmas, but real premises from which abstraction can only be made in the imagination. They are the real individuals, their activity and the material conditions under which they live, both those which they find existing and those produced by their activity. These premises can thus be verified in a purely empirical way.'[10]

The starting-point of a black theology of liberation is the actual, concrete existence and activity of black people within the South African social formation. In affirming this position a black theology of liberation necessarily realises that both the Bible and theology are themselves *arenas* of social conflict. Neither the Bible nor theological discourse is 'above' social structures and conflict. They are cultural and political products, which reflect the socio-cultural struggles of the societies that produced them. And to the extent that they are being appropriated within societies which are divided along lines of class, race, and sex, they constitute the locus of class, race and sexual struggles. A reading of the Bible and of the theological tradition from the perspective of the poor and exploited members of our society makes clear that:

Historically speaking, the church has been a church of the bourgeoisie, even when it claimed to transcend class barriers or laboured under the illusion that it pervaded all classes in the same way. Indeed, it has been a truly bourgeois church, if the notion of interclassism is taken as part of bourgeois ideology. . . . The church has been the church of the class which has identified itself with the history of the West, in which Christianity may be considered to have been a major force. Only those members of the working class who accepted this view of history attended church. But most of the working people never accepted this view and only gave the church the kind of formal allegiance subjects give to the claims of their rulers. They could not really belong to the church of another class.[11]

The historical-materialist sociological approach is not beyond critique but it does provide a good basis for a black theology of liberation, because it explodes the myth of homogeneity and classlessness in present society. According to this method:

In the social production of their lives, people enter into definite relations that are independent of their will, relations of production which correspond to a definite stage of development of their material productive forces. The sum total of these relations of production constitutes the economic structure of society, the real basis on which rises a legal and political superstructure and to which correspond definite forms of social consciousness. The mode of production of material life conditions the social, political and intellectual life process in general. It is not people's consciousness that determines their being, but their social being that determines their consciousness.[12]

Thus modern societies are divided into social classes on the basis of the economic system in which their members participate. A theology of liberation that does not take this factor into account is destined to be little more than liberal idealism.

Not only does a historical-materialist sociology explode the illusion of classlessness, but it goes further than liberal sociologies by connecting particular forms of religious faith and theology to particular kinds of classes in society. In other words it takes the notion of ideology seriously in social analysis. It recognises that:

People forget that every constitution, every law, and every philosophy belonged to a historical epoch. They think of ideologists as people outside history, scholars seated in the library working with thought. And the ideologists also forget. They forget how they make a living, who their enemies are, and the threats to their way of life. They forget their friends, their class position, and the struggles of their time. They study the writers of the past but ignore the classes, the nations, and the epochs. . . . All ideologists learn to write for their class. The prospect of fame and reputation, the desire for influence, the love of money and status – these motives work unconsciously as they write.[13]

The question of ideological framework is of vital importance in any attempt to participate in a theology of liberation. This is so because unless clear ideological choices are made, it is possible to claim to be a theologian of liberation while continuing to be a slave of the ideology of the ruling class, and drawing one's hermeneutics from that framework. This has in fact been the fate of some forms of black theology in this country. Some theologians have found themselves trapped by social and idealist structures in ways similar to the young Hegelians in the nineteenth century, who claimed to be overthrowing Hegel's philosophical system while in truth they capitulated to it. Similarly, with the exception of a few recent formulations, black theology has never really made an ideological break with bourgeois theological and biblical hermeneutics, and has not become a *liberation* theology. The starting-point for effecting such a rupture is to determine the relation of Christian theology and faith to bourgeois ideology and society. The process by which black theology can actually purge itself of the 'muck of ages' must involve, however, turning away from more theoretical and idealistic discourse, through prolonged, concrete engagement in the struggles of the black working class.

No reference has so far been made to cultural analysis. What has been said about sociological analysis applies equally to cultural analysis. Idealist liberal concepts of culture exist alongside historical understandings of culture. According to the former, culture is an entity which can be abstracted from historical reality, and analysed in a value-free manner. In contrast, the historical conception of culture defines it as 'the forms with which human beings produce, reproduce and sustain their lives'.[14] As such, culture is defined in relation to its historical, material basis. Culture is seen as a function of a people's location in the process of historical development. Like the use of the Bible or theology, it can be either reactionary or revolutionary, depending on the configuration of social forces in society and their corresponding degree of politicisation. To see culture in ethnic and static terms is to reify it, and empty it of its historical content.

Towards a black working–class theology
Consciously and unconsciously the different class forces in society evolve cultural forms that are relevant to their position, maintenance

and reproduction in the social order. It is thus necessary to speak of a ruling-class culture and a working-class culture. For this reason the task of a black theology of liberation is amongst other things to identify the distinctive forms of working-class culture and use them as a basis for developing theological strategies of liberation. One of the fertile areas for discovering such a culture is to be found in the African Independent churches. Till now, all the 'recognised' literature on these churches has reflected ruling-class interests and models of explanation.[15]

Studies of African Independent churches have missed this point mainly because they have tended to view these churches in terms of liberal anthropology, emphasising their 'Africanness' in some static, ahistorical form. A more helpful and liberating exercise would be to analyse these churches socio-historically, so that their social class character can be seen for what it is. When West, Sundkler and other liberal analysts raise the question of culture, they do so in relation to a mythical, monolithic, timeless African culture. The major theoretical weakness of this position is that it does not explain why, if 'Africanness' is the key feature of these churches, it is not the case that all Africans are members of the African Independent churches or even share the faith of the African Independent churches.

The African Independent churches and especially the Zionist churches are, in fact, in contradistinction to all 'mainline churches', strictly speaking black working-class churches. They are African to the extent that they are historically rooted in African precapitalist social formations, and are forced by their position of alienation within contemporary capitalist social relations to draw in the struggle for survival from the cultural resources provided by that historical past. The Zionist churches also defy most definitions of a Christian church by rejecting this channel of Western capitalist manipulation. This cannot be explained in terms of the fact that their members are Africans who still cling to some African traditions. Such an argument is tautological and lacks explanatory power, quite apart from being racist.

Looked at socio-historically, African Independent churches are religious-cultural organisations of the descendants of former African pastoralists. For one thing, the primitive accumulation stage of capitalist penetration, by which Africans were dispossessed of their means of subsistence, destroyed the material basis of African culture and religion. For another, the integration of dispossessed Africans in a subordinate position within the structure of capitalist production deprived black workers of access to the privileged areas of capitalist culture.[16] In fact black people became no more than mere tools in the development of capitalist culture, including its religious forms. In this situation black people could be neither Africans nor capitalists, on the one hand because the material basis for their existence as independent Africans had been eroded by colonial capitalism, and on the other because the new society into which they were integrated related to them as exploitable commodities, understood as labour power. In these circumstances the only available means of self-defence is cultural-ideological. Belief in God or gods becomes not a choice, it is a necessity. But cultural-ideological mechanisms of survival also require a material basis: they do not fall down from the sky. In order to understand the nature and function of the faith of African Independent churches, a thoroughgoing social-cultural analysis of the prehistory of the black working class, and the contemporary conditions of black working-class people in the townships and the rural areas, is a prerequisite.

Such a study is particularly important for those who want to develop a working-class-based black theology of liberation. The point of a study like that would be to show that culture is ultimately not ethnic. It is not African, Indian, coloured, white, English or Afrikaans. It is historical and class-based. The category of 'African culture' as an interpretative instrument for understanding African Independent churches has yielded meagre results. A black theology of liberation needs to move away from this category and towards the category of a black working-class culture, as the basis of liberating theological reflection and activity.

Culture is an arena of social struggle. For this reason, the ruling class leaves no cultural stone unturned. It extends its control and influence over such cultural areas as the streets of our townships, the family, education, the workplace, television, the church, health institutions, sporting activity, and the home. This is of vital importance for the ruling class, not because they want to feel powerful, but because the resultant character of the labour force is crucial for the stability and survival of the established order. It is significant for them whether the labour force is conformist or rebellious. To ensure that it is conformist, conditions of cultural reproduction must remain within the control of capitalist domination. This point is made succinctly by John Clarke: 'To grasp working-class culture as an empirical problem it is necessary to hold on to both ends of this chain – on the one hand, the broad movements of capital and, on the other, its specific, local consequences for the patterns of class reproduction.'[16]

A black theology of liberation, armed with a historical-cultural analysis, does not deny the usefulness of moral denunciations of the apartheid regime. It must nevertheless go further by identifying the connections between apartheid and the strategies of capitalist domination.

Theology in the service of the state: the Steyn and Eloff Commissions
CHARLES VILLA-VICENCIO

The self-identity of the present regime in South Africa has traditionally been grounded on a religious fervour that is unabashedly and aggressively political. However, from recent evidence, primarily that of the Eloff Commission, it seems that this brand of religiosity is giving way to a secular style of politics and a privatised form of religion.

Politico-religious fervour in South Africa is an inherent part of Afrikaner theologised nationalism. By contrast English-speaking members of the white group have been less doctrinaire and idealistic. Yet, over the years, they have moved into a closer alliance with their still dominant Afrikaner compatriots. They have allowed the Afrikaner to dictate the cultural ethos of the regime, doing little to modify or change the harsh manifestations of oppression, which are invariably attendant by-products of the traumatic preoccupations with a sense of divine mission.

There have been moments in this history of nationalism when deviant priests and others who proffered a different political gospel, have been told to keep religion out of politics. Yet without fear of contradiction it can be said that white nationalism in South Africa has been marked by a bold synthesis of religion and politics, giving rise to an uncompromising *white patriotic theology* – a dominant ideology that has persisted until most recently. Its persistence can be explained primarily by the fact that Afrikaners did not move to the cities in any significant numbers until the 1930s, the normal secularisation process emerging only after this time. In fact, in many instances, the present generation of Afrikaners is the first to have no link with rural living, and consequently the first generation to experience the full impact of religious and moral pluralism, cultural mobility, and a loss of existential self-identity, all of which are part of the harvest of the secular city.

With the shift to a city-centred ethos, a gradual change in the official attitude of the regime towards religion began to appear. This is nowhere more clear than in the report of the Eloff Commission of Inquiry into the South African Council of Churches.[1] Yet, the Steyn Commission of Inquiry into the Mass Media, filing its report only two years earlier, continued on the other hand to affirm a traditional patriotic theology, while arguing that 'a personal relation between the individual soul and the Godhead' is the essence of religion.[2] This apparent conflict between the recommendations of the two Commissions is probably an indication that *both* manifestations will continue to function in the official attitude of the state towards religion for the immediate future.

The difference is in part a variation of the dichotomy that has always been central to Afrikaner theology, founded as it is on two apparently conflicting theological approaches: pietism and theologised nationalism, or what in this essay are called *pietism* and *patriotic theology*. At times the adherents of these two traditions have been able to live harmoniously together. When pietism becomes a form of other-worldly preoccupation, the political stage is left to the political theologians of patriotism. Yet, when the latter falter in their patriotism, or are unable to substantiate their position against conflicting political theologies, the secular guardians of the nation, eager for what religious legitimation they can muster, opt for a form of apolitical pietism. What this essay suggests is that the complexities of the contemporary theology debate have undermined the once-unquestioned patriotic bent of political theology in this country, especially in Reformed theology circles.[3] It is this which compelled the Eloff Commission ultimately to affirm a gospel which addresses 'only truly spiritual purposes',[4] leaving politics to the secular forces of 'national interest'.[5]

The changing shape of religion

There is an obvious sense in which this shift, from an overt form of political and patriotic theology to privatised religion, is a particular manifestation of the secularising process which is reshaping religion throughout the West, involving the evacuation by the Christian churches from those areas of the social order previously under their control and influence. The effect of this trend is that while the influence of religion declines in the socio-political sphere, its influence continues, perhaps with renewed vigour, at the subjective introspective level.

Andrew Greeley, for example, describes secularisation as a shift from the corporate or political significance of religion to an increasing significance of religion at an individual or personal level.[6] Victor Lidz, in turn, relates secularisation to the separation of church and state, or the narrowing of the influence of religion to the personal realm.[7]

In South Africa this movement is seen most clearly by comparing the government's response to the Cottesloe Consultation of 1961, called in response to the Sharpeville shootings, and the report of the Eloff Commission a little more than twenty years later. The findings of Cottesloe were not in any way radical.[8] What is important, however, is that the secular and religious press interpreted the decisions of the consultation as having created 'an acute crisis of confidence within Afrikaner nationalist circles'. The Prime Minister, H. F. Verwoerd, rejected the decision of the consultation, making it quite clear that if Cottesloe represented the mind of the church, church members would be obliged to choose between church and party. The editor of the

Kerkbode, A. P. Treurnicht, even went so far as to accuse the consultation of an 'illegal coup d'état'.[11] Afrikaner Christians were, however, not ready to choose between church and state; the alliance between the Afrikaner churches and the state held firm. Patriotic theology was alive and well. Much has happened in both state and church since those heady days of encounter. Those churches which stood by the Cottesloe Statement – the non-racial English-speaking churches, together with the only black church represented (the Reformed Presbyterian Church), in unison with other churches, notably the Roman Catholic and the black Dutch Reformed churches – have taken an increasing number of bold steps into the political arena. This has been a process fuelled by developments in black politics, the advent of black theology, and major advances in the ecumenical movement. The opponents of Cottesloe were quite correct. The cautious and hesitant resolutions of that consultation heralded the beginning of a major theological confrontation with apartheid.

While this ecumenical consensus against apartheid was being forged, the homogeneity of the Afrikaner churches was disintegrating. Fragmentation was penetrating every sphere of this society – in both party and church. Each group would in time make its own theological claims of justification and legitimation. The Afrikaner church, once the ethos of Afrikaner unity, would begin to experience the disunity of a pluralism of theologies, ideologies and political persuasions.[10] When deviant groups both to the 'left' and to the 'right'of the government begin to assume *their* legitimation from these theologies, there is a need for the state to establish a different structure of legitimation.

The exact nature of this quest for a new legitimation cannot be discussed in detail here. Simply stated, it probably has to do with what is often called an 'alliance of moderates'. This means 'moderates' as seen from the perspective of the present order, formed around middle-class capitalist values, under the control of an elite within the ruling class. The only point that needs to be emphasised is that this group is unlikely to find its common centre or social legitimation in a theological identity. All the same, this theological motivation on both sides of the ideological divide is regarded by the government as disruptive of the alliance. Yet, because of the dominant role that religion and Christian theology have traditionally played in South African society, religious factors continue instinctively to be part of the sought-after legitimation. The social function of religion in this legitimation process is, however, vastly different from what it used to be. It is explicitly an apolitical and privatised one, while at the same time it is by implication a boldly political one, inasmuch as it abdicates all political responsibility to the secular forces of politics.

The Steyn and Eloff Commissions

From what has already been said, it is obvious why the social function of religion should be a matter of concern to the South African state. The task of the Steyn Commission was to investigate the function of the media in relation to those forces which it perceived to be disruptive of the prevailing order. These forces, according to the commission, include 'the Soviet, the ANC, terror and other onslaughts and objectives, as well as those liberals and radicals, who from pulpits, platforms or in writing, aim at the subversion of the social order and fabric of our society.'[11] As for the Eloff Commission, it was, in turn, established to conduct a similar investigation of these disruptive influences in relation to the SACC.

Similarities between the two reports abound. There is the selective use of sources, virtually devoid of any serious grappling with the classic texts on the topics under investigation. There are *non sequiturs*, involving long commentaries from select sources, followed by conclusions which do not necessarily follow, and substantial contradictions.

From the perspective of serious academic debate, the reports constitute poor scholarship and analysis. They were not, however, compiled by theologians, nor were they intended to meet the niceties of theological scholarship. At this very point a marked difference emerges between the Steyn and Eloff Commissions. The latter expresses a reluctance to involve itself in theological debate. 'No state', we are told, 'can take it upon itself to decide what the theology of the Church should be and the question, if ever it is to be settled, is to be resolved by theologians, not by this Commission.'[12] Later in the report, recognising that 'there may be differing theological perceptions' on matters of church and state, the commission insists that it dare only comment on these matters 'with diffidence', while ultimately it does make a theological choice, recommending that the government control the SACC's funds to ensure that they are used for 'only truly spiritual purposes'.[13]

It is this theological hesitation and qualification, despite the conclusions eventually reached, that distinguishes the Eloff Commission from the Steyn Commission. Yet, in the end, it is not what a commission says that counts, but what it does! At this level the two commissions reach different and yet complementary conclusions. The Steyn Commission allows for theological legitimation of the state, whereas the Eloff Commission promotes an overtly apolitical theology. Common to both reports is their rejection of theologically based dissent and resistance.

An attack on contemporary theologies

The major concern which emerges in the reports of both commissions relates to a gospel 'concerned with political, social and economic issues'. What is at stake is the nature of the Judaeo–Christian tradition. Dr Alex Boraine, participating in the parliamentary debate in response to the tabling of the Eloff Commission's report in the House of Assembly, argued that if the main charge of the commission against the Council were its involvement in the socio–political and economic issues of the day, 'then I must agree that the SACC must plead guilty as charged'. 'It is in fact my judgment', Boraine continued, 'that if they are not guilty of this charge, they would be found guilty in a higher court. In other words the essence of the SACC's defence is that they must obey God rather than man. In this instance they are faithfully reflecting the central message of both the Old and the New Testament.'[14]

The larger part of the argument in the Steyn and Eloff Commissions, on the other hand, attributes this involvement of the SACC not to the message of the Bible, but to a set of alien influences which impinge on the Council's understanding of this message. At this point the predispositions of both commissions towards liberation and black theology, as well as to the ecumenical movement, become most germane. Also pertinent is the fundamentally wrong understanding of the history of the SACC and the WCC. In this connection the summary statement of the Eloff Commission, for example, is grossly inadequate. We are told: 'From an organization whose main activity originally was the co-ordination of efforts to spread the Gospel, and whose principal interests lay in spiritual matters, the SACC developed into one largely concerned with political, social and economic issues. . . .' This development is ascribed directly to 'the acceptance of ecumenism' and 'the domination by black Christians of member churches of the SACC, and the emergence of liberation or black theology'.[15] The Commission's observation simply fails to do justice to the complex history of the ecumenical movement, or the multiplicity of programmes which constitute the work of both the WCC and the SACC, or the ethical teaching of traditional, and above all Reformed, theology.

Leaving aside the inability on the part of the two Commissions to understand what they are criticising, one may be tempted to conclude that the references to the more recent influence of black, liberation and ecumenical theology on the Council are more or less valid, until one begins to look more carefully at the definitions of these theologies provided in the two reports. The Steyn Commission's report, theologically less circumspect than that of the Eloff Commission, is preoccupied with the recurring theme of 'politicised theology and theologised politics',[16] which it describes as 'a particularly significant area of confluence wherein the Marxist, Third World and Western streams of anti-South African action meet, mingle and reinforce each other. . . .'[17] Under this definition the report considers the social gospel movement, the WCC and SACC, black theology, black consciousness, and the theology of liberation.[18] In each case the emphasis is the same – religion is used for revolutionary political ends.

At times the language becomes quite bizarre. In brief, it can only be concluded that the analysis is ideologically biased, the cited references highly selective, and that the findings of the Commission in this regard would not be verified by any but the most reactionary opponents of these movements. What makes this analysis most unacceptable is that this same rejection of 'politicised theology and theologised politics' is not applied when treating Afrikaner civil religion. While there is mild criticism of some aspects of Afrikaner nationalism, and while it is acknowledged, for example, that the Afrikaner Broederbond can be seen as 'extremely damaging of national unity', the report is totally devoid of the kind of judgment reserved for those theologies already identified when it deals with the theologised nationalism of Afrikanerdom.[19]

When attention is given to African theology, again one perceives a selective use of quotations to make the point that African theology is different from black theology. The latter, it is contended, has its origin within the 'sorrow, bitterness, anger and hatred' nurtured by the 'peculiar history of the negroes in America'. As such, it is argued, 'black theology cannot, and will not, become African theology'. Unlike black theology which is regarded as a 'vagrant culture element', African theology is said to be grounded on 'the African claim to a unique and different theological point of view' within a unique 'cultural, geographical, spiritual, social and temperamental background'.[20] These quotations from the work of John Mbiti and Gabriel Setiloane are used to affirm what the report refers to as 'differential theology' and 'differential development'.[21] Even Desmond Tutu, whose theology is in every other way rejected in an uncompromising manner, is quoted on the basis of a paper written a decade ago ('Black theology/African theology: soul mates or antagonists?') to support this argument.[22]

Setiloane is likewise co-opted on behalf of the Commission's cause: 'Professor Setiloane's great emphasis on traditional African religions is indicative of the urge to retain and develop own identity in own cultural idiom, which is widely present in African circles and which cannot be ignored by those working for a speedy and far-reaching change on the continent, and particularly in Southern Africa.'[23] It is here that the dominant ideological thrust of the report emerges in bold relief. There is, says the report, a 'striking accord between black [African] and Afrikaner thought'. 'These', it is insisted, 'are very weighty considerations deserving of earnest attention and when evaluating the moral and political worth of certain aspects of the concept of "separate development", based as it is on the "community principle" and on that of differential development.'[24]

Readily discernible in the Steyn Commission's report is a patriotic theology – conserving, legitimating and moderate. Any 'social conscience' which may be exercised as a consequence of 'a personal relationship between the individual soul and the Godhead' must be of a moderate kind, and never of such intensity that it distracts from or negates this spiritual centre. Here lies, according to the Steyn Commission, the essential failure of black and liberation theology.[25]

By contrast the language of the Eloff Commission is more qualified. Much of what has already been said about black, liberation and ecumenical theologies is reiterated in (as a rule) more restrained language. Yet the diagnosis of these theologies as well as of the WCC and the SACC is essentially the same. Most of the same sources are used in assessment, and many of the trite theological and historical judgments repeated. The marked difference between this report and that of the Steyn Commission is that there is no explicit support in it for any kind of 'political' theology, whether it be political theology 'for the state' or theology 'against the state'. The bulk of the report consists of a long chapter on the history of the SACC. This is followed by a shorter chapter in which it is argued that a credibility gap has developed during the course of this history between the Council and its member churches, as the Council has addressed itself with increasing directness to political issues, leaving it without 'significant grass-roots support for its actions'.[26] The *intention* of the report is thus not significantly different from that of the Steyn Commission. It is to isolate the SACC as a fringe organisation, which has allowed itself to be influenced by ideologies that are alien to the gospel. Then, in one of its more obvious contradictions, the Commission admits the extent of the support which the Council does enjoy from its member churches, in recommending that the SACC should not be acted against in terms of the Affected Organizations Act of 1974 because, it is argued, 'this step is not likely to halt member churches of the SACC in their pursuit of substantially the same sort of objectives as those endorsed by the SACC.'[27] It is, however, when one moves beyond the unsubstantiated rhetoric and questionable analyses of the Steyn and Eloff Commissions, that a more definite perception is gained of what function religion is being expected to serve in South African society. If the dominant emphasis of the Steyn Commission assumes a patriotic, legitimating function for religion, the Eloff Commission responds to the theological conflict more radically, in a shift towards a personalistic, privatised form of spirituality.

Church–state relations

Chapter four of the Eloff Commission's report addresses the theological relationship between church and state. In response to this debate, the commission recommends that religion be kept essentially out of the political arena. This is not a position adopted by the Commission in principle, but rather one that is pragmatically resorted to. It allows, for example, that 'in South Africa, where religious freedom exists and is indeed protected, the state is bound to recognize the right of the church, and church bodies such as the SACC, to express themselves on, to criticize and, if so persuaded, to condemn its policies or actions.'[28] It is also conceded, in response to the submission by David Bosch, that: 'We all read the Bible from a specific context and perspective, and this context becomes the filter through which we absorb biblical teaching, and by which our interpretation of the Bible is coloured.' It is further allowed, following Bosch, that the only way out of this dilemma is to enable people and especially leaders, both to the left and to the right, to become aware that their theological perceptions are contextually influenced.[29]

What is most interesting is the response of the Commission to Bosch's submission. 'In view of these circumstances', it is concluded, 'the SACC should take account of the fact that in addressing the state and requiring its voice to be heeded, there are the voices of other Christians and church organizations which also have to be heeded.'[30] This is ultimately used by the Commission, in spite of its recognition of the place of theological critique, as a basis for advocating steps by the government to ensure that the SACC confine its activities to 'spiritual' affairs. In so doing, the Commission opts for a classic secularist response to religion. In contending that because (a) there are so many conflicting religious views, (b) there is no obvious basis for choosing between them, and (c) there are no definite religious answers to complex political situations, it is therefore far better that religion be restricted to the private sphere out of harm's way.

The Commission fails completely to take Bosch's point, which is that it is precisely this religious pluralism and moral relativism that ought to be the basis of and the opportunity for a viable relationship between church and state.[31] In other words, there *is* a step beyond the acknowledgement of theological relativism, which does not plunge one into total scepticism and theological–ethical indifference. It has to do with acknowledging definite reservations about precisely what God is saying, while being sensitive and sensible enough to weigh the maladies of an ailing society. 'The church and its spokesmen cannot', Bosch recognises, 'provide detailed blueprints about how to solve these problems, but it may – indeed should – in fulfilling its prophetic role ceaselessly identify these anomalies in the body politic and help prepare a climate in which solutions become possible.' Given the plurality of perspectives already acknowledged there will inevitably be the possibility of a clash between church and state, and indeed between one church and another. Yet, it is this theological critique which ultimately enables the state to be the state. 'This', suggests Wolfram Kistner, 'is the most loyal service which the church can render to the state, to a particular government and to itself – it is to protect the government from itself and from unreasonable demands made by its people.'[32] To return to Bosch's submission, it is this which made some Old Testament kings grateful for the challenge of the prophets. Indeed, he argues, a wise government should do everything in its power to uphold the right of its subjects – and particularly of the church – to express their views and convictions.

An interesting and disconcerting omission from the submissions of Bosch and others on the question of religious pluralism is any reference to the broad-based theological consensus against apartheid which exists among Christians today, transcending denominational, cultural and ethnic divisions. To afford a small white minority theological opinion, declared heretical by every reputable theological grouping in the world, the same significance as is afforded to this major consensus, cannot be easily defended. No government can afford to ignore such consensus of opinion against it.

Privatised religion

The Eloff Commission has used the argument about contextual pluralism to substantiate a position that advocates steps being taken to limit theological opposition in the public sphere. If the Steyn Commission's report identifies political theology against the state as the enemy of the state, the Eloff Commission ultimately recognises *all* political theology, given its plurality of norms, as inimical to the establishment of the kind of 'alliance of moderation' to which reference has already been made.

The Eloff Commission's decision in favour of apolitical or privatised religion comes out most clearly in its final recommendations and in its lengthy discussions on what constitutes 'religious work'.[33] The Commission rejects what it calls 'the rather vague dictionary meaning of "religious work"'. Furthermore it shows that when the Minister presented the Fund-raising Act to Parliament, he allowed for the churches to be exempted from its requirements. The problem, suggests the Commission, is that 'he had a more conservative idea of what the proper sphere of interests of religious bodies should be'. The recommendation is therefore made that 'steps be taken to oblige the SACC to come clearly within the operation of the Fund-raising Act, 1978. To ensure that it cannot be argued that the SACC falls within the exemption, we recommend that the state law advisers prepare a suitable amendment reflecting the idea that only truly spiritual purposes are included. The substitution of the word "spiritual" for "religious" might be adequate.' The intention of this recommendation is to limit the influence of the SACC and individual churches, curtailing their social, economic and political involvement.

The South African Police submission to the Commission similarly insists that churches should focus their concern on 'personal salvation and conversion'.[34] The problem, it was contended, is that the SACC persistently moves beyond this sphere. 'It does not involve itself in its primary area, and does not undertake, for instance, large-scale campaigns for money in overseas countries for converting non-Christians in the Republic of South Africa to Christianity.'[35] It is this narrow understanding of ministry which is rejected in the SACC response to this submission.[36] Quoting from the work of Gerhard Ebeling, the SACC observed:

Christianity is constantly in danger of becoming pagan precisely where it seeks to be most pious. . . . The spiritual realm is then made into a world on its own, a separate reality which passes by the world as it really is, instead of engaging it.

. . . Could it be that separatist, unworldly talk of God which builds a world apart is likewise worldly talk of God in that negative, basically godless sense? It is indeed! The extreme possibilities of separation join hands: atheistic and, as it were, purely religious, purely spiritual talk of God. Both leave the world without God and God without a world.[37]

In spite of its many protestations a careful reading of the Eloff Commission does, however, reveal a number of concessions. It does allow, as already noted, that everyone, not only the SACC, 'reads the Bible from a specific context and perspective, and that the context becomes the filter through which we absorb biblical teaching.'[38] There is a sentence in the report which amounts to a further concession: 'Enough is said elsewhere in this report regarding the SACC and many of its member churches to show that its involvement in what is by many said to be purely political matters is considered to be biblically justified.'[39] The sentence indicates that it is the Commission which considers it to be such – or is that merely one of those 'indiscretions' which creep into most reports? Whatever may be the case, the Commission proceeds to reject categorically biblical justification as acceptable grounds for political involvement. The government, we are told, has a narrower understanding of what constitutes the proper sphere of religion, and the SACC's involvement in political resistance is 'not in the national interest'.[40]

Some options for a viable doctrine of church and state

There are fundamentally four options in the area of church–state relations which neither responsible church nor legitimate state can accept as justifiable.

The first is any form of either explicit or implicit theocracy. Theological and social ethical absolutes either do not exist or are too abstract to be of any direct political value. The complexity of politico-economic problems is such that they deny what is all too often the simplicity of priestly rhetoric.

The second is any form of political indifference by the church. To expect the church to do so is to ask it to surrender its theological integrity. Richard John Neuhaus, a conservative theologian, an opponent of the WCC, and a severe critic of ecumenical, liberation and black theology, in fact identifies a theological consensus about the church's political responsibility: 'the debate within and between the churches is no longer over *whether* religion should be politically relevant. Across the board, there is an emerging consensus that religion must be critical of societal patterns and must be engaged in advancing alterntatives.'[41] At the level of principle the Eloff Commission concurs: 'the state is bound to recognise the right of the church . . . to criticise and, if so persuaded, to condemn its policies or actions.'[42] The problem which concerns the Eloff Commission is the proliferation of theological perceptions in this regard, which causes it to suggest that it would be far better if the churches simply vacated the political realm.

The third option pertaining to church–state relations which is moral-ly and theologically unjustifiable, but implicitly present throughout both the Steyn and the Eloff Commissions, is resignation to a measure of social injustice and political oppression, on the argument that the consequences of a revolution may well be worse than the status quo.[43] The fourth option that cannot be theologically justified is the affirma-tion of revolutionary chaos. Theology is ultimately an option beyond both tyranny and anarchy, and this is surely the basis for a viable relationship between church and state, because ultimately neither church nor state can tolerate or legitimate either of these options.[44]

A viable doctrine of church and state, in rejecting these options, must ultimately do justice to three cardinal theological axioms which are central to the Christian tradition. The first is that *the prophetic function of the church is inherent in its evangelical mission*. The German title of Barth's classic statement on church–state relations published in 1938, *Rechtfertigung und Recht* (Justification and justice), makes this point with irrevocable clarity. The point of the statement is to ground social justice in the doctrine of justification by faith.[45] For Barth it is axiomatic that while 'the church cannot itself become a state, and the state, on the other hand, cannot become a church', each is under the authority of God, jointly responsible for realising the 'true character' of this world. In this task, Barth insists, Christians have no other means of knowing what the true function of the state is, or whether a particular state is legiti-mate, apart from measuring it against the declared intention of God for creation, as made known in Christ. 'If the state has perverted its God-given authority, it cannot be honoured better than by this [the church's] criticism.'[46] Theological interpretations of this declared will of God differ, and it is a presumptuous church that prescribes God's blueprint for political reform, as there are probably no final solutions to the variety of vexing political and economic problems facing society. Prophecy is not a political programme. Miguez Bonino's contribution to church–state relations becomes germane at this point. 'We urgently need a Christian ethics of politics', he tells us, 'precisely in order that we may avoid a wrong politicization of Christianity.' 'There is no *divine* politics or economics, but this means we must resolutely use the best *human* politics and economics at our disposal.'[47]

To recognise that theology is not politics is not, however, to suggest that theology ought to be apolitical. It is here that the Eloff Commis-sion becomes theologically and politically deficient. Horkheimer iden-tified the importance of the theological imperative for politics with clarity when he argued : 'A politics which . . . does not preserve a theological moment in itself is, no matter how skilful, in the last analysis mere business.'[48] Politics lacking this moment of radical cri-tique and debunking, as well as eschatological hope (however disturb-ing and annoying as this may at times become), has a tendency to close in on itself. Barth perceived the nature of this possibility when he observed that the state becomes 'demonic', not only by an unwarranted assumption of autonomy, but also by the *loss* of legitimate, relative *independence*. It is this which leads to Caesar worship and the myth of the state.[49] The state becomes a victim of its own power and is devoured by its own ideology. Prophecy is the radical negation of this possibility in the affirmation of transcendence, which protects the state from the state. Both Bosch and Kistner made this very point to the Eloff Commission.

The second axiom central to church–state relations is that *prophetic religion is not in contradiction to a personal, spiritual faith.* Personal religion is not equal to privatised religion. Prophetic religion, operative in the public square, is an indelible part of the Judaeo–Christian tradition, written boldly in the personal piety and praxis of the Catholic and Protestant traditions. This spiritual basis has throughout history, from time to time, compelled reluctant Christians, often at great personal cost to themselves, to oppose the state. This is not because they have deviated from the spiritual centre of their faith, but because of a spiritual experience of the majesty of God. Gregory Baum defines the nature of this spirituality when he observes:

in the major trends of biblical religion divine transcendence is inextricably linked with holiness and justice. God's majesty makes men tremble not only because God wholly transcends human proportions, but because God judges the sinful world, and God's holiness is attractive not only because it offers consolation but because it promises to turn right-side up a world that has been placed upside down by sin.[50]

It is this same spirituality which in different circumstances thrust a reluctant Thomas More and a Cardinal Wolsley, like Luther, Calvin, the French Huguenots and many other unwilling prophets, as well as dissidents and resistors in our own situation, into conflict with the state and other authorities. When Tutu informed the Eloff Commission, 'If we are to say that religion cannot be concerned with politics, then we are really saying that there is a substantial part of human life in which God's reach does not run,' he identified the pulse-beat of the conflict between church and state in the present situation.[51] As the Eloff Commission therefore recommends that the churches be compelled to confine their concern to 'truly spiritual purposes' it actually suggests that the church become even more dependent on that source which brings it into conflict with the state.

The third theological axiom of church–state relations is that *Christ is the Lord of both theology and politics.* In other words, theology and politics are inextricably bound together. For the state to endeavour to refute this is to take on more than a few turbulent priests. Rather, it is confronting a long and stubborn tradition.

It would, of course, be quite unrealistic to expect any regime to negate itself in responding to the demands of the church. When this critique and consequent vision is, however, part of the dream which constitutes the aspirations of a large black majority in the country, *politically* it dare not be disregarded. *Theologically*, on the other hand, the church dare do nothing other than speak on behalf of the poor, the marginalised and the voiceless, because this is part of its New Testament identity. It is obliged to show a special concern for the poor, because God is seen in the Scriptures to show a preferential option for the poor.[52] In this regard the Steyn and Eloff Commissions can be regarded as theologically complimenting the SACC when they argue that it is preoccupied with the political and economic aspirations of this section of the population. Again, Miguez Bonino puts this obligation in its correct context. 'The poor are not morally or spiritually superior to others, but they see reality from a different angle or location – and therefore differently.'[53] Here theology and politics overlap. The theological imperative to speak for the poor cannot be divorced from a political obligation to present their demands to a government that fails, by virtue of denying them the franchise, to represent their interests. Here the conflict between church and state is inevitable, a conflict between a government elected to represent the interests of a ruling class of whites, and a church theologically obliged to represent the interests of primarily the poor and marginalised of the land, who happen to be black. Ultimately, this political problem needs to be addressed by the state.

In spite of the church's prophetic timidity and institutional captivity to the forces of the status quo, the conflict between church and state is an inherent part of the encounter between those who represent the 'haves' and those who represent the 'have nots' – those who have political and military power, wealth, education, social privilege and an excess of resources, and those who have not these resources, except for a relentless will to overcome. For all the problems and difficulties involved, it is this confrontation which must be dealt with in South Africa by both church and state. What may appear to the ruling group to be impossible and non-negotiable is precisely what the politically and economically deprived majority are demanding. In the process a certain amount of fudging of principles and political compromise is inevitable. If the voices of black leaders in the churches and black organisations beyond the churches are to be taken seriously, few blacks will be prepared to settle for anything less than a qualitatively different society. Their quest is for the kind of society which is in contradiction to all that past white political experience has suggested possible.

Briefly, it means throwing off the tyranny of 'what is possible', and reaching towards new possibilities. In so doing the belief is not in the possibility of a perfect society, but in the non-necessity of *this* imperfect society.[54].

Historical determinism points to certain inevitabilities. If there is no qualitative change in South Africa political chaos and revolution are inevitable. Human ingenuity and utopian realism, on the other hand, insist that there is the alternative of a radically new political equation. This task is what Karl Barth called 'the great positive possibility', in contrast to Reinhold Niebuhr's more sober 'impossible impossibility'.[55] For Barth it is a possibility which 'ultimately declares the reactionary man to be wrong, in spite of the wrong that the revolutionary does.' For in so far as we love one another, 'we *cannot* wish to uphold the present order'. 'What we are talking about', insists Barth, 'is the breach in the wall of incomprehensible inaction, which is the still more incomprehensible action of love.'[56] In *Church Dogmatics* he is quite adamant: 'God stands at every time unconditionally and passionately on this and only on this side: always against the exalted and for the lowly, always against those who already have rights and for those from whom they are robbed and taken away.'[57]

It is this kind of theology which is part of the *political* conflict in South Africa. This does not mean that the state should necessarily be ready to capitulate to the demands of a church fired by such a theology. To address itself with dignity and integrity to the demands of this church may, however, be the first step in a larger and more important process of negotiation towards a just social order. This is the goal and the basis of both theology and politics at their legitimate best. Bluntly stated, there is a short distance between Christian spirituality and social action, between the pulpit and politics.

Towards a black theology of labour
BUTI TLHAGALE

The persistent use of the word 'black' to qualify a critical theological investigation has drawn much criticism from both black and white liberals, let alone the outright condemnation from the dominant Afrikaner group. The charge is that it perpetuates racism, distorts theological reflection and promotes a provincial mentality.

Black theology is a direct, aggressive response to a situation where blacks experience alienation at political, economic and cultural levels. The symbolic value of the word 'black' is that it captures the broken existence of black people, summons them collectively to burst the chains of oppression and engage themselves creatively in the construction of a new society. Black theology is aimed at the liberation of the black people and hopefully that of whites as well. Whereas the term 'contextual theology' remains an evasive expression in so far as it accommodates the self-justification of the oppressing group, 'black' in black theology underlines the unique experience of the underdog. Black theology is a radical, purposeful deviation from Western theology. It is suspicious of a Christian tradition that accepts uncritically the economic and political institutions of the day. It resists the 'ossification' of Christian values couched in the idiom of the dominant group.

But more seriously, black theology is an exercise in self-criticism. Meaningful faith in God is becoming increasingly difficult to sustain. The religiousness of black people is wearing thin. Christian symbols of brotherhood and love resound with emptiness. Images of God as a just, loving and merciful Father do not correspond with the harsh reality of racism, landlessness, economic exploitation and political powerlessness. Thus, because of the apartheid system, the credibility of Christianity is bcoming increasingly questionable. The mighty hand of God in human history, in the here and now of the black people, is hardly felt. Personal testimonies of the bountifulness of God are found wanting amongst those without food, housing, education, and work. If God takes sides at all, he must be on the side of wealthy whites, and not on the side of black people.[1]

Black theology can therefore no longer assume the presence of faith amongst the people nor can it complacently argue from the premise that South Africa is a Christian country, simply because reference is made to God in the preamble of the Constitution of the land. It is equally meaningless to continue to assert that blacks are traditionally a religious people. Socio-cultural changes have affected the traditional belief of the people. A more radical grounding of faith is imperative. It will not do to hold God by the scruff of the neck and plant him amongst the oppressed people. There is a need for black theology to validate the legitimacy of faith.[2] The approach that is gradually gaining the upper hand is the historical–materialist approach – not because this method is simply fashionable, but because this approach rests on the theory that beliefs and ideas are conditioned by the relations of production.[3] Marx put it this way:

It is always the direct relationship of the owners of the conditions of production to the producers which reveals the innermost secret, the hidden basis of the entire social structure, and with it the political form of the relationship of sovereignty and dependence. . . . [4]

If black theology is to talk meaningfully about Christian symbols, and how they affect the socio-economic conditions of the black people, it will have to grapple with the fundamental contradictions within present society.

The starting-point of this paper is the labouring black people.

The premises from which we begin are not arbitrary ones, not dogmas, but real premises from which abstraction can only be made in the imagination. They are the real individuals, their activity and material conditions under which they live, both those which they find already existing and those produced by their activity . . . [5]

Historical materialism

Labour is a 'fundamental category of human existence'.[6] Through labour, nature is transformed. It is cast into a form that will be of service to the community. Through labour human beings build their environment and their world, and in so doing they simultaneously build themselves. In a collective labour engagement, people build themselves together. In their collective labouring efforts they become co-creators. They are the 'effective subjects' of what they create.[7] Men and women, suggests Marx, are beings that exist for themselves. The activity of labour therefore enhances their mode of existence, their being. Through work they realise the meaningfulness of their existence. Labour activity leads to a collective growth. It leads human beings to become what they are meant to be.[8] It clothes them with dignity.

In an article, 'Human work: blessing and/or curse', Piano maintains that the Christian tradition has an ambivalent attitude towards work.[9] Work is seen as a 'liberating force' and at the same time a condemnation, a curse resulting from human sinfulness. The latter perspective, Piano argues further, is due to the influence of the middle class. Nevertheless, the value of work is increasingly becoming validated within the Christian tradition. Thus, through labour activity human beings are collectively seen as responding to God's call that men and women should become co-creators. The Christian tradition posits God as the first creator of the universe. People, through their labour activity, continue what God started originally. It is in this creative engagement that men and women experience a sense of fulfilment.

We cannot continue for long in this speculative vein without raising the question of relevance for our situation. This broad Marxian–Christian perspective has a bearing on South Africa. It is against this background that we must examine the material conditions of the black labouring class and consider whether blacks, through their work, realise themselves, construct their world, and appropriate the products of their labour – whether through their activity, they become co-creators with God. A historical perspective will enable us to understand the present struggle of the black working class.

Historical background

The purpose of this essay is to show that through the proletarianisation of the black people, work has become almost a curse. Without seeking to romanticise the past, the periods of communal production and of peasant farming seem to have augured well for many black people. Land, labour and the products thereof belonged to the people. Colin Bundy in his *Rise and Fall of the South African Peasantry* has shown that 'despite the limited land available to peasants, and despite the low level of accumulation and technology prevailing there, certain social and economic circumstances enabled African peasants to participate in the produce and labour markets on terms not wholly unfavourable.'[10] The rot set in when white magistrates replaced traditional chiefs in positions of control, when marginalised Africans were reduced to squatters or forced into locations, and when blacks could no longer acquire land because this interfered with the labour supply for white farmers. The rapid dispossession of the indigenous people culminated in the infamous 1913 Natives Land Act, which sought to lay down 'permanent lines of territorial segregation' between blacks and whites. All these factors, coupled with the growing demand for labour by the mining, industrial and agricultural sectors, stepped up the process of proletarianisation. The Stallard Commission, building on the recommendations of the Lagden Commission, emphasised the principle of territorial segregation:

The Native should only be allowed to enter the urban areas, which are essentially the White man's creation, when he is willing to enter and minister to the needs of the White man, and should depart therefrom when he ceases to minister.[11]

But the history of injustice towards the indigenous people did not stop there. The white dominant class set up coercive apparatuses to ensure the regularity of the labour supply, through the use of taxation, pass laws, etc. Furthermore, through the structures associated with the migrant labour system, 'capital was able to drive down the value of African labour power to the costs of reproducing the individual labourer from day to day'.[12] White workers were in turn fed, and thrived on, myths:

> The brain and industrial training are the whites' only superiority. Thus . . . work among whites must be confined to departments where the brain tells, and merely muscular work be apportioned to races willing [sic] to be considered inferior.[13]

The material conditions of 'poor whites' were improved in case they were tempted to identify with the African workers or other white militant groups outside the power bloc. It was for this reason, too, that white unions were set up along racial lines. The Industrial Conciliation Act of 1923 excluded blacks from the category of 'employees', the Act being changed only in 1979. A 'civilised labour policy' entrenched discrimination against the black worker.

Theological reflection

This historical–materialist background is absolutely essential for a discourse on black theology, otherwise it would be conducted in a vacuum. The narrative dimension pins theology to the ground and makes black theology an 'emancipatory reflection' relevant to a specific historical experience.

From the above account it emerges that, historically, black workers have been considered as objects, as part of the productive machinery organised in such a way as to bring forth surplus products only to be appropriated by the white ruling class. Under such circumstances, black labour can hardly be seen as an activity aimed at self-realisation. In the eyes of the black worker, work ceases to be the 'place of human growth' or the 'clearing' where the absolute manifests itself. Sheer drudgery and confinement to subsistence levels negate the concept of work as the continuation of the creative–redemptive work of God. The dimension of work as a 'liberating force' is completely subordinated to the negative dimension that shows human labour as the 'topos' where punishment is unleashed in its most painful form. What is produced by black workers does not enhance their living, but rather is claimed by those who own the means of production and benefit from the circulation of money on the market. Work, instead of building those engaged in it, brutalises them and reduces them to the level of servitude. The reduction of black workers to parts of the productive machinery, and the alienation of their products, form a counterposition. The task of black theology is to reverse it.

White theology, as well as more acceptable forms of it, abounds in its homiletic expression with phrases such as: opting for the poor, siding with the workers, sharing with the poor, or all are made in the image of

God. Black theology locates the 'solution' not in the gratuitous options of rich Christians but in the revolutionary awareness of the workers themselves. The image of God in which the workers are made is not a given, an already existent reality. It is something to be striven for, to be realised in meaningful human activity. The more workers labour in accordance with their free will, in response to their material needs, the more the image of God becomes a reality. The progressive self-assertiveness of the workers corresponds to the growing formation of the image of God. Work becomes creative and redemptive only if it enhances the quality of being.

Using Scripture as a source, black theological reflection underscores man's mastery over nature. Black workers and others ought to be partners in the creation of their environment and in the sharing of the benefits accruing from such an activity. Scripture is silent on endowments accorded along racial lines. Habermas notes in his commentary on 'Marx's metacritique of Hegel: synthesis through social labour': 'Through the labour process what changes is not only the nature that has been worked on but, by means of the product of labour, the necessitous nature of the labouring subjects themselves.'[14] The myth that 'the brain and training are the whites' only superiority' does not tally with reality. Lonergan in his work, *Insight*, has gone to great lengths to explain the function of the immanent acts within the cognitive structure of a human being.[15] There are no black and white cognitive processes, although consciousness may be culturally conditioned (hence the persistence of a black theological perspective). Blacks have been denied training in the various technical fields so as to prevent them as a racial group from competing with white workers. This has been a deliberate act of discrimination in order to keep white workers in a materially advantageous position. The fact that blacks are seen by whites as serving white needs in urban areas, and not their own needs, underlines the belief amongst whites that labour is at the service of capital and not vice versa. Social relations in a capitalist system have the appearance of a fixed nature. Workers seem destined to remain in the subservient order. The persistence of capitalism and its structures gives this impression and thus a fatalistic attitude amongst black workers prevails, just as the persistence of apartheid gives the impression that it is part of the right order of things. The priority of capital over labour crushes the worth of the black worker. The white worker has been cushioned from this broken human condition because of the allegiance he owes to the ruling class.

Labour in the service of capital runs contrary to the Christian understanding of justice. The idea of justice in the Christian tradition 'combines with the recognition of responsibility to society as duty and privilege of mutual dependence and service'.[16] The structures of capitalism, which allow for the appropriation of surplus value by a few, do not acknowledge the relationship of mutual dependence and service.

White theology, or, better still, Christian practice understands the responsibility of the 'haves' in terms of charitable concerns towards the downtrodden, the marginalised, the outcasts. The emancipatory reflection flowing from black theological discourse rejects the language of the rich white Christians, which describes the conditions of black workers from a white perspective. 'The poor', 'the marginalised', 'the outcasts', describe the conditions of those outside the 'gates of the city', those who hardly have a decisive role to play in the making of the history of their own communities or the history of mankind.[17] Black theology, deriving its insight from historical materialism, affirms labour as a fundamental mode of existence, not as marginalised but rather as being at the centre of history. How is it possible that armies of workmen in an industry can become marginal, subservient to the so-called factory owner and his handful of white helpers who occupy the upper level in the division of labour?

The workers enslave themselves in accepting the descriptive language of the oppressor. This language distorts reality and conditions the mind. To free the mind, a new language is imperative, a language that does not reflect the concerns of the capitalist owner but the preoccupation of the workers. Again, black theology, like the white Christian tradition, takes nature as a given, as a gift of God to be transformed and regulated for the benefit of all. Certainly whites were not given this gift first. All have a claim to it. Capital, created in an interaction with nature, is a communal possession. From this premise flows the conviction nutured by black theology that black workers have to restore the just order of things. The subversion of capitalism will not be a direct result of productive activity, but will come about as a result of 'the revolutionary activity of the struggling classes, including the critical activity of reflective sciences'.[18]

Solidarity

Revolutionary activity by the working classes presupposes solidarity. When Africans were forced off their land, denied the right to have farms or squat on white farms, they had no choice but to swell the urban areas in order to minister to the needs of the whites. When they left their original homes, they had their own deeply rooted sense of belonging, of togetherness, of solidarity. But this solidarity was to be transformed on the industrial plants into a new kind of solidarity. It was demanded of blacks in order to enable them to respond collectively to the challenges of the workplace. Solidarity comes about as a result of a collective consciousness. The victory of workers is only possible through solidarity. A class struggle against exploitation presupposes the forging of bonds of solidarity.

Christian perspective

Solidarity within the context of Christian social ethics, writes Dielmor Mieth, 'involves a double recognition, namely, that people belong together on the basis of equal worth and that people must stand together in order to overcome their problems'.[19] Human solidarity is also implied in the Christian symbols of God's Fatherhood, of brotherhood, of communion, in the homiletic declaration of St Paul, that there is neither Greek nor gentile, male or female, slave or freeman.

A black theological reflection, in the light of the collective experience of black people, understands universal human solidarity as a goal still to be achieved. It is not a fait accompli. The relations of production are presented in racial terms in order to safeguard the material and political interests of both the white ruling class and the white working class. As has already been pointed out, capital (especially in the mining sector) has avoided the social costs involved in the reproduction of the black workers by conserving pre-capitalist modes of production in the homelands. Homelands produce able-bodied workers and absorb the 'redundant African' and 'worn-out' African workers.[20] The 'civilised labour policy' prevented blacks from competing fairly in the labour market. For some 55 years blacks were excluded from the bargaining machinery set up by the state. Worker solidarity through unions was denied official recognition. Even in this era of black participation in trade unions, black workers struggle to enter into recognition agreements with companies. The Job Reservation Act has been phased out, but racial discrimination still continues on the grounds that blacks are not trained and do not therefore qualify for certain categories of work. Companies that are signatories to codes of employment conduct pay lip-service to their commitment. In short *baasskap* is still rampant.

It was the black consciousness movement that called for solidarity on racial lines because of the persistence of racial discrimination. Liberal whites, and those blacks who are immune to the pain and humiliation of racial segregation, fail to fathom the emancipatory role of black consciousness. The black theological perspective has been conditioned by black consciousness and the stark reality of racial segregation. Because of the long history of segregation and division, it is incumbent upon black workers to close ranks. Even if they kept them open they would only be open to a few envious liberals who acknowledge solidarity among black and white workers as a distant dream. The black workers' struggle is undoubtedly a *normal* struggle, which for tactical reasons is confined to black workers alone.

A critique of black consciousness

A critique of black consciousness shows that complete black solidarity is not possible. In fact it was never entertained even at the inception of the black consciousness movement. Ethnic divisions have been rejected outright as the work of the 'evil one'. By the same logic, those who participated in and promoted ethnic division were seen (and are still seen) as hostile to the total black struggle. This means therefore that total unity amongst the black people is a utopia. Secondly, the differentiation within the black community as a result of the emergence of a petite bourgeoisie, also tears apart the myth of total black unity. The petite bourgeoisie are traditionally known to shift between the exploited and the exploiter. Whether the continuation of racial discrimination will make them side with the black workers, or whether they will settle for the evolutionary change proposed by the ruling class, is still a matter to be verified. Desertion from the ranks of black people does not nullify the noble aspirations embodied in the black consciousness movement. A question that still needs to be faced is whether allegiance to the working-class struggle will transcend allegiance to ethnic groupings. The two are bound to remain artificially separate problems as long as some workers see the struggle in economic terms divorced from political issues. *A revolutionary consciousness is bound to see the two as inextricably intertwined.* Our theological reflection also shows this unity to be a key emphasis of Christian liberation.

For black theology, solidarity on racial lines is not in contradiction with Christian teaching. Solidarity, as has been pointed out, is a goal to be achieved. The immediate solidarity amongst the black workers is the result of the practice of discrimination. Solidarity as a moral attempt at realising justice must eliminate barriers amongst the workers – such as ethnic divisions, divisions between company unions and the workers' unions, or even ideological divisions (whether workers should be led by whites or by blacks themselves). Solidarity gives strength against uncompromising employers. Worker solidarity enhances the self-reliance of workers and their search for participation in decisions that affect their lives. Self-reliance, writes Dickinson,

is rooted in the conviction that genuine interdependence cannot be experienced until people are relatively equal, until those who have accepted their own inferiority and marginality rebel against such a self-image, until those who have come to accept their superiority have that illusion shattered. It is not possible to talk about interdependence with an interim period of self-reliance, a period when those who have been victimised . . . break that oppression and self-image.[21]

This is the perspective upheld by black theology. In consciously intensifying their class struggle, workers are actively presenting themselves as co-creators. Demanding recognition agreements, participation in industrial councils, staging strikes in protest against victimisation or arbitrary dismissals, organising legitimate unions while rejecting company unions, demanding better wages – all these acts are creative acts, acts modelled on the liberator-God who acts in history.[22] Co-ownership of industries, the right to participate in the policy-making machinery and eventually the right to have a say in the labour laws and all the laws affecting the lives of workers, will not be given, but are to be appropriated through a class struggle. As the struggle rages, the image of God becomes clearer and more convincing. The workers' partnership with God, as the result of the covenant, becomes more meaningful. Thus, for black theology praxis authenticates Christian claims. Self-assertive acts, in the form of strikes and work stoppages – despite expulsions, 'repatriation' and detention of union leaders – all affirm the dignity of workers. Segregation destroys human worth and is therefore in conflict with Mary's pronouncement in the Magnificat that God exalts the lowly.

The South African economic system has developed the metropolitan areas, and the peripheral areas are meant to provide the labour. By its nature the free-market system thrives on a cut-throat competitive system. In the South African context, the exclusion of the majority of the black people from sharing the benefits of 'stored labour', or capital, is a logical consequence.

A black theological reflection considers the tradition of entrenched privileges as incompatible with the true Christian spirit embodied in the gospel tradition. Christian symbols of brotherhood suggest a communalism that is in conflict with the rampant individualism of the free-market system. Both the Old and New Testaments underline the value of man-in-community. Material goods are for the enhancement of all, not for a selected few. This calls into being the need for a planned economy to replace the market economy. Black theological reflection underscores the corporate nature of man. This is also a value deeply rooted in African traditions. The quality of life for the black majority is likely to be enhanced in a planned economic system. Entrenched privileges of the capitalist system preclude any radical changes. The Christian ethos of charity also advocates a system of sharing. Paternalism is not recognised as a Christian value.

Whatever other limitations it may have, a socialist system harbours at its core the belief that humanity is by nature corporate, that labour is communal, that capital is the result of this social labour, and that justice demands an unconditional acceptance that all are equal before God.

Ecumenical vision and action

The ecumenical movement in Africa: from mission church to moratorium
GABRIEL SETILOANE

Christian co-operation to promote evangelism – for that is really what the ecumenical movement is all about – must have been a remote thought in the minds of the Christian missionaries on the African continent in the middle of the nineteenth century.

There was mutual assistance among the missionaries, born out of solidarity in the face of a strange and unfriendly environment. It became customary, for example, for missionaries of whatever nationality who went north of the Orange River to make their way first to Lithako (Kuruman), where Moffat and the London Missionary Society (LMS) group laboured, there to receive guidance as to which of the tribes would accept them and their services. In this way the first representatives of the French Evangelical Missionary Society in southern Africa found themselves at Motito among the Bahurutshe, the Americans under Lindley among Moselekatse's Ndebele at Mosega, and the Wesleyan Methodists among the Barolong at Pitsane. Casalis wrote home, giving expression to this solidarity, by referring to Mrs Archbell's hospitality – she mended his clothes and put him 'in touch with civilisation' whenever he visited Thaba 'Nchu to consult and compare notes with the Wesleyan missionaries. Soon, however, this kind congeniality gave way to rivalry, as a result of the journeys of discovery undertaken by Livingstone and others. The hunger for empires arose, and the 'scramble for Africa' following the discovery of diamonds in Kimberley and gold on the Witwatersrand engendered jealous competition. National and political goals took precedence over the altruistic desire to 'convert the heathen' and spread the good news. Societies like the LMS progressively developed a British face and lost the international complexion which attracted men like Van der Kemp. It is significant that missionary societies prospered best in the colonies of the countries of their own origin. Basutoland (Lesotho) and Barotseland (Western Zambia) are the exceptions – they were not colonies but protectorates, the missionaries preceding the arrival of the colonisers.

The beginnings of ecumenical consciousness
Conscious inclination towards working together on the mission field (for work among the European colonials was insignificant and fraught with imported denominational prejudice) comes to light very

late, and as a direct result of the work of the Students' Christian Movement in Great Britain and the United States during the latter part of the nineteenth century. The Student Christian Association (SCA) of South Africa was founded in 1896 by Luther Wishard and Donald Fraser[1] but its unity and existence were threatened by the political events which were to lead to the Anglo–Boer War of 1899–1902. At the Zeist World Student Christian Fellowship (WSCF) Conference, the General Secretary, John R. Mott, was persuaded by the members of the local SCA to visit South Africa, and the conscious effort toward ecumenical co-operation on the continent can be traced to this visit in 1906.

Mott addressed the Student Missionary Conference at Cape Town's Huguenot Hall. Students and churchmen destined to become leaders of their different groups, societies and churches heard Mott vividly express his life's devotion to Christian unity and co-operation. His name was to become a legend in South African mission circles. His vision of Christians of the world united across colour and creed and even national conviction remained to inspire and conscientise church leaders of all shades and conviction, until his return 30 years later.

Mott's visit served to link South African church life with world Christian thinking and developments, especially the development of an ecumenical consciousness generated by the Missionary Conference at Edinburgh in 1910, and the Church and Society Conference of 1925. The result was a quiet but sure growth of tolerance and of belonging to a united Christian movement, intent on conquering a 'pagan world'. Despite disruptive political events, in South Africa at the time, the first two decades of the twentieth century saw an extension of ecclesiastical co-operation. As a result of the formation of the International Missionary Council (IMC) with its programme of national church councils in member countries, together with Mott's second African visit in 1934, churches and missionary bodies in South Africa came to form the South African Council of Churches in 1936. The full participation by all Christians in South Africa was, however, marred by the political and nationalistic loyalties aroused by World War 2.

The conservative evangelicals

To the north of the Limpopo and the Zambesi Rivers, mission work began in the latter part of the nineteenth century. The field was vast. Missionaries worked in greater isolation in spite of the more enlightened ecumenical spirit they had experienced in the 'home country'. The pattern had been set in the south for missions to concentrate their work separately on certain groups and tribes, and mission work on the African continent proceeded in the classical manner: each little mission on its own, under the copious direction of its society 'back home'. These societies flourished, and massive organisations developed in all the cities, standing to this day as monuments to this era. This missionary empire-building hindered the development of an ecumenical consciousness in Africa.

A further deterrent was the arrival of conservative missionaries from the United States of America. Their missionary zeal was directed mainly at the countries of central Africa, the Congo, Kenya, Burundi, Chad and the Sudan. Armed with the dollar, modern technology, the radio and the aeroplane, they reached the yet untouched parts of the continent, together with the Bible and the medicine box. They were often fanatical, intolerant and uncooperative, on the doctrinal theological warpath. A revival movement soon appeared which was for three decades to hold sway in central and equatorial Africa, leaving a hard-to-erase stamp of 'conservative evangelicalism' on the indigenous African expression of Christianity – a matter to be reckoned with to this day.

Post-World War 2 developments

World War 2 created a new world outlook among the peoples of Africa. For the first time 'ordinary' Africans were cajoled into going to Europe and North Africa to defend 'democratic freedom' and 'self-determination'. They fought and died with their colonial masters. In the process, the elevated status which Africans had afforded their oppressors began to crumble, while their own self-esteem and self-worth developed. They returned home fired with a desire for freedom of their own. There was an explosion of ideas, and human possibilities seemed unlimited and boundless. A breath of air had blown through the continent, giving it new life and hope. In Francophone Africa this African nationalism expressed itself in the staid literary and philosophic tomes of Laye's *The African Child* and Leopold Senghor's *De la Négritude*. In Anglophone Africa, nationalism came wearing a rebellious and violently self-asserting face – the Mau Mau in Kenya, and in Ghana the Liberation From Colonialism Movement spearheaded by Kwame Nkrumah.

Things had not stood still in world church circles during the war. The vision transmitted by Oldham, Mott, Söderbloem and Visser 't Hooft, of one reunited Christendom moving towards a new world of Christian brotherhood, was too vivid to be dulled and tarnished by gunfire and the billowing clouds of smoke over the blitzed cities of Europe. Amid all that inhumanity and demonic cruelty of European to European, Christian hands and hearts which had come together at Edinburgh, Stockholm, Zeist and London did not altogether lose touch.[2] Witness to this was the Amsterdam Assembly, which took place just three years after the war. There was a renewed determination to stay together, which led to the establishment of the World Council of Churches (WCC). In the following decades this organisation was to influence the development of the ecumenical movement on the African continent. Earlier, in 1938, when the IMC convened its Tambaram Conference and the participation of 'people from the younger churches' had been a priority, this category was filled by missionaries and missionary executives who sought to speak on behalf of these churches. Twenty years after Tambaram, and ten years after Amsterdam, a new era dawned.

In 1958, there met in Ibadan, Nigeria, a conference which was to have much influence on the Church in Africa. Some 200 representatives of church bodies from about 25 countries attended the conference. . . . Here for the first time the Church in Africa found its voice. It was designed to be this way because the conference was called for the specific purpose of affording the African church leaders the chance to speak their minds on church matters.[3]

The days of 'Christianity by proxy' for Africa were over.

African churches come of age

The Ibadan Conference of Churches set in motion the machinery to create an African regional ecumenical body. One year later Dr Donald M'Timkulu, a South African educationist, was appointed general organising secretary with headquarters at the Mindolo Ecumenical Centre, while a strong provisional committee was elected to assist him. He travelled widely throughout the continent, his chief task being

to open the way and to prepare the ground and plant the seed which would ultimately flower as a strong co-operating body of Christian churches and other bodies concerned with the witness of Christ in Africa. Such a body would stand as a living witness to unity in Christ in Africa.[4]

Political 'winds of change' and the spirit of Pan-Africanism sweeping over the continent gave him a receptive and responsive audience. In April 1963 at Makerere University in Kampala the All African Conference of Churches (AACC) was constituted 'as a fellowship of consultation and cooperation within the wider fellowship of the universal church'.[5] The basis of its membership was confession of the 'Lord Jesus Christ as God and only Saviour according to the Scriptures'.

The ground for a programme of activities for the AACC had already been laid and tested through consultations and conferences on 'Christian Education in Africa' (Salisbury, December 1962–January 1963) and 'Christian Home and Family Life' (Mindolo Ecumenical Centre, Kitwe, April 1963).

The All Africa Christian Youth Assembly (AACYA) which was held in Nairobi at the end of 1962 and sponsored by the WSCF, and the Youth Department of the WCC, gave impetus to the Kampala Assembly of the AACC. Work done by the Rev. Hank Crane, Africa Secretary of the WSCF, had made the students of the newly established African universities aware of the challenges and opportunities which lay before the Christian community of Africa at the time.

At the AACYA they not only came to terms with themselves and the revolution sweeping through the whole continent, but they also set the tone for the Assembly of the Churches held at Kampala a few months later. They grappled with colonialism, African religiosity and African nationalism. Nobody could doubt their standpoint, and a few years later these young people would be the leaders of Africa: 'We are African Christians,' they declared, 'fully African and fully Christian. Therefore, we willy-nilly participate in the struggle of our continent for the attainment of our God-given freedom in Christ and full humanity.'[6] The theme of the Youth Assembly had given expression to this – 'freedom under the cross', while the inaugural assembly of the AACC was to have 'Freedom and Unity in Christ' as its theme.

Ecumenism in Africa

The ecumenical movement initially strove for Christian unity, which the churches had lost. In the 1950s the emphasis in the ecumenical movement was on 'unity', which was understood most of the time as 'organic'. The Faith and Order Commission was considered in the WCC to be the very marrow of the ecumenical movement, and the triumphs of these commitments were clear for all to see in the United Church of Canada, and the Church of South India. The decision by the Orthodox Churches at the New Delhi Assembly in 1961 to take up full membership of the WCC, and the decision of the IMC to be incorporated as a commission within the WCC (as the Commission on World Mission and Evangelism) were seen as a vindication of this concept.

African personality and understanding has never been intellectually eclectic, separating theory from practice and reality. Africa came of age in the ecumenical movement under the grip of a revolution aimed at shrugging off colonialism as a denial of human freedom and being. What someone like Kwame Nkrumah articulated on political platforms as hateful and oppressive, many a churchman had experienced within the church. For the first years, therefore, the commitment to African church independence was not only simultaneous with, but even emotionally and experientially analogous to, the transition from colony to independent state in the secular sphere. It was traumatic on all sides. Donald M'Timkulu looks back with a sense of great relief:

In spite of foot-dragging many of the Churches of Africa have attained autonomy. The movement from mission to church is almost complete. The older and larger overseas mission boards have handed over both leadership and financial control to the African Christians. Some of the smaller mission bodies, however, especially those who have come late into the field, have not gone this far. They still make in their own offices the final decisions on disposition of funds and use of 'their' personnel in Africa.[7]

The churches in Africa faced many issues in their relationship with the 'mother churches' abroad, which were in spirit and essence the issues and problems of the new African states with regard to their former colonial masters. In ecumenical circles the AACC voiced the problems and dilemmas not only of the churches but the new states of Africa. The organisation of the AACC and the role it played 'within the fellowship of the universal church' helped to sensitise Christendom to the problems of inter-state relationships, and to make the WCC a 'conscience to the nations'. Soon 'Third World' problems began to dominate the agenda of the WCC, as was seen especially at the Uppsala Assembly in 1966.

Concern for an African theological expression

Under the rubric 'The selfhood of the church', the inaugural assembly of the AACC in Kampala affirmed:

Christian freedom demands a great deal of tolerance towards and a sympathetic listening to those Africans who, while accepting Christ, find it difficult to accept also the Western concepts of Greek-Roman cultural origin which wrap Him up as He is handed to us. It is essential that such influences which are not of the *bene esse* of the Gospel should not be forced on people who have a totally different outlook and philosophy of life.[8]

Of primary concern whenever Christian Africans met during these times was the question of how Africa interpreted and appropriated to itself the Christian gospel brought by the missionaries. The question was raised at a consultation of African theologians held at Enugu, Nigeria, in 1965, which issued a book on African theology entitled *Biblical Revelation and African Faiths*.[9] After this, thanks largely to the work of E. Bolaji Idowu and much later John Mbiti, African perspectives on the Christian faith began to be taken seriously, taught in universities, and researched in church circles around the world. In fact it is at this level that African ecumenism has been openly inclusive and has crossed sacred barriers. The Association of African Theologians which has been formed is a comprehensive organisation in membership, drawing its members from all Christian denominations on the African continent: Protestant, Roman Catholic and indigenous (Independent) churches.[10]

Concern for society and community

African Christians were (and are still) too deeply steeped in the everyday life of their land not to feel even deeper than others the social traumas of the time. This was obviously evident in the period immediately before and after the attainment of independence by the African countries in the 1960s. During their struggles for independence it was Christians who had taken the lead in thinking, planning and interpreting the nature of the independence struggle. John V. Taylor, a sensitive observer of African church and Christian life, in fact expressed surprise at this in his *Christianity and Politics in Africa*.[11] This involvement was, however, inevitable as Christian leaders were about the best educated and most articulate members of the African population.

After independence they continued to be loyal to their Christian calling, and many ministers and pastors became leaders in the new governments they had helped to initiate. The most recent example is the President of Zimbabwe, the Rev. Canaan Banana. Unfortunately, political parties and governments are not always as altruistic in their motivations and schemes as Christians may desire, and many of the noblest dreams for independence were not realised. It was, however, a clear and stated policy of the ecumenical movement in Africa to serve, though not in a supine manner, the post-independent countries of the continent in their nation-building efforts and tasks. Samuel Amissah, then the General Secretary of the AACC, expressed it clearly before the Executive Committee of the WCC in 1965:

The African revolution gives churches the opportunity to serve people in a new situation and therefore with new needs. There are people who are taking on new responsibility who need to be helped to understand what it entails – cabinet ministers, commissioners, secretaries of governments abroad; youth who are continually attracted to the town; youth who are being resettled on the land; the growing school and college population; and women who are being urged by their governments to play a role in the life of their new nations through women's federations, etc.[12]

The AACC Youth, Home and Family Life Commission deliberately organised their programmes to this end. Nation-building and leadership training ranked high. Many leaders trained by the church were absorbed into their countries' civil services. Mindolo Ecumenical Centre in Kitwe became a training centre. Here people from all corners of the continent met to be trained not only to serve their churches but also to serve their developing countries.

This concern and participation of African Christianity in development and nation-building did not, however, mean a subservience to Caesar. Already in the preamble to the AACC constitution the emphasis is on 'Jesus Christ . . . as the *only* Saviour'. It was this confessional interpolation that declared as outright heretical the insinuations that Kwame Nkrumah – by the term *Osajefu* – should be regarded as Saviour. The leaders of the African countries – Nkrumah, Senghor, Nyerere, Kaunda – were greatly admired in church circles, and they appreciated the role of the church in their tasks. However, there was no question of any one of them ever being regarded as beyond reproach. This prophetic stance was repeated time and again during the period that Burgess Carr served as General Secretary of the AACC. The church in its African mould was not shy to intervene in quarrels between brothers, seeking to bring peace and reconciliation. When tyranny and despotism reigned supreme in Uganda, the AACC, after several interviews between Idi Amin and Burgess Carr, sent a delegation of churchmen to Amin 'to speak the prophetic truth of God'. Those critics are, therefore, wrong to have construed the AACC as no more than the Organisation of African Unity (OAU) at prayer, with the *sole* aim of condemning white racism. Under Burgess Carr, the ecumenical movement in Africa became recognised as an indisputable voice calculated to cast down evil, to uphold good, to guide the diffident, to nudge the shy, and to raise the hope of all. Of course, the AACC had a place in the ranks of the OAU, and rightly so, considering the contribution that the Christian church had made to African independence.

Contrary winds

Ecumenical development on the African continent did not, however, run smoothly. Not all the leaders of Christendom had the far-sightedness of Oldham and Mott. Although organisations like the WSCF, IMC and WCC had accepted and advocated Africa's right to develop its own Christian genius, the habit of Western European and American supremacy found the practice more difficult to accept than the theory. They would not let go. Tension within ecumenical courts rose. The fact that for a long time the budget of ecumenism in Africa was underwritten abroad did not improve the situation. M'Timkulu states:

The Church getting help from abroad faces exactly the same problem as the new nations that continue to receive foreign economic aid. How do they gain real independence and free themselves from this new form of colonialism? The problem is encircled with subtle and complicated issues.[13]

The executives, moderators, presidents and administrative secretaries of the new churches of Africa were frustrated, and confidence between them and their counterparts in the churches and ecumenical councils abroad was at an all-time low.

The moratorium debate

As if to make matters worse, all this happened at the time when the church in Africa was seeking to develop an African face. Négritude, African socialism, African personality and African humanism were the new philosophies being advocated and experimented with on the continent. The church was deeply involved in this search for 'an African way'. Frustration in organisational and administrative areas hampered its contribution in the search for an African personality. It is out of this frustration that the idea of a moratorium on funding and mission activity was born. Significantly the idea first found expression in the mind of John Gatu of Kenya, General Secretary of the Presbyterian Church (offspring of the mission work of the Presbyterian Church in the USA).

The argument for a moratorium was that the continued flow of funds from First World countries to churches in Africa compromised these receiving churches and hindered their initiative and originality, as regards their planning for the future development of the church. The principle, 'he who pays the piper calls the tune', was not forgotten by those who provided the funds. Inordinate pressure was felt by African church leaders to plan the development of the church in Africa along the lines dictated by Europe and America. Gatu's suggestion was to with-draw from Western ecclesiastical demands, in order to seek in quiet continental isolation to cultivate an African answer to the development of the church. Moratorium meant an end to foreign personnel and funds for the work of the church in Africa. The idea was to activate and stimulate self-help from the African churches themselves, and if not self-help, at least a mentality and ability to ensure that development was dictated by African concepts of life. The church and secular institutions in Africa had enough experience of foreign aid with strings attached, and felt itself smothered by it. Resentment was felt in both church and state. The reaction from the church, which held moral sensitivity and honour dear, was extreme.

Moratorium as a strategy in church development was first publicly discussed at the Commission of World Mission and Evangelism Conference in Bangkok in 1973. It was also debated at the Lusaka Assembly of the AACC in 1974. African arguments that moratorium was envis-aged as a short-term goal were not convincing. Moreover, the likeli-hood of missionaries having to leave Africa, and the prospects facing executives and office workers in the missionary houses for whom moratorium would mean cessation of work and a means of livelihood, were awesome. Yet for Africans moratorium had portended a period of real growth dependent on their own initiatives. However, in the debate African resentment towards the churches of Europe and America be-came evident. The church in Africa considered itself as having come of age.

World confessional movements

Almost parallel with the ecumenical movement of Oldham, Mott and Visser 't Hooft was the development of confessional ecumenism. The World Methodist Council often claims to have been the first to employ the term 'ecumenical' in modern times to describe the fellow-ship of Methodists all over the world. After World War 2, the Luther-ans established a World Federation (LWF) in an attempt to redress the estrangement which had arisen in its midst as a result of its having been on both sides of the enemy lines. Then followed the founding of the Alliance of Reformed Churches. Regrettably such world confessional organisations have hindered the development of ecumenism on the African continent. Some churches in fact felt uneasy in the fellowship of the African churches and preferred to have fellowship in a world confessional setting, for example the Dutch Reformed churches of South Africa. Although the Lutheran churches on the continent partici-pated in the formation of the AACC, they have gradually withdrawn, hardly ever participating in that organisation's programmes. There is, however, a bright side to this coin. The world confessional movement, functioning within an atmosphere charged with a desire for co-opera-tion and rapprochement, has been able to expose the scandal of churches of common doctrinal origins working separately merely because they were started by missionaries from different countries.

Ecumenism, African style

For many the most important goal of the ecumenical movement is the attainment of unity despite doctrinal differences. For this reason the few achievements of unity are acclaimed and revered. In the minds of many forward-looking missionary planners the Church of South India was the norm, surpassing even the United Church of Canada. Throughout Africa, talks were held by the missionaries seeking church unity. Except for Zambia where in 1964 unity of sorts was attained between Methodists, the Paris Evangelical missionaries, the Baptists and the United Church of Canada Mission to the Copperbelt, church unity on the continent seems to have proved unsuccessful. Here and there some small struggling missions have rationalised their work and come together out of financial considerations. In some cases it has happened because of non-theological pressures. In all cases where church unions have been achieved on the continent, the initiators have been white and often missionaries. Why does it seem as if the fervour for 'organic' unity of the church does not burn in the African bosom with the same intensity as it does among some whites? Furthermore it seems that since the 'younger churches' of Africa joined the WCC, the emphasis in the ecumenical movement has moved from the concerns of the Faith and Order Commission to those of practical human predicaments: Church and Society, Development Aid, the Programme to Combat Racism, and Dialogue with Other Faiths.

It may well be that Africa, having inherited the divided church from abroad, has not felt the pangs of this division as deeply as have European Christians: 'the sin of our divisions' is not felt as Africa's sin, and therefore there is no inner compulsion to repent of it. Yet tolerance, mutual acceptance and co-operation between the churches are more evident on the African continent than elsewhere, and denominational barriers are criss-crossed with amazing ease, especially at the congregational level.

A feature that has developed over the years in many African towns and cities is the fraternal organisation of ministers and pastors. In South Africa it has even given birth to a national organisation which holds its gatherings annually, the Interdenominational African Ministers' Association of South Africa (IDAMASA), whose membership is open to all denominations. An undeclared taboo reigns over discussion of doctrinal differences, and the emphasis of IDAMASA, and its women's wing called IDAMWASA, has been on practical matters related to the function of the church and its agents in the black communities of the land. The burdens imposed on such work by the policies of the country have come up for discussion and confrontation, while for the safety of its members, straight political issues have been eschewed. Still, IDAMA-

SA's programme has been clearly aimed at the amelioration of the situation of blacks. In most towns and cities there is a ten-day observance of prayers for church unity conducted in the member churches, where pulpit exchanges are practised. This occasion often culminates in a church unity service for members of all denominations.

African ecumenism is also present at a more obvious grassroots level. Donald M'Timkulu describes it adequately:

The social ties binding the African Christian to his extended family and clan have always been stronger than the forces of separation that arise from membership in different denominations. The important family occasions like births, marriages, funerals and clan festivals bring together in one place of worship relatives with different confessional backgrounds. On these occasions they not only share in common acts of worship with gay disregard of denominational differences, but they also take part in symbolic acts of family and clan unity that have their roots in the traditional past.[14]

Perhaps this is the reason for the lack of fervour for so-called 'organic unity'. There are other forces at work in the African soul that continue to reduce the dividedness of the church as planted in Africa from abroad.

Ecumenical vision and reality in South Africa
MARGARET NASH

There is a time coming, and it is not far off, when the church buildings in the townships (which are now so often closed to community and worker organisations) will no longer be used for religious services. They will be taken over as fortresses for storing arms and waging war. And only the church that will survive is the church of the houses and the streets, where Christian people are gathering and living out their faith in solidarity with all who struggle against oppression.
Black preacher at a Heroes' Memorial Service, Cape Town, 1984.

We live on a small, fragile planet – a minute but unique part of the universe. This much we know from the discoveries, experiences and electronic communications of our space age. Technology has made of this planet a global village in which no part can expect to exist in isolation from another.

If history means not only what has happened, but how we organise our memory of what has happened and thereby provide a higher organisation of events, then we live in an age of universal history. We face a common destiny, a common fate. For there to be a future for ourselves, our children and our children's children, present generations will have to find ways of holding at bay the forces of destruction now being unleashed by sectional greeds and fears. Nuclearism, chemical and biological warfare, and the destruction of the environment through technology for profit not people, threaten our future. To avoid this we have to generate attitudes and relationships of dependence on one another and on the ecological balance of all creation.

This existential truth confronts all sectors of human society, whatever their nationality, religious tradition, ideological persuasion or human condition. It challenges all belief systems that claim universality and uniqueness, and all movements that claim to be ecumenical. The question is whether in a world of division and conflict talk of unity, community and wholeness can ever be more than rhetoric? Can the striving for it have any real meaning and usefulness in the lives of people, communities and nations?

In South Africa destructive division and conflict stemming from racism constitute reality. Three-hundred-and-fifty years of European aggrandisement and thirty-five years of apartheid have brought the country to the brink of civil war. The entire subcontinent is threatened with a fate like that of Vietnam, with immediate and long-term social and environmental devastation caused by hi-tech warfare, waged in this case by a potent but strangely necrophiliac minority. Christians in South Africa face the bitter irony that this has been and is perpetrated in the name of Western Christian civilisation.

In such a situation it is a luxury and an irrelevance to survey the global scene and reflect on what it means to live in an age of universal history. We need to focus instead on the black preacher's challenge, for if we believe God is the God of the poor, then we must throw all our efforts into the people's struggle for national liberation. Would this not mean developing a 'Confessing Church' (of committed individuals) and leaving the institutional churches to their fate?

Let us look more closely at the consciousness of South African church people, whether ordained leaders or laity. No matter how escapist our privatised religion may be (and that can apply as much to a small and impecunious African Independent church as to a large middle-class white congregation), we all live amidst tension and fragmentation, incompleteness and insecurity, contradiction and cut-throat competition.

This is true at the level of the personal and social, the political and economic, the national and global. It is painful. But we also have glimpses of beauty, experiences of acceptance and belonging, resonances of a universal and even cosmic heartbeat. For ease of pain, comfort of soul, realisation of our creative human potential, we yearn for wholeness and harmony, we gravitate towards offers of healing and more abundant life.

For all our brokenness and frustration we are not yet burdened with the fear of extinction as a human race. Apartheid isolates us and locks us into an intense narcissistic absorption with our own struggles. We are not part of nuclear *angst*, nor the intercontinental network of anti-nuclear movements in Europe, North America and the Pacific, where the spectre of nuclear annihilation has begun to penetrate the consciousness of millions, including young children. Yet apartheid is an international issue, and we are part of a global struggle for justice, peace and ecological balance. So the pain and longing for wholeness, the struggle for a better alternative, is a matter of species survival and planetary destruction, not just the easing of pain. It calls into question the meaning of human life itself. For Christians it calls into question the meaning of faith, the nature of the God revealed in Jesus Christ as source of life and Lord of history. It is an *ikon* of hope beckoning us towards an open future.

When suffering under and struggling against apartheid interact with the suffering and struggling of this first generation 'to live with a recurrent sense of biological severance, ... a radically impaired imagination of human continuity' (Lifton), then participants begin to experience solidarity and bonding in place of the numbing, disabling effects of isolation and separateness. With that sense of solidarity comes empowerment. Latent or suppressed resources of initiative and creativity emerge and seek expression in images, relationships and activities that affirm and generate life.

The ecumenical movement is very much a twentieth-century phenomenon. William Temple termed it, in the 1940s, the 'great new fact of our time' and Pope John XXIII in the 1960s described it as the 'opening of the windows of the church so that the winds of the Spirit can blow freely and renew its life'. But the ecumenical vision that motivated and inspired John R. Mott, Oldham, W. A. Visser 't Hooft, William Temple, M. M. Thomas, John XXIII, Cardinal Bea and Don Helder Camara, cannot simply be inherited. Powerful as are the Vatican II declarations that, 'By her relationship with Christ, the Church is a kind of sacrament or sign of intimate union with God, and of the unity of all mankind', and that 'The joys and the hopes, the griefs and the anxieties of the men of this age, especially those who are poor or in any way afflicted, these too are the joys and hopes, the griefs and anxieties of the followers of Christ', we cannot simply adopt them as slogans. The ecumenical vision has to be sought, received and obeyed anew in the midst of this period of intensifying national struggle and of planetary crisis. We still have to wrestle with the questions: What is God doing in history? How can we recognise and co-operate with God as we strive, in the face of threat and despair, to be makers of our own history and stewards of our children's future?

Ecumenical vision

In this era and on this interconnected, pluralistic and profoundly threatened planet, ecumenical vision can be nothing less than apocalyptic. It must offer a cosmic vision of God's sovereignty and power to terminate this historical order and rebuild a new creation. It must address the direst realities of human deprivation and destructiveness, frustration, meaninglessness and dread of annihilation. And it must enable these to be acknowledged and expressed, accepted and integrated psychically and spiritually into a dying and rising to new life that is both personal and corporate, mundane and cosmic.

For religious faith to be salvific, to be authentically and effectively healing, it must offer the believer, seeker and all humanity a 'sense of the whole' that can embrace the desperate polarities of human experience, historically and in our own era; a sense of the whole that can generate and sustain such ways of feeling, thinking, choosing, sharing, living as might enable the global family to die to the old and be born into an epoch beyond our present imagining – an epoch of co-creativity with the awesome recurring redemptive Presence that countless generations have learned to call God.

Mundane reality

All this must seem academic, utopian and far removed from the mundane realities of church life in South Africa. At parish level there is, in addition to financial pressures and struggles with inflation, the treadmill of pastoral ministry to people with so many different needs: among the affluent, the problems of loneliness, drugs, broken marriages, death and bereavement, neglected old people, and underneath it all a deep gnawing anxiety about the future of this country and themselves in it. Among the poor those same problems exist, but they are immensely aggravated by hunger and homelessness, pass laws and unemployment, crime and communal violence, political alienation and unvented rage.

In the denominations there are the usual problems of institutional inertia, the lack of fit between traditional patterns that worked tolerably well in the past and the kinds of ministry now needed in so many amorphous, unstable agglomerations of people, whether in suburbs or townships or proliferating rural slums. Not to mention the trauma of being asked to face the near-genocidal implications of population removals into homeland ghettoes and concentration camps.

At the level of the South African Council of Churches there are problems of interface: member churches with one another; local churches with overseas churches and donor agencies; local activities and organisations seeking moral and financial support from the Council and through it from overseas churches and donor agencies; internally between various personnel, programmes and priorities.

The 'little ship' is also buffeted by the storms of political pressure: from the state and the conservative white community on the one side, and from rival liberation movements (AZAPO, UDF) on the other. Add to these the problems of exercising the power of patronage, a power which may subtly corrupt or mislead even the most highminded.

The SACC and, particularly since 1976, its General Secretary have come to be seen by the needy (and the covetous) as a source of or means of access to all manner of benefits. These range from bursaries for rural school children and other education assistance, legal aid, maintenance of dependants of political prisoners, publicity and intervention in cases of threatened removals, to opportunities for overseas theological study and conference travel, and grants for relief and development projects undertaken by local churches and community groups.

Yet the Council is not by definition a welfare body, a service agency or a financial conduit. Nor is it a marriage of convenience. It exists to promote the unity and mission of the church in this country and indirectly throughout the world. Such a raison d'être is different from and in tension with that of any of its component parts, participants or beneficiaries. Implementing that vocation requires more than programme maintenance and good honest administration. It requires the kind of theological perspective, consensus and mutual commitment that grow out of shared pain, that can nurture and sustain dialectical relationships between all who take part – a mix of affirmation and acceptance in spite of difference; encouragement and critical solidarity; experiment and mutual correction – in fact, what the Bible terms covenant relationship (*berith, diatheke*).

Given the tensions and crises of church–state relationships and the outbursts of violence that are coalescing into undeclared civil war, in which the divisions are within as well as between us, within as well as between races, classes, churches, what hope is there of making ecumenical progress, of developing and expressing a renewed sense of the whole? If we confine ourselves to the nitty gritty that answer is, little hope, if any. But if we escape into some nebulous utopian scenario where angels sing in harmony and all problems have melted away there is even less hope. For ecumenical renewal precisely consists in and comes through creative tension, through learning to live the coming future now, constantly moving between what is and what could be, what God wills to be. The future, if there is one, belongs to those who know what it is to pray –

> Let us see now with truer sight, O God
> Of root and sky; let us at last be faithful
> In perception, and in action that is born
> Of perception, even as we have been faithful
> In the green recklessness of little knowledge.

The future belongs to those who then 'plod out' the vision they are granted in answer to such prayer, until 'the vision at last will find its people'.[1]

In other words, the ecumenical issue is not an ism or an ideology, not a set of bargaining points and procedures for religious businesses negotiating company merger. Nor is it a matter of intellectual concepts and theological perspectives to which some people and groups do or do not subscribe. Rather, it is a basic question of obedience to God. A question of action and a way of life stemming from a faith that builds on, yet moves away from and beyond, what has been and is, in order to fulfil what could be, to fulfil what God wills to be and to become. It is a life of faith that does not deny the reality of evil but integrates it, a way of living that accepts cruelty, suffering and frustration not fatalistically but in union of spirit with Christ crucified (who experienced the ultimate horror of God-forsakenness), and in so doing puts to test the promise that the seed which falls into the ground and dies will bring forth a rich harvest (John 12: 24).

Beyers Naudé

Such has been the ecumenical obedience of Beyers Naudé, who in his lifetime has had to undergo not only severe institutional and social hardship but also, and more painfully, a psychic and spiritual travail that could have broken him but instead became the means of strengthening. As he completes his biblical span of years and hopefully enters a new decade, Naudé brings to the SACC, to the South African churches and to the world church the orientation and commitment of a pastor who is also a prophet, a servant who is also a *baanbreker*. On him will fall in a very particular way the gift and task of leading the church in southern Africa into costlier ecumenical obedience.

On the one hand, he is called to hold before us a vision which is nothing less than apocalyptic in setting forth God's will and power to reconcile, to reintegrate in Christ all persons, all principalities and powers, in the country and throughout the cosmos. On the other hand, he has the prophet's unenviable task of unmasking deception (of self as well as of others), proclaiming divine judgment, and calling for the repentance that leads to demonstrable amendment of life – and so will attract renewed persecution. On the one hand, he will be drawing on his own experience and understanding of southern Africa: on the other, he will surely be mediating the perspectives and challenges of the pilgrim people of God throughout the world.

Covenanting for justice

With others in South Africa and further afield he will be grappling with the practical question, How in the face of rising militancy and intensifying repression can we link our own local struggles for survival, justice and human dignity with those being waged elsewhere? How can we link them in ways that are not artificial, burdensome or onesided but rather are synergistic, that generate a surplus of energy because they allow the resources of the divine grace (*charis*), of the trinitarian communion of love (*koinonia agape*), to flow more fully and freely through and between one another?

This practical question was sharply focused at the Vancouver 1983 Sixth Assembly of the World Council of Churches on the theme, 'Jesus Christ – the Life of the World'. It has since been developed in relation to a major ecumenical study-action thrust on 'Justice, Peace and the Integrity of Creation' (JPIC). The Assembly, representing some 400 million people in 300 member churches, affirmed that life is God's gift, intended in its fullness over against the misery and chaos of a world that rejects God's design; it also renewed its commitment to the ecumenical vision: 'The Lord prays for the unity of his people as a sign by which the world may be brought to faith, renewal and unity'; and it offered an image that even the simplest can understand: 'The tree of peace has justice for its roots.'[3] In his keynote address near the beginning of the Assembly Allan Boesak challenged the churches not to allow the issues of peace and justice, the struggles against militarism and threat of nuclear annihilation and the struggles against racism, to be separated:

Peace is never simply the absence of war, it is the active presence of justice. It has to do with human fulfilment, with liberation, with wholeness, with meaningful life and wellbeing, not only for the individual but for the community as a whole. And the prophet Isaiah speaks of peace as the offspring of justice.[3]

Boesak warned against using the gospel to escape the demands of the gospel. 'One cannot use the issue of peace to escape from the unresolved issues of injustice, poverty, hunger and racism. If we do this we will make of our concern for peace an ideology of oppression which in the end will be used to justify injustice.' To this challenge the Assembly responded clearly and firmly in its Statement on Peace and Justice:

Peace cannot be built on foundations of injustice. Peace requires a new international order based on justice for and within all nations, and respect for the God-given humanity and dignity of every person. . . . The churches today are called to confess anew their faith, and to repent for the times when Christians have remained silent in the face of injustice or threats to peace. The biblical vision of peace with justice for all, of wholeness, of unity for all God's people, is not one of several options for the followers of Christ. It is an imperative in our time.[5]

A conciliar process of covenant

Building on the work of the Vancouver Assembly and of a May 1984 consultation to develop an integral approach to issues of peace and justice, the WCC Central Committee, meeting in July 1984, called on the churches and Christian action groups, basic communities, and 'grassroots' organisations to 'enter into a conciliar process of covenant to justice, peace and the integrity of all creation'.[6] In secular language this could be translated as a process of consultation and mutual commitment in regard to the interrelated threats to personal, societal and planetary existence.

Put that way the call raises an immediate practical problem. How can squatters under plastic on the outskirts of Cape Town, residents of a threatened 'black spot' in south-eastern Transvaal, trade unionists or beleaguered township–dwellers in Eastern Cape towns like Cradock and Kwanobuhle (Uitenhage) be expected to do more than concern themselves with their own basic struggles for survival against forced removal, retrenchments and unemployment, crippling rent rises, and repression of community organisation? In the short run, the answer is negative. Those who seek to be in solidarity with the poor and the oppressed have no right to arrive with high–flown analyses and theological treatises regarding what is happening in various parts of the world, and how this or that particular trouble spot fits into the wider pattern.

However, the history of many specific struggles reveals a paradox. Where there is real empathy and the building of communication links between an embattled but resistant group and a wider fellowship of solidarity, local resistance can be strengthened, and the political costs of an oppressive programme, whether it be the bulldozing of a squatter camp, proposed legislation or the detention of trade unionists, can be considerably raised. In 1979 Crossroads squatter camp was spared, and has lived under threat ever since; in 1983 Cabinet Minister Piet Koornhof's draconian Orderly Movement and Settlement of Black Persons Bill was withdrawn; in February 1984 Mogopa was razed in a swift military-type operation – and became a household word throughout the Western world, as Prime Minister Botha found to his cost when he visited Europe in mid-1984 to solicit moral and material support for his 'reform' plans.

However, oppression takes covert as well as overt forms. To deceive with ambiguity and false promises, to subvert, manipulate, vilify, to divide and estrange the oppressed (the struggling community and its supporters) is integral to domination. Unless the oppressed and their partners in struggle develop a shared awareness of this fact, and constantly seek to nurture and express humane values in the service of humane goals, they soon become vulnerable to the subtler forms of oppression. They fall victim to rumour-mongering and suspicion, agents provocateurs, bribery and corruption, and the displacement of frustration into debilitating internal conflict – whether about ideology, strategy or tactics – and struggles for power. In this context it is evident that pastorally and politically the concept of ecumenical covenant to justice, peace and the integrity of all creation is not as utopian or irrelevant as might first appear.

Rather, the conciliar process of entering into covenant stimulates people and groups in diverse situations to discover their common humanity and actualise their interdependence as fellow inhabitants of spaceship earth. It encourages them to wrestle with the biblical question, 'Have we not all one father? Did not one God create us? Why do we violate the covenant of our forefathers by being faithless to one another?' (Mal. 1: 10) It strengthens them against privatised and other-worldly religious teachings that either promise prosperity in this life as an inevitable sign of God's blessing or relegate salvation to the great hereafter, and in both cases induce pious complicity with social evil. It also brings to light unrecognised structures of oppression among and within the oppressed and their partners, for example, sexism and male chauvinism among black nationalists struggling for political liberation, zeal (in Europe or North America) for the SACC and for the black liberation struggle in faraway South Africa while ignoring or evading the call to support 'controversial' Third World priorities such as the Special Fund of the Programme to Combat Racism, the New International Economic Order or the New World Information Order.

A way of building commitment

The conciliar process of convenanting is seen by the WCC and those who are already working on it as not so much requiring new programmes but 'as a way of building our commitment to one another in the struggles for justice, peace and the integrity of creation. It is being built *solidly on the foundation of God's covenant relationship with his people and on the covenant relationships of the churches with one another in the WCC.*'[7] Consequently the whole of the WCC activity should be permeated by a theological and pastoral dimension that would be energising as well as cohesive in its effect. We in South Africa need to ask ourselves how the elements in the process are being taken up by the SACC and its constituents (member churches and regional councils of churches), and how 'activists' can share in these without feeling they are being diverted from essentials. The elements include:

Biblical, theological, historical and socio-ethical studies on justice and peace; and on the nature and meaning of covenant related to justice, peace and the integrity of creation.

Case studies to highlight what is complementary and what is contradictory in the different struggles, for example the question of armed struggle in national liberation struggles in southern Africa and the emphasis on non-violence and disarmament in the anti-nuclear movements.

Ecumenical visits which bring together churches with 'very different starting points' in the struggles for justice and peace. This is also needed internally in South Africa where local churches, even within the same denomination, are often worlds apart.

Monitoring and analysing the experience of people and groups who are consciously trying to link the struggles for justice, peace and the integrity of creation (JPIC), and sharing their experiences with the churches.

Analysing the effects of programmes of service and development (agricultural, home industries, famine relief, health care, literacy) on the struggles for justice and peace.

Giving specific support to and acting in solidarity with groups trying to link Justice and Peace struggles, and to develop networks among groups, churches and the World Council of Churches. Strengthening the elements of Christian initiative and voluntary ecumenism is much needed to energise the official ecumenism of the ecclesiastical institutions.

Workshops, consultations and conferences to explore the conciliar process of entering into covenant for justice and peace. The emphasis is on rooting the process in suitable specific situations; the concern is lest the word covenant should become a cheap promotional slogan.

A world conference, possibly in 1989, which would enable the sharing and deepening of experiences.[8]

Sharing as justice and solidarity

Linked with all this is the problem of relationships between haves and have-nots, even within the ecumenical fellowship.[9] Reference has already been made to the 'power of patronage' that is to some extent available to the SACC (and to certain member or observer denominations) through overseas funding. The question is how dominance /dependence patterns can be minimised and relationships of equality and mutuality between donors and receivers be nurtured. In other words, how can the sharing of resources (especially material and personnel) take place as an expression of justice and of solidarity with the poor. Changes in this sphere will require a great deal of analysis, honest communication, patient working out of alternatives and experiential education. While the state could alleviate the problem by cutting off the flow of funds from abroad, that seems unlikely in view of the politically counter-productive effects such intervention would have in Western Europe and North America.

'Christians for Justice and Peace'

How does all this relate to the South African ecumenical process, becoming known as 'Christians for Justice and Peace'? This programme to 'mobilise Christians' was called for by Durban's Catholic Archbishop Denis Hurley at the June 1983 SACC National Conference. Hurley challenged the churches to recognise the urgency of the South African situation (dramatised in the quotation with which this essay began) and to react to it as a government would react to a declaration of war. They should mobilise their members and resources as widely and thoroughly as possible to wage an all-out sustained campaign to dismantle the structures of oppression and help to build a society that would enjoy the peace that flows from justice.

Such a campaign would have to be multi-level and multi-denominational, carried out within and between churches and promoted by all manner of initiatives – from grassroots organisations and Christian action groups as well as from official church bodies.

Aggiornamento

This challenge was Archbishop Hurley's way of trying to feed into the wider South Africa church scene a process of *aggiornamento*, renewal, that has been going on systematically in the Catholic Church since Vatican II. Over the past fifteen years the Southern African Catholic Bishops' Conference (SACBC) has developed a body of insight and *authoritative* church teaching on social issues that is unique in this country. It has also invested resources in programmes of conscientisation, organisation building and leadership development that enable these teachings to be evoked and applied in various sectors of society. This process has been a dialectical one, with challenges coming to the bishops as much from their own people (youth, workers, black priests' solidarity group, women, rural poor), from the collapse of white minority rule in Angola, Mozambique and Zimbabwe, and from the ferment in Latin America (basic Christian communities, liberation theology) as from Vatican II and post-conciliar theological reflection.

Responding to the Archbishop's challenge is of necessity an untidy and uneven process. It does involve church leaders and official church bodies, but unless and until it directly involves 'activists' at local and regional level nothing is likely to happen (apart from meetings and meetings-about-meetings, and minutes of same). One of the problems confronting ecumenical leadership is how to encourage and facilitate a chicken-and-egg process in which a whole variety of necessary activities will happen. These range from hard slog within denominations to get them to build into their constitutions the authoritative teachings most of them presently lack regarding the *contextual* meaning of Christian faith and witness in southern Africa in the closing decades of the twentieth century, to encouraging Christian initiative groups to tackle at local level whatever for them are the burning issues. Both ends of the spectrum are needed. By themselves doctrinal statements change nothing; but without them the denominations cannot give the direction and support needed by local Christian action groups.

Between them lies the ill-defined work of building an infrastructure of functional communication and relationships that will enable conscientisation, community organisation (mobilisation of human and other resources) and leadership development to be promoted in spite of institutional inertia, or preoccupation with the overwhelming demands of trying to provide traditional church structures at a rate equal to population increase (doubling every 22 years) and demographic shifts.

This again is a chicken-and-egg affair. Begin with an act of justice and you soon trip over obstacles – inadequate information about available resources, ill-developed contact networks, the binding force of habitual customs and expectations. Work on these and you find that so much time and energy is required that the original issue (increased bus fares, wages, detention without trial) tends to get lost. Begin with the question: How can our church become more faithfully and effectively involved in God's mission to heal and renew our society and you must quickly turn to the people who are being hurt – the poor, the squatters, the families of detainees – to hear their stories and be discomforted by their importunate demands.

We can muddle along and move crabwise; or we can consciously recognise that the means is as important as the goal, that we are called to become the church (*ekklesia*, called together) as a working model of the reconciling and transforming mission of God to all persons and the whole of creation. On Sundays we break bread in church and in so doing affirm the vision that we are to be and to become the covenant people of God, transcending all human frontiers, proclaiming and demonstrating to the world the essential unity of humankind.[10] What we do with bread the rest of the week tests the reality of our affirmation. In action lies freedom (Bonhoeffer); in obedience we become one – with God, within ourselves and with one another.

Spirituality: Christian and African
DESMOND TUTU

I do not suppose that there are many today who are so blatantly racist and dismissive of black intellectual and other abilities as in the past, but negative attitudes are still far too prevalent. Indeed it is astounding that in the closing decades of the twentieth century a Cabinet Minister could state from the floor of Parliament that 'blacks are slow thinkers'. It is true that we no longer hear such arrogant pontificating as issued from the seventeenth-century ethnographer Olfert Dapper who declared that 'No one, however thoroughly he has enquired, has ever been able to find among all the Kaffirs or Hottentots or Beachrangers [*sic*] any trace of religion or any show of honour to God or the Devil.' This sentiment was to be echoed in the nineteenth century by no less a person than the great missionary Robert Moffat when he asserted that 'Satan has employed his agency with fatal success in erasing every vestige of religious impression from the minds of the Bechuanas, Hottentots and Bushmen; leaving them without a single ray to guide them from the dark and dread futurity, or a single link to unite them to the skies.'[1]

Those are incredible statements to have been made in the light of what is known about the religious life of Africans, namely that many of their spiritual insights have a remarkable affinity with those found in the Bible, especially in the Old Testament. As Robertson Smith has said:

No positive religion that has moved men has been able to start with a tabula rasa to express itself as if religion was beginning for the first time; in form if not in substance, the new system must be in contact all along the line with the older ideas and practices which it finds in possession. A new scheme of faith can find a hearing only by appealing to religious instincts and susceptibilities that already exist in its audience, and it cannot reach these without taking account of the traditional forms in which religious feeling is embodied, and without speaking a language which men accustomed to these forms can understand.[2]

Indeed, informed anthropologists recognise precisely 'how profound and refined' African religious concepts are.[3] There are still those who argue that blacks cannot hold their own in discussions about religious and other matters, that they are incapable of making any significant contributions to the development of social and religious thought. After all, it is argued, Christianity is an occidental phenomenon in substance and in expression. Anything else must be uprooted completely to be replaced by that which is essentially 'Christian'. And in this way we suffer from the cultural imperialism that absolutises Western ways of theologising, of worshipping this God, conducting church business, and ordering the common life of the church. Few are even consciously aware that these presuppositions are Western, for they are regarded as simply 'Christian'.

Contextual theology

I recall that when I wanted to do my doctoral studies on a black theology topic, my likely promotor said he did not think that there was enough material in existence to provide a viable doctoral thesis. The black American theologian Gayraud Wilmore observed that whenever people ask 'What is black theology?', they are really articulating an unspoken question, 'Is black theology theology at all?'

Others appear to be sympathetic to the concerns of blacks, and yet, while not being black themselves, want to determine the agenda for blacks. This stems from the old view that others know best what is good for us. It is very instructive, for example, to note that even in the debate regarding disinvestment there is a sudden rash of white altruism. All of a sudden there are people who are concerned that if economic sanctions were to be applied in respect of the South African government, it is the poor blacks who would suffer most. It is no coincidence that those who speak in this manner happen to be beneficiaries of the oppressive and exploitative status quo, who have hardly uttered serious protest against current black suffering, while professing concern about possible future suffering.

Surely we need not again argue here that Christianity did not precede the working of God and the Holy Spirit among Africans. We have always been a deeply religious people. This was so long before the advent of Christianity and the African worldview is at many points more consistent with the biblical worldview than that emanating from the West. There can never be only one theology, that of the West: the Bible itself presents us with a plethora of theologies. In the Book of Genesis alone we find a mosaic of as many as three different theologies speaking about God. Theology that suffers from the limitations and imperfections of those theologising, and has relevance and validity only for a particular context, is simply inadequate. Theology should glory in a particularity that gives it relevance. The price for contextuality, particularity and relevance is, however, that it cannot lay claim prematurely to universality. There is a plurality of theologies, jostling and competing with, complementing and challenging one another. Because each seeks to address specific issues arising from the contexts of particular communities of faith, it is possible that a particular theology may become obsolete when the issues it was addressing have ceased to be burning ones. What is true with such a theology will remain and can be integrated into the abiding tradition of the entire Christian family.

Theology is not the same thing as the gospel. Theology is temporary and particular, whilst the gospel is eternal and universal.

These are critical times, and we must respect the contextual differences between us, for the integrity of the gospel of Jesus Christ is at stake, and we cannot afford to be merely 'nice' to each other. Our maturity must be tested by how well we can handle points of view which are not only at variance with our own but which may call in question whatever we have held to be dear and sacrosanct. We must remember that we do not have a monopoly of truth. We must remember that truth belongs to God, and he is its ultimate guardian and guarantor. God's truth does not need us to protect it, and the church is God's church. Truth has as, what is for us, a humbling attribute, that it has managed to survive for 2 000 years in the face of some remarkable hostility, both intellectual and political. Those who thought that it was moribund and on its last feet are no longer around. Not even the gates of hell can prevail against the church of God. It is important that we maintain a sense of proportion. I want to suggest that a key concept we could well use to advantage is *relevance*. I do not mean that we should engage in the frenzy of yesteryear when we rushed about trying to be faddish and in fashion, proving just how relevant we were. I refer much more to the relevance of the gospel as demonstrated by our Lord. He came preaching good news. Good news to a sick person is healing, to a sinner it is forgiveness, to the hungry it is being fed and to the self-righteous and complacent it is judgment. For Jesus the good news spoke to the real, not to the imagined need.

An agenda for African spirituality

As an African and as a Christian, I need to contribute to the emergence of a relevant spirituality. The spiritual, it goes without saying, is central to all that we do. The God we worship is an extraordinary God, who dwells in light unapproachable, He is high and lifted up, and His train fills the temple. The angels and archangels and the whole host of heaven do not cease to worship and adore Him. Heaven and earth are full of His glory. He is the transcendent one who fills us with awe – the *mysterium tremendum et fascinans*. But He does not allow those who worship Him to remain in an exclusive spiritual ghetto. Our encounter with Him launches us into the world, to work together with this God for the establishment of his kingdom. This is a kingdom of justice, peace, righteousness, compassion, caring and sharing. We become agents of transfiguration, transformation and radical change. When Moses encountered God at the burning bush he heard the command, 'Go down to Pharaoh.' When Isaiah saw the Lord high and lifted up, it was to hear the summons 'Who will go for us?' When Jesus was baptised, He received the Spirit of God and it was this Spirit which propelled Him into the wilderness to do battle with the evil one, and being anointed by the Spirit of the Lord meant being sent to preach the good news to the poor, the proclamation of release to those in captivity, and the year of the Lord's favour – a time when release was proclaimed to those indebted to others, and the return of the land to its rightful owner.

Spirituality as praxis

The Bible insists that religious exercises, however meticulous the concern for their ritualistic correctness, which have no beneficial consequences for the way worshippers live, are totally unacceptable and an abomination to God. God shocked His people when He told them through Isaiah that He would not accept their sacrifices, nor heed as they prayed with uplifted hands because these were full of blood. Repentance, He insisted, could be authenticated only by doing justice to the widow, the orphan and stranger, the most marginalised of the marginalised (Isa. 1: 10–17). He rejected their fast, because the fast he required was for them to undo the fetters of the imprisoned, to feed the hungry and to clothe the naked (Isa. 58: 5–7). This point is reiterated in Jesus' parable of the last judgment (Matt. 25: 31f). It is quite impossible to love God, whom we have not seen, if we hate the brother or sister, whom we know. Loving God and loving neighbour are two sides of the same coin. Our love of God is expressed and authenticated in our love of our neighbour. This is a message central to the Bible, and it is a cornerstone of African religions.

Biblically there can be no false dichotomies between the spiritual and the material. Archbishop William Temple argued that Christianity is the most materialistic of all the great religions. When God intervened in our human affairs He came not as disembodied spirit, but as a human person, flesh of our flesh, and bone of our bones. He communicates His life, divine, holy and utterly spiritual through mundane, secular things such as bread and wine, water and oil.

Spirituality as liberation

If our worship is authentic and relevant, it prepares us for our combat with the forces of evil, the principalities and powers. It prepares us to be involved where God's children are hurt, where they spend most of their lives: at work, in the market place, in schools, on the factory floor, in Parliament, in the courts of law, everywhere they live and work and play. Jesus refused to remain on the mountain top of the transfiguration. He came down into the valley of human need and misunderstanding.

I have not yet heard victims of oppression, those who live in deprived ghettoes or are uprooted and dumped in resettlement camps, or the banned and those detained without trial, accuse us of mixing religion with politics. If anything, they are concerned that the church is often not involved enough. It is almost always those who benefit from the socio-political and economic dispensation who accuse religious people of mixing religion with politics.

For the oppressed the most vital part of the Christian gospel is its message of liberation from all that would make us less than the children of God – sin, political and economic deprivation, exploitation and injustice. It is also liberation to be people who enjoy the glorious liberty of the children of God, which must include political empowerment to determine the shape of one's destiny.

And we are witnesses to His sovereignty. We will go forth imbued with the zeal to proclaim Jesus as Lord, inviting others to accept Him as their Lord and Saviour to whom they owe absolute allegiance. A church that is not missionary and evangelistic is a disobedient church, ignoring the commission from its founder to make disciples of all people. We are that body which exists for the sake of those who are not its members. Our greatest proclamation comes from our lifestyle.

We must also show that we are members one of another because we are members of the Body of Christ. We are brothers and sisters of all those who have been baptised into Christ, and therefore we have a responsibility for them, especially those with whom we disagree. Whether he and I like it or not, Mr P. W. Botha and I are brothers, members of the same family. I cannot write him off, I cannot give up on him because God, our common Father, does not give up on anyone. What is the consequence of this fundamental and disturbing theological fact? How do I carry out my responsibility to the oppressed and to the oppressor when both are my kin?

As the body of Christ we must become what Harvey Cox called a *verbum visibile*, a kind of audio-visual aid for the world to demonstrate that we are the first fruits of the kingdom, showing forth what human society is meant to be – a forgiving community of the forgiven, a reconciling *koinonia* of the reconciled. We must show forth in our community life that Christ has broken down the middle wall of partition, that there can be neither male nor female, Greek nor Jew, rich nor poor, slave nor free but that we are one in Him. We have a rich diversity, even a bewildering diversity, precisely because of our fundamental unity, so that the Babel in black churches when we sing in all kinds of different languages is the reversed Babel of Pentecost. We must surely go ahead to encourage our people, black and white, to worship together, to pray and play together more often without having to wait for the permission of secular authority.

We should so order the life of our churches that others do not feel they are God's stepchildren and that God's home-language is English, and that the British parliamentary procedure is necessarily the best way of doing our business. Other options should be given a real chance. Our church structures should reflect the reality that blacks form 80 per cent of our church population. We are indigenised in the bad sense of being conformed to the ways of the world we inhabit. Our churches, whilst seeking to move away from the ways of the past, have been bastions of the very policies for which they have condemned the government. We need more non-racial appointments to church positions, especially to parishes. We should work out how to circumvent the evil laws of apartheid that make it difficult for the church to be the true church. We have been told that we should rather obey God than man, and the government should be challenged on this basis. We must move away from splendid resolutions and rhetoric, important as these are, to more effective Christian action. We must be ready to learn from our sisters and brothers in other parts of the world, such as in Latin America where the church has been revitalised as it has become involved in the people's struggle for justice and dignity.

Spirituality as theology

Our theology is to become relevant and authentic. We should rehabilitate great Christian words such as *reconciliation* and *peace* which have fallen on bad days, being thoroughly devalued by those who have used them to justify evil. Christ is our peace, who bought at a great price His own death on the Cross. That is what real reconciliation has cost. We have been given the privilege of a share in Christ's ministry of reconciliation. We are serious about human liberation. It must be total human liberation. That includes our attitude to the place of women in the church. I am myself fully in support of the ordination of women for I have not been persuaded by theological or non-theological argument that there are any compelling reasons why we should not ordain women. We impoverish ourselves in depriving them. Our language in theology and in society must be inclusive language. Language is not merely descriptive. It creates the reality it describes.

Theology is, in addition to all else, also ethics, addressing questions of war, peace and conscience. When can Christians use violence? When can they justifiably go to war? These are matters of considerable concern to many. How do we hold together those whose sons, brothers and sisters, and fathers and mothers end up facing each other from opposite sides in internecine strife? What must our people do when they are sent as soldiers against unarmed fellow South Africans? I speak here as one who is pastor to both blacks and whites. We have occupied theological backwaters, because we have allowed ourselves to be bypassed in debates about nuclear warfare, surrogate parenthood, the permissive society, the new morality, homosexuality, transplants and death. In many of these areas we have not helped our people.

These are some of the issues which we ignore at our peril. We do so only at the cost of sleeping through a revolution – fit only to be spewed out by the Lord, for being neither hot nor cold, but waiting to find out which way the wind is blowing.

Spro-cas revisited: the Christian contribution to political debate
PETER RANDALL

Karl Rahner has warned that the church runs risks in attempting to translate its ethical norms into concrete proposals. 'But', he adds, 'this is a risk that must be taken if the church is not to be seen to be pedantic, to be living in a world of pure theory, remote from life, making pronouncements that do not touch the stubborn concreteness of real life.'[1] Clearly the church has to play a role in the political, economic and social life of the community if it is to be relevant to the needs of people, even if that role is largely confined to making proposals for consideration and experimentation, proposals that obviously must be theologically motivated.[2] This process is likely to involve the formulation of models for a just, or responsible, society. As Richard Turner has said, a model for such a society 'must remain a relatively distant hope. But it does have a function, both as a critical tool for analysing existing social reality and as an ideal that can help to encourage South Africans to work towards a better future.'[3] In this essay both the phases of Spro-cas, as 'Study Project on Christianity in Apartheid Society' and as 'Special Programme for Christian Action in Society' (Spro-cas 2), will be taken as one example of the church at work in this way.

A venture of faith

Spro-cas began early in 1969 with an office, a director, a secretary, and warm encouragement from the leaders of the bodies which had undertaken to sponsor it and to seek the necessary funds. They were the Rt. Rev. Bill Burnett, General Secretary of the South African Council of Churches (SACC), and the Rev. Beyers Naudé, Director of the Christian Institute of Southern Africa (CI). In the event, the CI was to be the senior partner in the Spro-cas venture, with Beyers Naudé playing the central role. In turn it is probably true to say that Spro-cas had a far greater influence on the Institute than on the Council, due in part to the close working relationships that developed between their respective staff members, and in part to the greater flexibility and adaptability of the CI's structures and its generally more open and receptive style.

The intention behind the setting up of Spro-cas was clear enough: to examine the economic, educational, legal, political and social implications, and the implications for the church itself, of the *Message to the*

People of South Africa, a theological critique of apartheid drawn up by a commission of the SACC and issued in its name in September 1968. The means by which this intention was to be realised were, in the beginning, hazy in the extreme. In retrospect, it seems extraordinary that such an ambitious project – or series of projects under the general name of Spro-cas – could have been given such an apparently informal and casual beginning. It was to last nearly five years, involve in its first phase some 130 members of six study commissions, and employ at its peak 25 staff workers. It resulted in the publication of more than twenty substantial reports and other books as well as a host of background papers, dossiers, posters and study-aids on a wide range of South African issues and cost in the region of a quarter-of-a-million rand (in today's terms probably equivalent to several millions).

There were no pilot projects, no feasibility studies. There was no guarantee of funds, no attempt to establish a clear methodology. The director literally sat at an empty desk and wondered how to go about things. But perhaps it was right that there were none of these things: it is possible that the whole project, which was soon to grow in directions totally unforeseen by its initiators, might have floundered before it was launched, submerged in a welter of conflicting advice and 'expert' opinion.

In the end it was, perhaps, a venture of faith on the part of a small group of Christians who were convinced that such a project was both desirable and necessary in order to help the church move from mere denunciation of apartheid, no matter how eloquent and even passionate, to a more meaningful and concrete involvement in the hard issues facing those church members who opposed the policy.

It soon became apparent that the central issue for Spro-cas to deal with concerned social change. This was spelled out in the first of five biblical principles underlying the project:

Concepts like 'a new order', 'new creation, 'all things new', are basic to the biblical message. The good news is the call to change from evil to good, and the possibility of this change taking place. In the Bible both man and society are seen to be in need of redemption. Our society too needs continual renewal. Christians should not fear such renewal or change, but welcome it, and see themselves as active collaborators in change.[4]

'Active collaborators in change': that in essence was what the participants in the various Spro-cas programmes hoped to be. It is, of course, very difficult to estimate how effectively that hope was met, or to evaluate the extent of the contribution made by Spro-cas to political debate in South Africa. It is probably particularly difficult for me, since I was so intimately involved in the project throughout its existence. However, after the passage of more than a decade, it should be possible to identify some of the features of that contribution.

In the first place, there can be little doubt that the church – broadly intrepreted – had not previously, and has not since, embarked upon so focused an attempt to contribute to the country's social existence. In drawing together such a representative group of South Africans – interdenominational, interdisciplinary, interracial, even interfaith – these groups pooled their collective gifts to give concrete expression to their desire for social renewal. I believe that Spro-cas, at its point in history, performed an important function on behalf of the Christian church by helping many people to clarify and articulate their ideas about the proper ordering of their society. In so doing it threw up a mass of evidence about the unjust nature of that society and identified those areas most urgently in need of change in the light of the gospel imperative, moving on also to a consideration of the strategies that might be employed to achieve this change. There can be little doubt that if the temporal authorities, the central government and its ministries in particular, had considered the work of the Spro-cas commissions more seriously as a genuine attempt to apply the Christian ethic to our society, rather than seen it as part of some leftist plot to subvert the existing order, certain important changes would have come about both earlier and more easily. The series of government-appointed commissions of the late 1970s and early 1980s, set up in the face of crisis situations particularly in the economy and in education, to some extent traversed similar ground to the Spro-cas commissions and in some cases arrived at similar though less courageous recommendations of change.

In terms of its own structure and methods, which evolved organically as the project got under way, Spro-cas may still be something of a model for change-oriented programmes, as distinct from 'institutions' and 'organisations'. There is no intention to suggest that this model may be applicable to the church itself, for example, although there may well be features of it worth considering. The essential features of Spro-cas were described in the final report of the project as follows:

1. Spro-cas has been a programme, or a series of interrelated programmes and projects. It is not an organisation.

2. It has been temporary and short-term, with its own death envisaged from the start.

3. It has been a sustained and reasonably systematic effort (theological reflection, study commission, action programmes).

4. Its structure has been very simple and flexible, and its work has not been hampered by a hierarchy of committees.

5. It has operated, in its action phase, through clearly demarcated black community programmes and white consciousness programmes. This has in fact resulted in a very high degree of co-operation between black and white staff members. The basic assumption underlying this structure was that a 'multi-racial' programme would not effectively meet the differing needs of black and white.

6. It has developed a number of spill-over effects which have been

allowed to develop or, if they have not proved relevant, to die.

7. It has been able to take risks and to risk failure. It has adopted tactics of confrontation where these seemed right.

8. It has set itself realistic objectives and has tried to clarify its objectives.

9. It has followed an action–reflection model.

10. It has, in the process of its work accumulated skills and resources which could provide the basis for on-going activities.[5]

It is 5 on this list that might cause raised eyebrows today, but it should be remembered that the list was drawn up in a particular historical context in which black consciousness was at its height, as was black rejection of liberal multi-racial enterprises. The outcome was the separation of the white and the black programmes – one aimed at raising the consciousness of whites to the need for change and the other at community development in the broadest sense. This led quite logically to the establishment of the Black Community Programmes (BCP) as an autonomous body which was to carry out very significant work in the black community until its banning in 1977.[6]

Black consciousness

In the early 1970s black consciousness appeared as a new and vital force in the complex interplay of forces in South African politics, and its long-term significance may have been overemphasised. The final Sprocas report, however, attempted to place it in its historical context, seeing it as part of the cultural and intellectual ferment in the black community:

We are in the early stages of a new historical phase in South Africa, in which the initiative for change is passing into black hands. The tempo of this process can only accelerate, no matter what temporary setbacks black initiatives may receive and no matter what efforts are made to thwart it . . . .[7]

The report singled out 'the growing ability of black labour to press its demands in a militant and coherent manner' as a particularly important feature of this process. Events over the past decade, including the black student uprising of 1976, which forced certain, admittedly inadequate, changes on the system of Bantu Education, and the dramatic and widespread demonstration of the potential power of black trade unions in the 1980s, suggest that in broad terms this analysis may still stand.

Sam Nolutshungu has provided a critical evaluation of the BCP:

It was politically important from the start, since it published most of the material produced by and about the black consciousness movement, and provided employment of key SASO militants after they left university and a framework within which they could continue to work towards their political objectives in contact with the masses. It also provided a model of politically minded, public action independent of white South African liberal patronage and hostile to official policies and plans.[8]

This model was also important in confronting the Christian churches, as well as the SACC and the CI in particular, with such issues as black autonomy and leadership and with questions of strategy which had to be faced and thought through.

What is significantly different now is the public resurfacing of a progressive non-racial movement, expressed most clearly in the United Democratic Front, as a focus for opposition by both black and white. While still an important force, represented for example by the National Forum, black consciousness has to some extent been forced on to the defensive by this new development.

Apartheid and the church

The earlier, study project, phase of Spro-cas, like the subsequent development of the BCP, also confronted the 'English' churches, and the SACC and the CI, with often uncomfortable choices, helping to clarify some of the fundamental intellectual and strategic issues involved in a theological and theoretical rejection of apartheid. As Paul Rich has said:

Politically, the Christian Institute began to move towards a more committed radical liberalism which involved a shift in both economic as well as political resources from the entrenched white ruling class to the black majority within a federal political structure.[9]

Peter Walshe has made much the same point.[10] It is clear that Spro-cas, through its commission reports, its white consciousness programmes, and the establishment of the BCP, played a major role in the evolution of the Institute during the years from 1970 until its banning in 1977. This evolution essentially involved the formulation of a strategy designed, in Walshe's words, 'to encourage black consciousness and to prepare for a future in which blacks would exercise predominant political power',[11] while at the same time becoming more critical of the country's economic system in addition to its racist political structures.

Walshe sees this as 'yet another reminder of the common ground that can be shared by democratic socialism and a prophetic Christianity when the latter has been galvanised by the praxis of a liberation struggle'.[12]

The influence of Spro-cas on the SACC, and thus indirectly on the main body of the English-language churches, was much less obvious. In general terms these churches seem to have found the more radical appproach to social change espoused by the CI and Spro-cas 'to be in direct conflict with their more cautious programmes of persuasion, consultation and reasoning with the authorities'.[13] The 'average' white English-speaking church member was not prepared to accept demands for movement towards a new political dispensation in which the majority would play a decisive role, or the creation of a new economic structure. The 'English' churches chose rather, as Villa-Vicencio describes it, 'to continue to opt for a more passive liberal stance, idealistically hoping that God would somehow miraculously heal their land without involving them too deeply in too many sacrifices or in the agony of the healing process'.[14]

The Spro-cas church report, *Apartheid and the Church*, was heavily critical of this very approach. It pointed to features in the life of the church which could not be supported from a biblical point of view, and called for, among other things, a more determined and vigorous programme of black advancement within the churches themselves. It is of course impossible to assess here the extent to which this report may have influenced synods and other decision-making bodies. But, on the surface at least, there has been marked change in the decade since *Apartheid and the Church* was published, the most obvious illustration of which is the fact that archbishops, bishops, moderators and other leaders in the 'English' churches are now far more likely to be black than white. This is obviously more than just a skilful use of tokenism, but it is interesting to speculate on the outcome, were the Spro-cas Church Commission to investigate the matter now in terms of the extent to which meaningful change has actually taken place. Villa-Vicencio has some cautionary words in this regard:

A quiet *quid pro quo* is being agreed. Conservative whites 'tolerate' black leadership and black leaders are compelled to allow grassroots whites to continue in their former ways. . . . Black leaders are replacing white leaders while the white congregations continue to cling to the habits once delivered to them by their fathers in the faith.[15]

At another level, the Spro-cas Church Commission failed to move the South African churches towards a more radical style of confession, towards the creation of a genuinely ecumenical movement seeking true obedience to Jesus Christ within apartheid society. As John de Gruchy has pointed out, the conclusions of *Apartheid and the Church* would, if put into effect, have led to the emergence of a Confessing Church in South Africa.[16]

A future scenario

The analyses of South African society undertaken by the Spro-cas study commissions in the early 1970s inevitably led to several assumptions about the future. It did not require particularly strong prophetic gifts to arrive at these, but it is nonetheless an instructive exercise to consider the extent to which they have been borne out. The scenario for the next decade or so was summed up in 1973 in these words:

As the forces of change grow in scope and strength so they evoke, and will increasingly evoke, counter-forces of repression and reaction. We are thus in a period in which the immediate future is likely to be marked by continued intolerance of dissent, whether by black or white, and increased hostility towards activity aimed at socio-political change. This will in turn accelerate the processes of polarisation and confrontation in the society, with all the dangers and challenges this entails.[17]

A cursory review of events and developments since then – the steady diminution of civil and personal liberties, the uprisings of 1976 and their bloody aftermath, the banning of the black consciousness organisations and other bodies in 1977, the death in detention of Steve Biko and others, the regular procession of 'security trials', the township riots of 1984, the escalation of urban terrorism – all these suggest that the Spro-cas commissions had correctly identified the quickening spiral of violence and counterviolence, of protest and suppression.

At the same time it was apparent by 1973 that the response of the white power structure to initiatives for change was of a dual nature:

On the one hand there is the intransigence, the attempt to stifle and destroy. . . . On the other hand, however, there are some accommodations to meet a changed reality.[18]

These 'accommodations' have become evident, to greater or lesser extents, in each of the societal areas in which the Spro-cas study commissions operated. In education, for example, there has been a marked increase in the state's per capitum expenditure on black pupils, a stated commitment to the principle of equality of educational provision, acceptance of the right of church and other private schools to admit children of different races, parity in salaries for qualified teachers, and – in response to the students' revolt of 1976 – significant changes in the policy governing the medium of instruction in black schools. And in the economy, even more striking changes have taken place, from a uniform application of the previously racially discriminatory income-tax system to acceptance of black unions and the right of black workers to engage in collective bargaining, including, under certain conditions, the right to strike. In the political system, the most obvious 'accommodation' has been the attempt to draw at least the Indian and coloured communities into the government of the country by means of an ethnically based tricameral parliament.

But the fundamental structural problems remain. These include segregated school systems, the reliance of the economy on the migrant labour system, the denationalisation of Africans and their exclusion from the central processes of government, and the continued entrenchment of racial discrimination in important areas of the legal system.

Spro-cas was not alone in being unable to effect any meaningful change in these structural features. A pessimistic view may be that they will in fact be amenable only to violent and revolutionary change.

The Spro-cas contribution
At the level of personal growth and involvement, Spro-cas must have made a very real contribution to the lives of many individual South Africans. This would have applied most directly to the staff

members, many of whom were to pay dearly through banning orders, prosecutions, withdrawal of passports, and exile. Less directly perhaps, many of the commission members and those who were involved as participants in the Black Community Programmes, the Programme for Social Change, and other ventures initiated by Spro-cas, would have found their participation a significant factor in their own development. The harnessing of the gifts of a wide range of theologians, sociologists, economists, educationists, lawyers and political thinkers was in itself a memorable venture. Spro-cas 'old boys' and 'girls' have made notable contributions, in a variety of fields, to the broad political debate in this country, amongst them Bishop Desmond Tutu, Professor Francis Wilson, Sir Richard Luyt, Professor John Dugard, Professor André Brink, Chief Gatsha Buthelezi, Mr Bennie Khoapa, Professor Fatima Meer, Mr E. A. Saloojee, Professor Lawrence Schlemmer, Dr F. van Zyl Slabbert and Professor Nancy Charton.

For others, sadly, their involvement in Spro-cas was almost a final act of participation in the public life of the country. They include Dr E. G. Malherbe, Professor Donald Molteno, Dr Edgar Brookes, Mr Leo Marquard and Dr W. F. Nkomo. The gifts of others again were lost to South Africa prematurely, through death or through exile: Rick Turner, victim of an assassin's bullet; Justice Moloto, Bennie Khoapa, Horst Kleinschmidt, Theo Kotze, Donald Woods and others living in exile abroad; Barend van Niekerk, André Hugo, and David Poynton, each the victim of an untimely death.

Happily there are also those who, like Beyers Naudé, having endured their sacrificial penalty, are free again to provide inspiration and leadership.

The reports and other publications that came out of Spro-cas remain as concrete evidence of the intense activity that was generated during the project's short life-time. Some of them have gone through several editions and printings and remain in demand, particularly the report of the Political Commission, *South Africa's Political Alternatives*, which has been prescribed at several universities, and it seems fair to believe that its analyses and recommendations have influenced a generation of South African students.

Spro-cas was never envisaged as more than a short-term project. Inevitably the dynamics it created had longer-term effects. One can only guess at the contribution that would have been made by the Black Community Programmes if the state had not systematically harassed its leaders – Bennie Khoapa, Steve Biko, Bokwe Mafuna and others – from 1972, culminating in its outright banning in 1977.

The BCP and the other Spro-cas undertakings clearly identified a need for the kind of publishing they had developed. The direct outcome of this was the establishment, as Spro-cas itself was coming to an end, of Ravan Press, staffed initially by several Spro-cas workers. The original aim of Ravan Press was to continue to provide a publishing forum for alternative theological, literary and political work on South African issues. While it was never intended that Spro-cas should have any memorials, its own publications and the establishment of Ravan Press may perhaps be regarded as its continuing contribution to our conflict-ridden society.

As South Africa moves into a new phase of struggle for liberation and social justice, with the politics of 'reform' replacing the politics of repression, and as its society becomes less blatantly racist, with the mechanisms of control becoming ever more subtle, the need for another initiative along the lines of Spro-cas must grow. In the words of Villa-Vicencio, 'the English-speaking churches will repeatedly need to reconsider their position and the extent to which they are promoting the spiritual, psychological, social, economic and political liberation of their people – or merely giving credence to and 'baptising' reform politics ultimately designed to ensure the future hegemony of whites in this country.'[19]

Spro-cas took place in a particular historical context. In each age the church needs to renew its understanding of the political and social implications of its theological commitment.

The churches and the trade unions
JAMES COCHRANE

Against enormous odds, faced with repeated attempts at control and repression, the independent non-racial or 'black' trade unions in South Africa have nevertheless made their great mark on the last decade and more. Indeed, many would see in this growing movement the most significant force challenging apartheid's structures of power. What impact has this had on the churches of South Africa? What impact have the churches had on the worker movement?

The former question is easier to anwswer. Beginning with a focus on migratory labour practices, particularly the resultant tragedies of broken, disunited families, the churches in South Africa have been forced to recognise the signs of the times. After decades of being relegated to the periphery of Christian interest, workers have again acquired status in the halls and departments of the denominations.

But what kind of status? How serious is the concern? To what extent are Christian leaders, like the captains of industry, responding to pressure and crisis with tense jaws, and clenched teeth, hoping that things do not 'go too far'. Put differently, is the church-at-large equipped or ready to deal with the implications of worker movements, which are increasingly oriented to macro-issues and not only to shop-floor concerns?

Of course, the industrial relations picture is not two-dimensional. More than enough contradictions invade every aspect of South African society at present, including the worker movement itself. A process of unresolved struggle exists, battles being waged on several fronts simultaneously while negotiations in many cases allow for a temporary resting place. How are the churches to make sense of this? Where are the means to understand the process? On what basis are decisions taken, resolutions made, resources allocated, and actions initiated to intervene in the struggle? What interventions are in any case legitimate for the church, and do those involved know how to assess the implications of intervention?

These are no mean questions. Perhaps a look into the past, and a reading of the range of present responses of some churches to these issues, may help to clarify the central issues.

The church and the ICU

One easily assumes that contemporary concerns are just that – contemporary and therefore new. But in the second decade of this century, and into the 1930s, a black trade union movement of substantial proportions arose to challenge the dominant powers of South Africa, as well as the witness of the churches. But for certain political and organisational errors, it might have changed the face of South Africa.

As it was, the Industrial and Commercial Workers' Union (ICWU, or often simply the ICU), launched nationally in 1920 after some years of organisation by Clements Kadalie in the Cape, rapidly developed a powerful mass base. Its potency and its militancy led even a startled Father Huss, well-known as an ardent reformer, to call the ICU a deadly threat to the peace of the country.[1]

The ICU was a child of its times. Industrial resistance as a whole had been on the increase after the First World War, over one hundred strikes occurring in the two years beginning with 1918. Anglican Canon Hodson thus noted that 'there is nothing to gain by fighting the trade unions but everything to be gained by working with them.' Moreover, the leading Anglican newspaper saw clearly that at the root of much of the discontent and restlessness of labour lay the struggle of the worker to achieve 'the position due to him as a human being'. More commonly, the reaction was one of fear and deep disquiet. In any event, the church was forced to face a new situation.

Documents of the time reveal that the contradictions already inherent in the South African political economy were not exorcised from the church. Thus, whereas labour and labour issues were discussed seriously for the first time, no coherent understanding of specific situations emerged. Consequently, lack of insight and frequent oversights prevented any effective relationship between the churches and black worker organisations.

This is clearly evidenced in responses to the ICU. One writer expressed in 1927 a conviction, borne out by subsequent records, that the ICU was 'fast becoming a gigantic question to the whole of Christian South Africa'. Noting its cry for justice, the commentator pointed out the ICU's 'unquestionably legitimate demand that every race, regardless of colour, shall be allowed to enjoy the good things it helps produce'. 'Will the churches move', he asked, 'regardless of the consequences?'

Sympathy for the aims of the ICU was in fact expressed in several quarters, particularly with regard to the right of workers to organise for collective bargaining and a decent standard of living. But almost always accompanying these church statements were numerous negative demands made upon the ICU.

Among other things, as the price for church support, the ICU was told not to attack whites and to cease provocative speeches. Moreover, it was felt that black unions should be white-sponsored, that reform should be recognised as an incremental process, and political activities rejected. Above all, 'socialism should be avoided, drunkenness and vice given up, and decent homes and family life built before the church could count the ICU as allies,' announced Bishop Carey of Bloemfontein.

Clearly, given the daily realities of black working-life and the constraints of the pass system, migratory labour and land reserves, let alone other aspects of conquest and colonisation, such sentiments were bound to miss the mark entirely.

One may conclude, therefore, that with rare exceptions (one being James Henderson of *South African Outlook*), the few church statements of support that one may find only emphasise the inability of the church to respond to the challenges presented by the ICU. Solidarity proved to be without substance, where it was at all considered. This has not been without consequence for the relationship of workers to the denominations, or for the ability of churches to deal with labour and industrial relations ever since.

The contemporary era

Besides a residue of historical events which distinguish the contemporary context from that of the 1920s, significant structural changes have recently occurred in the political economy of South Africa. Signalled by the Wiehahn proposals on trade unions and the related Riekert proposals streamlining influx control, these changes have, above all, given some recognition to blacks as rightful participants in the industrial relations system. Though the new legislation clearly attempts also to enforce more sophisticated controls over labour, blacks have access, for the first time, to legal channels for organisation, bargaining and powers of association. A rapid rise in black worker-controlled trade unions has occurred.

It would be wrong, however, to see this development as the fruit of legislation. On the contrary, the new legislation has been a response to necessity, as government and business have attempted to cope with a situation running out of their control. Resistance from black workers to their exploitation and oppression, as never before, has become a central part of the modern South African equation. For these reasons, the churches too have had to come to terms with the worker movement and the emergent independent, non-racial trade unions. The challenge is too great to ignore.

Have churches succeeded in meeting this challenge? Some experiences provide key pointers to the answer, and it is to these that I turn. Each one allows a particular point to be addressed. Taken as a whole, they provide as well a reasonably comprehensive view of the kinds of responses evidenced by the churches over the last decade.

At its eighth National Conference in July 1976, the South African

Council of Churches, focusing on economic exploitation, adopted a resolution calling on the church as a whole to be 'an exemplary society', and to investigate institutions in which they invest in respect of wage practices, collective bargaining, discrimination in promotion of staff, and the making of excess profits. This was followed at the 1982 conference by a resolution specifically addressing the question of trade unions. It affirmed the right to organise and to demand bargaining rights, while deploring the harassment and persecution of trade unionists. Churches were encouraged to promote fair employment practices, to make buildings available for trade-union meetings, to protest against victimisation, to inform trade unions outside South Africa via sister churches about the situation, to pressure employers and help make them aware of grievances, to assist strike-affected families, to contribute to leadership training among unionists, to organise workshops for clerics on industrial relations, and to encourage them to learn about mediation practices. The Methodist Conference of the same year also accepted this resolution at denominational level.

The SACC's interest in trade unions had clearly increased after 1976. Financial support was provided in the form of relief grants, strike aid, and conference costs for trade unions, which the Council began to regard as significant agents of change with a just cause. Its first major intervention, however, came in 1979 with a strike at Fattis and Monis food factory in the Western Cape. The SACC General Secretary was approached to back a community boycott of the company's products. After discussion, he decided that the SACC should sponsor mediation, at that time a new concept in South African industrial relations. The SACC's services were then offered to the company, and a Methodist academic was approached to act as mediator. His job was to meet with an elected spokesperson from both sides, and to pursue common ground. Both parties agreed and met from time to time. Negotiations proceeded on the basis of a set of demands issued by the workers via the Food and Canning Workers' Union, and ultimately resulted in the company re-employing the dismissed workers.[2]

This 'success story' created widespread interest round the country, especially because of its strategic implications in somewhat uniquely incorporating many external organisations in support of the workers. Trade union, community, religious and political forces came together, establishing a precedent since developed many times elsewhere. More specifically, the boycott tactic was invoked, and the implicit threat of the SACC General Secretary coming out in support of the boycott remained an important bargaining tool, although the threat was in fact never issued.

Additionally, the experience demonstrated that processes of mediation were undeveloped in South Africa – nobody was quite sure what a third party was meant to do, and reliance was therefore made on gut-level, intuitive techniques. Although people in industrial relations work outside of the church had already begun to think about mediation practices, the Fattis and Monis process, in hindsight, thus played a role in the development of a now-established independent (but secular) mediation service.

A subsequent strike within the red meat industry of the Western Cape, this time involving the Western Province General Workers' Union (now the General Workers' Union), took things a stage further. A similar strategy emerged to the one developed during the Fattis and Monis strike, but with significant differences. A mediator was not sought from the churches, the meat bosses turning down an offer from the SACC. Union officials were detained. Moreover, the Union correctly wished to retain some control over the direction and implementation of supportive actions. At the same time community organisations, fired by the earlier success, were much more ready to intervene. This resulted in a confusion of roles, and certain actions taken by other parties which turned out to be at cross-purposes with the Union's desire at least partly to oversee activities related to the strike.

Tensions grew, bolstered by the detentions and resultant absence from crucial discussions of key union officials. Two church-based community organisations affiliated to the Western Province Council of Churches (WPCC) subsequently became embroiled in controversy. Both had staff members playing key roles in the events surrounding the strike. In the judgment of many, among them members of the two community organisations, staff interventions began to assume proportions unbefitting the support role required by the union.[3]

The consequences were unfortunate, to say the least. For this and a number of other reasons, the strategy failed. Bitter recriminations followed as various parties attempted to understand what had happened and why. The Union itself twice issued public statements denouncing the role played by the two church-based community organisations, going as far as to say:

by failing to act in the democratic manner towards the community we [the Western Province General Workers' Union] did not allow the community to be arbiters of the activities of certain profoundly anti-democratic tendencies in the community. These tendencies – in the shape of two church-based community organisations – entered into the Union without the sanction of the rest of the community and succeeded in severely disrupting the meat boycott.[4]

For the churches and related organisations, the primary lessons to be gained from the unhappy direction matters took in this affair concern the whole issue of intervention itself and the consequence of unwise strategies. To this we shall return.

Entirely different and also worth considering is the role of churches in support of the South African Allied Workers' Union (SAAWU), one of the most well-known of the emergent unions. Perhaps more than any other large grouping of workers, SAAWU considers trade-union issues to be intimately and fundamentally connected with broad political issues in the struggle against apartheid. It has developed, therefore, a highly politicised model of trade unionism, in the process presenting a challenge to many groups who are not worker-based, as well as to other trade unions who for various reasons have restricted their energies to shop-floor concerns. SAAWU has suffered regular hammer-blows from the state, including repeated detentions of its leaders, strong police intervention, and co-ordinated employer measures against it.[5] Having been ejected on several occasions from various office premises in East London during 1980, and prevented from acquiring premises in the township of Mdantsane, SAAWU turned to the Methodists. A disused church hall in Duncanville was offered for their use. A major help to the union at the time, the church also gave support to a nationwide boycott of Wilson–Rowntree sweets manufacturers, a boycott launched because of unfair actions by the company against SAAWU members.

The most prominent churchman involved, the Rev. Gawe – newly elected head of the Border Council of Churches – remained in close contact with SAAWU. His relationship with the Union continued until 1982 when he died in suspicious circumstances in a car accident. That foul play was suspected indicates the level of tension and of risk attached to trade-union activities during this period. That some churches nevertheless regarded it as correct in terms of their Christian responsibility to support worker struggles in a highly charged atmosphere demonstrates two points. Firstly, resistance on the labour front had clearly become sufficiently forceful to press interested third parties – in this case the church – into a rethinking of their role from the ground up. Secondly, many denominations and church groups have consequently begun to reformulate their self-understanding in the political economy of South Africa and to develop appropriate theological insights.

Chief among those who have promoted a new awareness of the labour movement, of worker issues in general and of the resultant claims upon the church, is the Young Christian Workers movement (YCW). Roman Catholic-based, YCW's extensive influence is no small reason for the far more advanced level of Catholic involvement in these issues as a whole than that of any other denomination.

YCW itself began after the First World War. Belgian priest Joseph Cardijn, son of a small-time coal merchant and domestic worker, felt keenly the rift between church and workers at parish and institutional level. Leaving normal priestly activities, he spent time waiting outside factory gates, asking young workers about their work and life. His concern was not proselytisation, but rather conditions of work, safety in the factory, overtime demands, wage rates, and so on. Out of this arose groups of Young Christian Trade Unionists, later YCW.

In South Africa YCW was introduced after the Second World War by Eric Tyacke – a lay Catholic worker who had encountered the organisation on a trip to England. Like so many church-related organisations involved in controversial secular issues, YCW stood apart from the institutional Roman Catholic Church, and had to raise most of its funds itself. Ordinary priests paid little attention to it or its concerns, and meagre support was forthcoming at parish level. A small group of sympathetic priests had to be depended upon.[6]

Meanwhile Tyacke had moved directly into trade-union work. At first based in the conservative white-dominated Trade Union Council of South Africa (TUCSA) with the portfolio of African Affairs, his position was finally eroded to the point of futility by union leaders unwilling to deal with the growing awareness and power of black workers. Towards the end of this time, Tyacke received financial help in crisis situations when attempts were made to crush a coloured transport-workers' union for which he then worked. The help came from Ffrench–Beytagh, then Anglican Dean of Johannesburg.

After his later deportation, the Dean assisted Tyacke through the Community of the Resurrection (CR) in launching the Urban Training Project (UTP) in 1971. The UTP committee included a priest of the CR and a member of the Christian Institute, while YCW helped in establishing contact with workers on the East Rand. A Workers' Rights calendar was distributed through churches, occasional addresses to Sunday congregations were made, and here and there permission was given to set up an advice table for workers outside churches.

But above all, the UTP sought to train workers in unionism and to provide back-up educational services, thus helping revive some African unions as well as establishing a handful of new ones. Over time this deliberately led away from the initial oligarchical role UTP played in relation to the workers' organisations themselves, to the formation of more democratic structures under worker control, with the establishment of the Council of Unions of South Africa (CUSA).[7]

The story of the UTP is one of the clearest examples of a common phenomenon within the churches of South Africa – the key role played by motivated and sensitive individuals on the interface between church and worker, often in conjunction with small pressure groups treated by the institutionalised church as rather peripheral to the main body. This is not a healthy situation. It demonstrates to the workers, the vast bulk of Christians in South Africa, a relative lack of concern on the part of the churches for their world. Inversely, it indicates the preoccupation of churches with institutional matters, whether liturgical, clerical or material, and with a gospel removed from the experiences of millions of South Africans. Statements of concern, declarations of support and the appointment of the occasional cleric or lay-worker to the task do not detract from the predominant reality – the minimal, sometimes pitiful allocation of resources, energy and activity which is currently the norm. The problem becomes particularly apparent where church groupings are suddenly faced with a situation demanding their response, and the insight and experience necessary to cope.

A recent strike by members of the Retail and Allied Workers' Union (RAWU) in Cape Town allows the point to be illustrated. Initiated by an external community organisation, the Churches Urban Planning Commission (CUPC), RAWU was a young union at the time when two workers were unfairly dismissed at a Grand Bazaars store in Cape Town. A further 48 workers from RAWU went on strike and were dismissed. RAWU unsuccessfully attempted to organise the large number of remaining workers in support, and failing in this, called for a boycott of the Bazaars. Several individual clergymen were called upon to assist in intervention, but no clear continuity of action was developed. Finally RAWU formally approached the Western Province Council of Churches (WPCC), asking it to intervene on moral grounds. Partially successful, this strategy resulted in most of the dismissed workers being reinstated, but not all.

Several points emerge from the experience, as described by a WPCC organiser. The Union, in approaching the Council, appeared to be unclear about what they wanted from the WPCC. No in-depth discussion of issues and strategy took place between the Union and the church representatives. Moreover, the Union appears not to have established itself among the majority of the workers before launching the strike and the boycott, a fact that perhaps reflects its external origins and early stage of development. Nor did it have a recognition agreement from the company. Nevertheless the churches poured money and energy into a situation they did not fully understand, a problem displayed again in their approach to management where proper intervention and negotiation skills were absent. The danger of counter-productive actions was thus very high, as evidenced in the premature use of the press.

Overall, the experience was not a wholesale disaster, but it has left many questions unanswered. Above all, the lack of a critical ability to assess the situation knowledgeably and to grasp the implications of intervention strategies implies a profound need in the church to educate itself, its clergy and its lay-workers appropriately before leaping into the dark. This is especially true in a very fluid labour scene, characterised by complex legislation and endemic crises.

Church and class

Ultimately, when facing the question of the church's relationship to trade unions, one cannot avoid the fact of class. Whatever theoretical and practical weight one lends to the concept of class, it must be recognised that trade unions are in principle institutions of the working class and not of the ruling elite, the management strata, or the bourgeoisie as a whole. In a conflict-overladen context like South Africa, where worker aspirations contrast starkly with the prevailing ethos, the factor of class is moreover enormously potent and easily grasped in terms of notions of oppression and exploitation.

This the church must face fairly and honestly, recognising that class struggle exists in South Africa – not because it is demanded or sought, but because the structures of our political economy entrench and extend practices based upon contradictory and competing interests between the ruled and the ruler. Another implication may be added: trade unions are not necessarily democratic organisations or free from involvement in oppression and exploitation, as is obvious in the case of the history of many white-dominated, ethnically organised unions in South Africa. Moreover, trade unions are not the whole of the working class. Often only a certain percentage of the working class are collectively gathered. In short, the church needs to view trade unions in context, as well as look well beyond their memberships in responding to the challenge of the worker. At the same time, trade unions are no fly-by-night affairs – they are the most important working-class organisations, having demonstrated their ability to survive great pressures.

There will be no attempt here to argue the case for the church's involvement in the life and world of the worker. Recent theological tradition, beginning with the Christian socialists in the middle of the nineteenth century, is rife with discussion and ultimately consensus on a large number of issues concerning the significance of labour and the legitimate demands of workers upon society and the church itself. Central figures such as Tillich and Barth have lent their weight to the tradition. Barth, for example, spent formative early years at Safenwil. Here, he says,[8]

Class warfare, which was going on in my parish before my very eyes, introduced me almost for the first time to the real problems of real life. The result of this was that my main study was now directed towards factory legislation, insurance, trade union affairs and so on, and my energies were taken up in disputes sparked off by my support for the workers, not only in the neighbourhood but in the canton.

So specialist theological books now gave way to books on economics.

Moreover, Barth believed, such involvement had nothing to do with providing worker movements with a 'religious line'. On the contrary he conceived of his support for workers as a necessary condition of preaching the gospel. 'Jesus was a worker, not a pastor,' noted Barth; and Jesus' own associates were from a similar stratum. 'That was not a cheap pity from above to below,' he wrote, 'but the eruption of a volcano from below to above.' For Jesus, therefore, 'the opposite to God is not the earth, not matter, not the external, but evil, or as he put it in the forceful manner of his day: the demons, the devils who live in man.' The 'great momentous apostasy' of the church consequently rests for Barth in saying that social misery ought not to be, but not in order 'to summon all her power for the sake of this conviction that *it ought not to be.*' He concludes: 'The Church has often performed her service badly. That is quite certainly true of our church and of myself. Of the church, therefore, I can only say to you [the workers' organisation at Safenwil]: "She is there in order to serve you. Do what you think is right." [9]

These themes, as illuminated by Barth, parallel in one way or another central points in the theological debate conducted about the church in its relation to the working class ever since. They have been introduced not via the young Barth, who is merely one representative of this stream of thought, but through a wide variety of traditions and impulses. [10] Black theology in South Africa, too, has increasingly turned its attention to questions of class. The Economics Commission of Spro-cas, though itself only touching on the issue, generated one of the most influential local publications on the subject to date, Richard Turner's *The Eye of the Needle*. [11]

The most comprehensive declaration yet to appear in South Africa, however, is that of the official representatives of eight church bodies from the greater Durban area who met in 1982. Entitled *Worker Rights: A Statement of Christian Commitment*, the document makes clear their belief 'that in South Africa both *legislation* and *general industrial practice* are so heavily loaded against workers that the church has no option but to come to their defence, as a first priority in industrial mission.' [12]

Basing themselves on briefly clarified theological themes (human rights, the *imago dei*, sin, kingdom, rebirth, discipleship and restoration), the declarants promise co-operation 'with all efforts to establish the fundamental rights of workers in South African society', as part of the greater task of creating 'a society of sharing, solidarity and freedom'. The statement proceeds to outline what are regarded as fundamental workers' rights outside and at the workplace. Finally, a series of twenty commitments are made, focusing on employment practices; worker representation in the church; victimisation and exploitation; training, education and public support measures within the churches; practical help; and ecumenical and international contact.

In many respects *Worker Rights* could be a watershed in the life of the church in South Africa. Its claims and commitments are far-reaching, and deserve entrenchment at all levels of mission, education, pastoral life and organisation in the denominations. At the same time, it is important to note that the statement has not treated with any depth a central issue, highlighted by Turner's book: to what extent is the entire political economy to be made transparent to worker participation? Questions about ownership and the breadth of democratic decision-making structures are begged. That consideration aside, a further central issue arises, this time one painfully clear to the authors of the statement themselves: 'we are very aware that a statement by itself cannot achieve very much.'

What shall the churches do?

Industrial relations in South Africa are obviously not straightforward. They are loaded with a very high degree of political content and a long history of deeply embedded legal structures of racism. Trust levels are usually markedly low, and harsh repression by state officials and police has for decades characterised the lot of black workers attempting to organise themselves. In any case, as one analyst has pointed out in a University of Stellenbosch Business School paper reflecting on the role of trade unions in South Africa:

The essence of industrial relations is not peace – it is conflict. The question is not 'Conflict, Yes or No?' Conflict cannot be eliminated. The question is 'How?' How will conflict be dealt with? . . .

Particularly, it is inherent in industry within the free enterprise System, in a capitalist, market economy.

Managements should recognise that conflicts of interests and conflicts of rights are both inherent in the management–worker relationship.

What is true for management is also true for the churches. That conflicts are inherent in our contemporary structures of polity and economy does not allow one to draw the conclusion that mediation between two parties in order to achieve a reconciliation of interests is the chief concern of the church. Such reconciliation is not a question of goodwill or right intention, but of the institutions of society which are engendering conflict.

Consequently, a demand such as that made by the Anglican Bishop of Natal in a critical response to *Worker Rights*, that 'the Church needs to address itself to both sides', to reflect as well on the duties and responsibilities of workers to their employers, is only half-serious.[14] This is especially true if one notices that the relationship between worker and employer in South Africa is hopelessly imbalanced in terms of power. Legislative, financial, political, educational and organisational sources of power are heavily against workers. One is not dealing with equal contractual partners, but with a legacy of oppression and exploitation.

Intervention

Church people have great difficulty accepting the reality of the conflict situation without feeling driven to establish and secure a harmony of interests and rights between conflicting parties. This line of approach must be recognised for what it is in the present context – it is idealistically naive and potentially damaging. This is so whatever biblical and theological arguments may be thrown around in defence of the neutral role.

Consequently, we may say of intervention strategies that those involved should take great care to understand the general nature of conflict in industrial relations governed by the South African racial capitalistic system.

Secondly, the specific conflicts of interests and rights characterising a particular intervention situation cannot be read off from other situations. A detailed grasp of the unique context is a prerequisite for any reasoned intervention capable of producing insight while avoiding calamitous oversights.

Thirdly, any third-party intervention must avoid decision-making processes in which affected workers do not play a key role or at least provide a clear lead. Here church workers, and especially clergy, may be particularly prone to move too quickly and inappropriately into directive roles, either because they are used to taking initiatives and articulating themselves in groups, or because they conceive of themselves as those who can and should guide others. The theological concept of service in solidarity, so powerfully captured in the story of Jesus' washing of the feet of his disciples, is in this case misconstrued or simply not recognised.

Fourthly, those asked to or wishing to intervene should do so only after considering the implications of any and every strategy of intervention, given the dynamics of the relevant situation. The ill-prepared, uncritical reformer, however committed to a cause, is a danger both to himself or herself as well as to those whose need occasions their generosity of heart, mind or purse. For churches and related groups or individuals resolved to rally to the just cause of workers in South Africa, this condition necessarily implies a far greater state of readiness to turn resolution into response than is presently apparent. More is called for than a member of a committee or department given over to monitoring labour issues, as well as much greater imagination and courage in supporting the few bold individuals and groups in the church already working at the heart of the matter.

In this respect all denominations and other Christian groupings in South Africa may learn a great deal from the YCW. Their starting-point is the life of young workers and the conditions they experience at work, at home and at school. They live out of the reality of workers and place themselves within that reality as a movement of education, action and theological reflection, in a complementary role to trade unions or other similar worker organisations. In YCW groups, workers are able to express themselves, to listen, to take decisions, and to start assuming responsibility for their own lives. Consequently, with by far the longest and most penetrating experience in South African denominational life, YCW's insights are not just interesting but the firmest touchstone for the involvement of other Christians in working-class issues. Consultation, dialogue, and debate with YCW whenever possible, particularly when interventions are being considered or requested, are to be recommended.

What differentiates YCW from more conventional practices of industrial mission is its stance against the denominational institution or church body acting independently or on behalf of the workers. YCW rejects the notion of the church taking the initiative ahead of workers, for this more often than not results in an undermining of the status of *worker* representatives. Instead, YCW encourages help, support and strengthening of worker leadership. Of course, its very locus among workers provides YCW at the outset with the right base for judging how these things may be achieved.

For similar reasons, YCW does not favour the usual concept of industrial mission (especially the dominant British model). Again, industrial mission chaplains, almost by definition, often short-circuit worker representation and trade union procedures, especially when they assume a so-called 'neutral' stance in a loaded situation. Thus, if there is to be a chaplaincy, it should be conceived of as a pastoral and theological responsibility by one who 'accompanies' the workers themselves on their journey.

By this, however, YCW speaks not of the well-known idea of the worker-priest. To regard such a priest as the logical type of appointment in industrial chaplaincy to accompany workers is insufficient. For there is often an unconscious kind of deception involved in 'playing' at being a worker when one is really far more at home with organisational and relational skills and ultimately independent of the need for employment outside of the church. The worker-priest objectively holds a position of power not available to the average worker. Consequently, YCW believes that the desire to avoid alienation from the worker, and to follow one's flock into the world of work, may indeed be important, but not when this means taking on an intervention role in lieu of worker leadership.

Education

Throughout this essay, the massive need for education within the church on industrial relations structures in South Africa and on the world of the worker has been repeatedly noted. Particularly where interventions arise or are demanded, the need for appropriate education and training on a systematic basis has already been demonstrated.

More than this, however, Christian workers themselves need educative assistance, especially in respect of their struggle to claim dignity, rights of participation in decision-making concerning their lives and work, and freedom to organise. Not for nothing has a union representative, in discussing how the church could help worker struggles, stressed the need for help in research and investigative journalism – tasks unionists overloaded with day-to-day affairs usually cannot undertake.[15]

But the church also needs assistance. As Archbishop Hurley remarked after hearing accounts from trade unionists of their situation: 'Our great regret was that we had known so little about the privations, indignities and humiliations to which black workers are subjected in their work situation.'[16] Concerned Christians in management have also acknowledged their ignorance, despite being on the interface of industrial relations.

Structures of support

Ultimately the contradictions and ambiguities, the fears and the contrary interests that plague the churches of South Africa, are likely to remain. The problems of the alienation of workers from the church and of the church's inability to relate with effective potency to the world of the worker, may be expected to continue in force. However, the acceptance of this reality should not occasion despair or apathy.

What is possible is a concerted attempt to develop new structures of support for workers and their organisations where these structures do not exist, and to back up those that do. The allocation of significant resources is implied, as is the willingness to free as many suitably motivated and skilled (or trainable) church workers as possible to handle the task. The final condition is the determined creation of a theological and organisational climate by which the required task can be elevated into the centre of church life and accorded the necessary seriousness.

That this is no utopian set of recommendations may be witnessed in the remarkable boldness with which the South African Catholic Bishops' Conference (SACBC) has set about constituting its Church and Work Commission. Following on the work of YCW and prodded by the 1973 wave of strikes in Natal, the SACBC established a Church and Industry department to deal with the growing challenge. At first concentrating on keeping the bishops informed and publishing a regular periodical to generate local support for workers, the department reached the point where more was required than could be managed. At a plenary session of the SACBC in 1977, a Declaration of Commitment was issued and given force. The decision was made to engage in well-judged solidarity actions in support of workers rather than merely issue pastoral letters of moral concern. As an expression of this commitment, the department of Church and Industry was then upgraded to a full Commission on Church and Work.

Members of the Commission are often directly connected to the world of workers, thus ensuring the necessary insight and capacity to avoid the kinds of mistakes documented earlier. Moreover, some re-thinking of theological concepts and understandings has resulted, to a large extent because of the voice of the worker which had previously been absent from direct representation.

The Commission has opted to shift the church away from 'neutrality' (meaning cautious disengagement) towards responsibility to those most affected by oppression and exploitation in our context – a direct result of a rethought understanding of Christian love expressed in the corporate notion of justice. That the gospel is not thereby restricted to a specific class, the Commisssion expresses by incorporating movements based among young middle-class as well as management-level Christians.[17] However, all groups begin with the presupposition of a commitment to workers similar to that made by YCW, and thereafter consider its implications for the world in which they live, play and work.

In short, the SACBC has exposed itself to a profound learning experience. Above all, it has done so systematically, by establishing appropriate systems of learning and response, backed by the full authority of the SACBC, and given the muscle to carry out the task. The gospel as hope to the downtrodden and simultaneously a potent challenge to the privileged is made partially visible in structural form.

The option for the poor in South Africa
ALBERT NOLAN

'This phrase [the option for the poor] burst upon the ecclesiastical scene only a few years ago. Since then it has become the most controversial religious term since the Reformers' cry, "salvation by faith alone".'

These are the opening words of Donal Dorr's recent book on the option for the poor and Vatican social teaching.[1] He is not exaggerating. I should say that the challenge to the church, to almost all our churches, represented by this term 'option for the poor' goes far beyond anything envisaged by the Reformers. It challenges both Catholic and Protestant, and it challenges us in a very fundamental way.

In this essay I should like to do little more than open up the debate about the option for the poor in South Africa. The question has been raised here and there in a variety of forms, mostly without the term 'option for the poor'; but in South Africa there has been no systematic Christian practice based upon it and not much research and reflection around this controversial phrase. Dr Beyers Naudé would be a good example of someone who could be said to have taken this option and suffered the consequences; but the biblical grounding and contextual implications of such an option for every Christian in South Africa (black and white, rich and poor) has not been systematically worked out.

My intention, then, is to open up the specific approach implied in this new theological term for further research, reflection, debate and practice.

There is a great deal of confusion and misunderstanding about the meaning of the phrase itself, and even a measure of deliberate distortion of its meaning. Hence, in the first place, it will be necessary to state quite clearly what we are talking about and even more importantly what we are not talking about. Then we shall have to give some account of how this new theological theme is grounded in the Bible. And finally we must venture some suggestions about what it may mean in the struggle for liberation in South Africa today.

Option for the poor: what does it mean?
One of the most common misunderstandings is that an option for the poor means a choice or preference for preaching and ministering to

the poor rather than to the rich. The more recent phrase 'preferential option for the poor', made popular by the Puebla Conference of Latin American bishops, has tended to reinforce the idea that all we are talking about is a pastoral preference in the distribution of the church's services, resources and preaching. We must give more of our attention to the poor and work with them by preference. Some would argue that the church should serve *only* the poor and have nothing whatsoever to do with the rich. Others would respond by saying that the gospel and its message is for all and we cannot abandon the rich. But all of this misses the point.

The option for the poor is not a choice about the *recipients* of the gospel message, *to whom* we must preach the gospel; it is a matter of *what gospel* we preach to anyone at all. It is concerned with the *content* of the gospel message itself. The gospel may be good news for the poor and bad news for the rich but it is a message for both the poor and the rich.

The opinion that the preferential option for the poor is simply a way of emphasising the all-importance of almsgiving, charity and relief work need not delay us here. The poor are not people who are deprived because of bad luck or misfortune. The poor are the oppressed, the victims of the social sin of injustice. The option for the poor is concerned with the *sin of oppression* and what Christians should be doing about it.[2]

One sometimes hears the objection that the poor are not all saints and the rich are not all sinners. There are indeed people who understand their option for the poor in a way that simply romanticises the poor and imputes guilt to everyone who is not poor. It is thought that anyone who is poor and oppressed is incapable of doing wrong and that anyone who is rich must have knowingly and willingly chosen to make the poor suffer. But this again misses the point. The option for the poor is not a preference for some people over other people. It is a matter of taking up the *cause of the poor* as opposed to the cause of the rich. The moral judgment involved here is not a judgment about individuals who are rich or poor, but a judgment about the morality or rightness of two conflicting causes. The option for the poor is a judgment about the rightness of the cause of the poor and a condemnation of the cause of the rich, whatever the measure of personal guilt of those involved may or may not be.

It has also sometimes been thought that the option for the poor is a matter of *lifestyle*: an option for poverty. We do not necessarily help the poor and oppressed by imitating their deprivation. The option for the poor may indeed influence our lifestyle, it may even have a very profound effect upon our material and economic life, but all of this will be determined entirely by the exigencies of the struggle for liberation as it is being waged at any particular time.

The option for the poor then is an uncompromising and unequivocal taking of sides in a situation of structural conflict. It is not a matter of preaching to some people rather than others, or a matter of being generous to the 'underprivileged', or a judgment about the personal guilt of the rich, or even, in the first instance, a matter of lifestyle. It is the assertion that Christian faith entails, for everyone and as part of its essence, the taking of sides in the structural conflict between the oppressor and the oppressed.[3] Nothing could be more threatening to the cherished beliefs of so many of today's Christians. Nothing could be more threatening to so many of our churches in the way they operate in the world today. Nothing could be more controversial and challenging for our theology and our practice as Christians.

Those who feel threatened will say that this is not the gospel, it is politics. The gospel, they will argue, is about peace and reconciliation and not about taking sides in a conflict. Yes, but surely the gospel does not require us to reconcile good and evil, justice and injustice? Does it not rather demand that we take sides against all sin and especially against the all-pervasive sin of oppression?[4]

These are weighty assertions, though. They call for a solid biblical grounding. In other parts of the world, and by no means only in Latin America, a great deal of biblical research has been done around this topic. We shall need to be well acquainted with their research as we try to develop our own South African perspective on the poor in the Bible.

The option for the poor in the Bible

The option for the poor is not a biblical phrase but it does sum up very neatly and succinctly one of the most central themes of the Bible. We know that the concept of the poor is central to the whole biblical revelation, but it is so easy to 'spiritualise' all that is said about the poor in the Bible by quoting texts that refer to 'spiritual poverty' as the attitude of total reliance upon God and having a humble and contrite spirit. There are obvious ulterior motives for this kind of interpretation but the real point is that what is said in different parts of the Bible about the poor must be interpreted as far as possible in terms of the *different historical contexts*. Any generalisation that ignores the different historical contexts is sure to be arbitrary and biased.

The option for the poor in the Exodus story

Exodus was the original and paradigmatic saving act of God. It was the foundational revelation of Yahweh, the God of the Hebrews. As Rubem Alves puts it: 'The exodus was the experience that moulded the consciousness of the people of Israel . . . determining the logic with which Israel assimilated the facts of its historical experience and the principle by which it organized them and interpreted them.'[5] The story was told and retold, celebrated each year at the Passover, and used as an interpretative framework for understanding all God's saving activities including the death and resurrection of Jesus – the new Passover.[6]

The outline of the Exodus story is clear enough. We are introduced to a group of people in Egypt doing forced labour as slaves, building cities and prestigious buildings for the Pharaoh (Exod. 1: 11). Their cruel oppression and broken spirit (Exod. 6: 9) is described at some length. The scene was as common in the ancient world as it is today.

The new thing, the new revelation, was the appearance of a God called Yahweh who actually took notice of them, who saw their oppression, heard their cries and helped them to escape from their oppressors. Here was a God who actually sided with them rather than, like all other gods, siding with the kings and Pharaohs who oppressed them. Later they recognised Yahweh to be the only God, the creator God, the God of their Fathers.

What does this tell us about the option for the poor?

Here we have the original poor people of the Bible, the Hebrew slaves in Egypt. Their poverty is obviously material and economic but what is far more striking is that their poverty is the direct result of the structural oppression of Egyptian society. The poor here are the oppressed and what is described at length is precisely their oppression. Recent studies on the meaning and usage of the Hebrew words for oppression have proved beyond any doubt that almost the whole Bible is concerned with the political problem of oppression, and that poverty is seen consistently as the result of oppression.[7]

In the Exodus story the option for these oppressed Hebrews is taken in the first place by Yahweh himself. God takes sides with the oppressed and against the oppressor in no uncertain terms. And this is precisely what counts in Exodus as the fundamental revelation about Yahweh.[8] There is no sense whatsoever in which he can be seen as a God who tries to reconcile or make peace between Pharaoh and his slaves. God rescues or liberates the oppressed from the oppressor, and this is what he continues to do throughout the Bible. As we read in Psalm 103: 6 (JB): 'Yahweh, who does what is right, is always on the side of the oppressed.'

The other interesting thing about the Exodus story is that it is the poor and oppressed themselves who must take an option for their own cause. The work of Moses was precisely to persuade the Hebrew slaves to take up their own cause, and that is what faith and trust in Yahweh meant for them in practice.[9]

The option for the poor is almost always thought of today as a commitment which the non-poor have to make to the cause of those who are oppressed. But what is far more fundamental in the Bible is the option of the poor for their own cause. It cannot by any means be taken for granted that all poor people will take up their own cause. Some of them will be too broken in spirit and too lacking in hope of success. Others will abandon the cause of the oppressed as a whole in order to promote their own private cause of moving upwards into the ranks of the oppressor. This is the sort of option for the oppressor that enables the oppression to continue. The option for the poor is not intended only for those who are not poor and not oppressed.

Of course in the Exodus story Moses himself would be the example of someone who, though not himself oppressed, took sides with the oppressed workers of Egypt.

The option for the poor in Canaan

Exodus was only the beginning of the liberation story in the Bible. When the descendants of the Hebrew slaves reached Canaan they joined forces with oppressed peasants and other rebels most of whom had a common ancestry. Together they began to build the new nation of Israel. With their background of oppression and with the new hope based upon Yahweh, the liberator of the oppressed, it is not surprising to discover that they built a nation in which there were no rich and no poor, no kings, princes or even chiefs, and no slaves. It was a federation of twelve tribes and the land was divided equally amongst the families or clans (Num. 33: 54; 34, 18).

Recent scholarship has shown beyond doubt that the Israelite society of the twelve tribes was indeed an *egalitarian* society and that this structure was based upon belief in Yahweh, the liberator of slaves. In this respect, Israel was unique among the nations of the ancient world.[10]

What does this tell us about the option for the poor? It makes it quite clear that the option which God takes, and which the poor themselves take for their own cause, is an option for an egalitarian society in which there will be no oppressor and no oppressed. It is not fundamentally an option for some people and against other people, but an option against all oppression and injustice in favour of a world in which all people will benefit from a just freedom and equality.

The option for the poor in the Prophets

For reasons that would take too long to explain here, the egalitarian society of the twelve tribes did not last. Gradually inequality set in, despite the attempts of the Jubilee legislation (Lev. 25: 8–55) to stem the tide, until eventually the people began to ask for a king in order to be like other nations. The prophet Samuel resisted and warned them that the king and his officials would become rich at their expense and they themselves would become slaves again. But the people insisted and as the Bible understands it, God allowed them to have a king (1 Sam. 8: 1–22).

This was the beginning of oppressive structures within Israel itself. Saul did not become rich but he proved to be a jealous tyrant. David was a pious and benevolent dictator who began slowly to take on the trappings of an oriental monarch. But it was Solomon and his successors who fulfilled Samuel's worst fears. The majority of the people were reduced to much the same poverty and oppression as that from which Yahweh had once liberated them in Egypt and Canaan.

Hence the rise of the great prophets. Although most of the prophets probably did not come from the oppressed classes of Israel, they took up the cause of justice for the poor as Yahweh's cause. The result for almost all the pre-exilic prophets was persecution, imprisonment and martyrdom (Matt. 23: 29, 33; Luke 6: 22, 23, 26). Their identification with the cause of the oppressed led eventually to their own oppression. It was when Jeremiah himself was hunted and persecuted that he could count himself as one of the poor (Jer. 20: 13).

The prophets were almost by definition those who took an option for the oppressed. The kings were almost by definition the oppressors.[11] And it would not be unfair to say that the prophets failed most of all, because the oppressed themselves had not taken an option for their own cause. The result was the destruction of Israel as an independent nation, the deportation of its elite (middle and upper classes) to Babylon (Jer. 29: 1–2) and the disappearance of its poor and oppressed classes into the surrounding nations.[12]

The option for the poor during and after the exile

During the centuries after the fall of Jerusalem and the monarchy, in exile in Babylon and after the return to Jerusalem, the remnant of Israel remained a small colony oppressed by a succession of empires: Babylonian, Persian, Greek and Roman. There was suffering but on the whole, even in exile, it was not remotely as bad as the oppression experienced originally in Egypt. There was a measure of persecution but now it was mostly a religious persecution. With the exception of the Maccabees and later the Zealots, there was no attempt to struggle for liberation. Israel became submissive and opted for a kind of religious independence.

It was during this period that they developed that very special form of Jewish piety that we call *spiritual poverty*. The scrolls of the law and of the prophets had been taken into exile by the elite. These they read, interpreted and rewrote in terms of their present experience.

The poor and oppressed were central to the written tradition they had inherited. The poor were God's favourites. Thus they read the texts about the poor as applying to themselves, the oppressed remnant of Israel (Zeph. 3: 11–13; Isa. 49: 13). But now being a member of the remnant of Israel and remaining faithful to Yahweh becomes a matter of personal choice and individual responsibility. And if we also remember that the warnings and condemnations of the prophets made the remnant feel guilty and repentant, we can understand how poverty comes to be thought of as a moral category rather than a social category. To be God's chosen people the religious remnant of Israel must imitate the 'virtues of the poor', which are understood to be the virtues of being humble, meek, contrite, patient and totally reliant upon God (Isa. 57: 15; 66: 1–2; Ps. 34: 18; 51: 17; Mic. 6: 6–8; Dan. 3: 39; Zeph. 2: 3; 3:

11–13). To be truly poor becomes a matter of the heart and of the spirit: a humble heart and a contrite spirit.[13]

How does this relate to the option for the poor?

The Jews who developed this spirituality of poverty were indeed oppressed, but they regarded themselves *alone* as the 'poor of Yahweh'. This was the beginning of the detachment of spiritual poverty from its roots in material poverty and in the social category of all the oppressed classes. Instead of taking an option for the poor one can then take an option for the 'virtues of the poor' in a way that enables the status quo of oppression to continue unchallenged.

However, some aspects of the piety of the poor that was developed during this period can be of value to us in our commitment to the cause of the poor. It was Jesus and his movement that brought the piety of the poor down to earth again and rooted it firmly in an option for the materially poor and politically oppressed.

The option for the poor in the gospels

In the time of Jesus and his disciples, the remnant of Israel was very conscious of being oppressed by the Romans. But, like the prophets in previous times, what Jesus draws attention to is the internal structures of oppression. Oppressor and oppressed, rich and poor, could also be found within Jewish society and religion. The Sadducees and the Pharisees, the scribes, the chief priests and the elders (that is, the nobility and rich landowners) were in various ways oppressors; while the poor, the blind, the lame, the crippled, widows and orphans, the 'sinners', the tax collectors and prostitutes were all in their own way oppressed people.[14]

In this situation Jesus took sides quite clearly and unequivocally. He spoke of a God who blessed the poor and the oppressed and brought the good news that they would be set free and that God's kingdom belonged to them (Luke 6: 20–23; 4: 16–22; 12: 32).

Jesus' option for the poor included a determined effort to get the poor to take an option for their own cause. He insisted again and again that it was *their faith* that would heal them and save them.[15] He used his position to restore their dignity and confidence in themselves by telling them that they were 'the salt of the earth' and 'the light of the world'. In short, he told them not to bow down or lie down but to stand up and walk (Luke 17: 19; Mark 2: 11–12). His preaching of the kingdom gave them hope for the future.

Jesus' option led him to identify himself totally with the poor: 'whatever you do to the least of these you do to me' (Matt. 25: 40,45). It was for his stand in favour of the poor and against the oppressor that he was, like the prophets, persecuted and eventually killed.

There is no way that one could argue that the category of people Jesus was opting for were the morally or spiritually poor. They included sinners, prostitutes and tax collectors. They included people who were hungry and thirsty and begging on the streets. What moved Jesus to identify with them was not their *piety* but their *suffering*.[16] That is not to say that there is no idea of spiritual poverty in the gospels. There is. But it is different from the piety of 'the poor of Yahweh' in exilic and post-exilic Judaism. The essence of the distinction between material and spiritual poverty in the gospels has been summed up very simply and concisely by Nicholas Berdyaev: 'If I am hungry, that is a material problem; if someone else is hungry, that is a spiritual problem'.[17]

The central challenge in the gospels is the challenge that Jesus presented to the rich and the powerful and to all who had sided with them. He faced them with a simple and uncompromising option – the choice between God and money (Matt. 6: 24 par.; compare Mark 4: 19 par.). Those who chose God would have to sell their surplus possessions (Matt. 6: 19–21; Luke 12: 33–34; 14: 33) and join with the poor in a sharing community in which no one would be in need (Acts 2: 44–46; 4: 32, 34–35), that is to say, where there would be no rich and no poor, no master and no slave. They would not be poor in the sense of destitute (Greek *ptochos*) but they would be poor in the sense of having rejected all avarice, greed and oppression (Greek *penes*).[18] Or, in Matthew's words, they would 'hunger and thirst for justice' (5: 6; compare Luke 6: 21); they would not be destitute but they would be 'poor in spirit' (5: 3; compare Luke 6: 20).[19]

Here then is the new spirituality. There is no glorification of poverty but a determination to overcome it. There is no denial that we have enemies but a determination to love them too (Luke 6: 27–35). There is no refusal to recognise the reality of sin in the world but a determination to be forgiving (Matt. 18: 21–22). There must be a struggle against all forms of oppression but there must be no revenge (Matt. 5: 38–39).[20]

This would be the spirit of the new community that takes an option against suffering and oppression. It would be sign or symbol of the new Israel, the kingdom that is to come.

The option for the poor in South Africa

In our situation of a cruel and relentless oppression that is perpetrated in the name of God and the Bible, it becomes imperative to preach about God as the one who has taken sides, here in South Africa, with all who are oppressed – and to preach this to everyone. It will then be necessary to spell out, work out and live out the consequences of this for the various groups amongst the oppressed and the oppressing or exploiting classes.

The oppressed must take a clear option for their own cause, for the cause of *all* the poor and oppressed. An option to become upwardly mobile by oneself or with a small group that abandons the rest of the oppressed is not an option for the poor but an option to join the oppressing and exploiting classes. People in South Africa are oppressed in many different ways and to different degrees. Workers are oppressed, some much more than others; blacks are oppressed, but some suffer considerably more than others; women are oppressed but not all to anything like the same extent. It becomes possible therefore to be oppressed on one account while being part of the oppression on another account. An option for the poor is an option against every form of oppression and exploitation. An analysis of the relationship between the various forms of oppression is helpful here. But a Christianity that does not challenge the poor and oppressed themselves, including women, to take an option and join in the struggle for liberation is simply unbiblical.

Many of the churches in South Africa, especially through their official statements and sometimes in Sunday sermons, are beginning to take a prophetic stance. But in view of what we have seen of the option for the poor in the Bible, we may well ask whether the stance of these churches has gone nearly far enough. There is a growing denunciation of injustice but there is no clear annunciation of hope for a future liberated society. There are challenges to the government and to whites in general but there is no clear statement that the oppressed should take up their own cause as God's cause. The stance of the churches is not clear. If whites are supposed to take an option against oppression, what does this mean in practice? Not many of them are likely to want to take an option for the poor but what do we say to those who do want to do so?

Those who profess a willingness to side with the oppressed in South Africa will have much to learn. It is obvious that siding with the poor is easier said than done. A purely theoretical decision that apartheid is heretical and sinful is not enough. In religious terms, what is required is a deep conversion, an experience of being born again and a long spiritual journey. Before one's option for the poor can become a truly practical reality, there are ingrained prejudices to be overcome as well as other emotional and cultural obstacles.

One of the more serious emotional obstacles is based upon the fact that we do not experience the same daily sufferings and insecurities as the poor. When you are not humiliated at every turn and regularly beaten up by the police, you do not experience the same emotions of fear, frustration, anger and indignation. You may side with the oppressed but you will not easily feel the same way about the oppressor. And that makes it more difficult to share God's anger at what is happening daily in our country. However, as we get involved in a practical way and as we begin to risk our own security and comfort, our reputation and even our lives, a certain sharing of the experience of oppression and of God's anger becomes possible.

And then there are the cultural obstacles. It may be that a new culture is being born within the struggle for liberation in South Africa, but at present we have to face the fact of cultural differences and try to transcend them as part of our option. The cultural differences are not merely African and Western. There are also cultural differences between the working class and the middle class of any race, between youth culture and adult culture, and between people of various backgrounds: Afrikaners, Indians, Portuguese. These differences are not significant and they can easily be overcome by people who have taken the same option but there is no value in pretending that they do not even exist.[21]

Taking an option for the poor is like setting out on a new spiritual journey.[22] It is so easy to get stuck along the way, at the liberal stage of paternalism or at the romantic stage of glorying the poor. It is so easy to think that one has all the answers because of one's superior education or analysis. A thoroughgoing option for the poor includes the willingness to question one's assumptions and to learn from those who are oppressed. It is only after one has learnt to have confidence in the ability of the oppressed to promote their own cause and bring about their own liberation that one can begin to share that struggle with them and to make a contribution in real solidarity with all those who have taken an option against oppression.

Centuries of apartheid or racial capitalism have left their mark upon all classes and groups in South Africa. Only the self-righteous will claim to be immune. We need to be redeemed, liberated and cleansed.

What I am suggesting is that we might try to do this by exploring together in practice and in study and research, a common option taken by all classes and races for all the oppressed. The term 'option for the poor' itself does not matter.

We might choose to call it something else. What matters is the uncompromising commitment to the cause of the oppressed as the cause of God.

References

Charles Villa–Vicencio: A life of resistance and hope

¹ P. Randall, 'Not without honour: the life and work of Beyers Naudé', in P. Randall (ed.), *Not Without Honour: Tribute to Beyers Naudé* (Johannesburg, 1982), pp. 1–50.
² C. Villa–Vicencio, 'A source of hope and despair', in Randall (ed.), *Not Without Honour*, pp. 82–97.
³ G. Bryan, *Naudé: Prophet to South Africa* (Atlanta, 1978), p. 12.
⁴ See T. D. Moodie, *The Rise of Afrikanerdom* (Berkeley, 1975), p 62f.
⁵ B. J. Marais, *Kleur Krisis in die Weste* (Johannesburg, 1952).
⁶ T. Lodge, *Black Politics in South Africa Since 1945* (Johannesburg, 1983), p. 225.
⁷ A. Luckhoff, *Cottesloe* (Cape Town, 1978).
⁸ Bryan, *Naudé*, p. 13.
⁹ C. F. B. Naudé, *My Beslissing* (Johannesburg, 1963); also in Randall (ed.), *Not Without Honour*, pp. 99–105.
¹⁰ Randall (ed.), *Not Without Honour*, pp. 1–50.
¹¹ See essay in this volume by J. W. de Gruchy on the Christian Institute; also P. Walshe, *Church versus State in South Africa* (Maryknoll, 1983).
¹² This biographical comment is based on a personal interview conducted with Beyers Naudé in October 1984.
¹³ Quoted in J. J. Ansbro, *Martin Luther King, Jr.: The Making of a Mind* (Maryknoll, 1982), p. 91.

John W. de Gruchy: A short history of the Christian Institute

¹ See R. J. Shorten, 'The Pre-history and Establishment of the Christian Institute of Southern Africa with Particular Reference to the Response of the Dutch Reformed Church' (unpublished Hons. project, University of Cape Town, 1982).
² For a detailed study of the history of the Christian Institute see P. Walshe, *Church Versus State in South Africa: The Case of the Christian Institute* (Maryknoll, N.Y., 1983).
³ On Cottesloe see A. H. Luckhoff, *Cottesloe* (a Town, 1978), and J. W. de Gruchy, *The Church Struggle in South Africa* (Cape Town, 1979), pp. 62–9.
⁴ See J. W. de Gruchy and C. Villa–Vicencio, *Apartheid Is a Heresy* (Cape Town, 1983), pp. xvi, 148ff.
⁵ A memorandum dated 27 September 1963.
⁶ Undated document, but clearly issued sometime towards the end of 1963.
⁷ Walshe, *Church Versus State*, p. 35.
⁸ Walshe, *Church Versus State*, p. 49.
⁹ On *The Message* see J. W. de Gruchy and W. B. de Villiers, *The Message in Perspective* (Johannesburg, 1968).
¹⁰ See the essay in this volume by P. Randall, 'Spro-cas Revisited: the Christian Contribution to Political Debate'.
¹¹ See De Gruchy, *Church Struggle*, pp. 127ff.
¹² See B. Khoapa (ed.), *Black Review* (Durban, 1972); P. Randall, *A Taste of Power* (Johannesburg, 1973), pp. 186ff.

[13] Walshe, *Church Versus State*, p. 149.

[14] Mimeographed address, 26.10.1974.

[15] See International Commission of Jurists (eds.), *The Trial of Beyers Naudé* (London and Johannesburg, 1975).

[16] *Pro Veritate*, February 1976, p. 5.

Jaap Durand: Afrikaner piety and dissent

[1] T. D. Moodie, *The Rise of Afrikanerdom* (Berkeley, 1975).

[2] Cf D. J. Bosch, 'The roots and fruits of Afrikaner civil religion', in J. W. Hofmeyr and W. S. Vorster (eds.), *New Faces of Africa: Essays in Honour of Ben Marais* (Pretoria, 1984), pp. 25–32.

[3] D. Bonhoeffer, *Ethics* (New York, 1963), p. 206; cf. also J. W. de Gruchy, *Bonhoeffer and South Africa* (Grand Rapids, 1984), pp. 12–43.

[4] See *inter alia* H. G. Stoker, *Die Stryd om die Ordes* (Potchefstroom, 1941), pp. 250–1. For the Kuyperian influence on apartheid theology, see I. Hexham, *The Irony of Apartheid: The Struggle for National Independence of Afrikaner Calvinism against British Imperialism* (New York, 1981), pp. 96–100; A. J. Botha, 'Die Evolusie van 'n Volksteologie' (unpublished doctoral dissertation, University of the Western Cape, 1984), pp. 406–36.

[5] Botha, 'Evolusie', pp. 195–200.

[6] P. Huet, *Eene Kudde en een Herder: Verhandeling over de Toebrenging van Heidenen tot de Christelijke Kerkgemeenskap* (Kaapstad, 1860); cf. Botha, 'Evolusie', pp. 265–8.

[7] *De Volksbode*, 14 March 1889.

[8] Such as Professor Lex van Wyk.

[9] P. Randall (ed.), *Not Without Honour: Tribute to Beyers Naudé* (Johannesburg, 1982), p. 15f.

[10] *Op die Horison*, 1939, p. 113.

[11] *Die Kerkbode*, 7 December 1949, p. 1047.

[12] B. B. Keet, *Christian Principles in Multi-racial South Africa* (1954), pp. 8–19; Botha, 'Evolusie', pp. 476–82.

[13] B. B. Keet, *Waarheen Suid-Afrika* (Stellenbosch, 1955).

[14] Cf. C. J. Botha, 'Ben Marais se stryd in die sinodes teen die "Bybelse fundering van apartheid" ', in A. C. Viljoen (ed.), *Ekumene onder die Suiderkruis* (Pretoria, 1979), p. 15.

[15] Randall, *Not Without Honour*, p. 6.

[16] In an interview with Prof André du Toit on 19 November 1984, to be published in a forthcoming issue of *Die Suid-Afrikaan*.

[17] Ibid.

[18] Ibid.

[19] Bosch, 'Roots and fruits', p. 26.

[20] W. S. Vorster, 'The use of an appeal to Scripture and the NGK: a shift of paradigm or of values?', in Hofmeyr and Vorster, *New Faces*, pp. 1–16.

Willem Saayman: Rebels and prophets: Afrikaners against the system

[1] D. F. Malan, *Afrikaner Volkseenheid en My Ervarings op die Pad Daarheen* (Kaapstad, 1959), p. 178.

[2] Ibid., p. 164.

[3] Cf. C. Villa-Vicencio, 'An ideology in transition' in A. C. Viljoen (ed.), *Ekumene onder die Suiderkruis* (Pretoria, 1979), p. 157.

[4] D. J. Bosch, 'The roots and fruits of Afrikaner civil religion', in J. W. Hofmeyr and W. S. Vorster (eds.), *New Faces of Africa: Essays in Honour of Ben Marais* (Pretoria, 1984), p. 31. Cf. also H. Giliomee, *The Parting of the Ways: South African Politics 1976–82* (Cape Town, 1982), p. 18.

[5] W. A. de Klerk, *The Puritans in Africa* (London, 1975), p. 178.

[6] Malan, *Afrikaner Volkseenheid*, p. 11.

[7] Giliomee, *Parting*, p. 113.

[8] The paper was published in *Pro Veritate*, March 1977, pp. 6–7.

[9] De Klerk, *Puritans*, pp. 113–20.

[10] Cf. the chapter by Jaap Durand in this volume.

[11] Cf. L. Newbigin, *The Other Side of 1984: Questions for the Churches* (Geneva, 1983), pp. 30–1.

[12] Cf. W. A. Saayman, *Unity and Mission* (Pretoria, 1984), pp. 41–2, 46.

[13] Cf. J. H. P. Serfontein, *Brotherhood of Power: An Exposé of the Secret Afrikaner Broederbond* (London, 1979); also I. Wilkins and H. Strydom, *The Super-Afrikaners* (Johannesburg, 1978).

[14] Viljoen, *Ekumene*, pp. 88–90.

[15] H. Giliomee and H. Adam, *Afrikanermag: Opkoms en Toekoms* (Stellenbosch, 1981), pp. 97–8.

[16] Ibid., p. 95.

[17] Cf. A. du Toit, 'No Chosen People: The History and Significance of the Myth of the Calvinist Origin of Afrikaner Nationalism', unpublished essay, 1981: also Bosch, 'Roots and fruits'.

[18] Bosch, 'Roots and fruits', pp. 26–7, 29.

David Bosch: The fragmentation of Afrikanerdom and the Afrikaner churches

[1] Published in J. W. Hofmeyr and W. S. Vorster (eds.), *New Faces of Africa: Essays in Honour of Ben Marais* (Pretoria, 1984), p. 14–35.

[2] This principle, first explicitly formulated at the Peace of Augsburg (1555), may be freely translated as 'each country has to follow the religion of its ruler'.

[3] Ninian Smart, 'Christianity and nationalism', *The Scottish Journal of Religious Studies*, 5,1 (1984), pp. 37–50.

[4] T. D. Moodie, 'The Dutch Reformed Churches as vehicles of political legitimation in South Africa', *Social Dynamics*, 1,2 (1975), p. 158.

[5] Cf. G. D. Scholtz, *Die Geskiedenis van die Nederduitse Hervormde Kerk van Suid-Afrika*, vol. 1: 1842–1885 (Cape Town and Pretoria, 1956), pp. 273–4.

[6] For some references to Milner's ideas and ideals, cf. Scholtz, *Die Geskiedenis van die Nederduitse Hervormde of Gereformeerde Kerk van Suid-Afrika*, vol. 2: 1885–1910 (Cape Town and Pretoria, n.d.), pp. 122–4.

[7] Quoted in J. R. Albertyn, *Kerk en Stad* (Stellenbosch, 1947), p. 15.

[8] Cf. Scholtz, *Geskiedenis*, vol. 2, pp. 124–37.

[9] For a brief survey and evaluation of the churches' attitudes during the 1914 armed revolt, see C. F. A. Borchardt, 'Die Afrikaanse kerke en die Rebellie, 1914–15', in I. H. Eybers, A. Konig and C. F. A. Borchardt (eds.), *Teologie en Vernuwing* (Pretoria 1975), pp. 85–116.

[10] Cf. Moodie, 'Dutch Reformed Churches', p. 162.

[11] Cf. A. N. Pelzer, *Die Afrikaner–Broederbond: Eerste 50 Jaar* (Cape Town, 1980), pp. 187, 191.

[12] Albertyn, *Kerk en Stad*, p. 110.

[13] Ibid., p. 291.

[14] Ibid., p. 294.

[15] M. D. C. de Wet Nel, 'Enkele vraagstukke van ons sendingtaak onder die Bantoe', *Op die Horison*, 20 (1958), pp. 7, 25. My translation.

[16] Johannesburg, 1959.

[17] Cf. E. van Niekerk, 'Church-centredness: an ideology among ideologies', *Theologia Evangelica*, 13 (1980), p. 9. 'In a South African context it is interesting to note that – as far as I can see – criticism of apartheid and racism has tended to come from the 'descendants' of Andrew Murray rather than the orthodox 'school' of the Koot Vorsters.' Cf. also Jaap Durand's contribution to this volume.

[18] For a survey and evaluation on the events, cf. A. H. Luckhoff, *Cottesloe* (Cape

Town, 1978).

[19] Quoted in A. N. Pelzer (ed.), *Verwoerd aan die Woord* (Johannesburg, 1963), p. 404. My translation.

[20] Beyers Naudé, in an interview with André du Toit, Hermann Giliomee and Rykie van Reenen, November 1984.

Proclamation and protest:
Allan Boesak: The lost sons
Wolfram Kistner: Outside the gate

[1] J. Moltmann, *Politische Theologie/Politische Etiek* (München, 1984), pp. 116–17, 121.

John W. de Gruchy: Theologies in conflict: the South African debate

[1] See D. Tracy, *The Analogical Imagination: Christian Theology and the Culture of Pluralism* (London, 1981).

[2] See D. J. Smit, 'What does *Status Confessionis* mean?' in G. D. Cloete and D. J. Smit (eds.), *A Moment of Truth: The Confession of the Dutch Reformed Mission Church 1982* (Grand Rapids, 1984), pp. 7ff.

[3] See J. W. de Gruchy and C. Villa–Vicencio, *Apartheid Is a Heresy* (Cape Town and Grand Rapids, 1983).

[4] N. Lash, *A Matter of Hope* (Notre Dame, Indiana, 1982), p. 291.

[5] For a perceptive discussion of this problem within the South African context, see J. S. Kruger, 'Theology as response to social change: a case study', *Missionalia*, 7, 1 (April 1979).

[6] See A. Konig and H. Keane (eds.), *The Meaning of History* (Pretoria, 1980).

[7] See W. S. Vorster, 'The Bible and apartheid 1' in De Gruchy and Villa–Vicencio, *Apartheid*, and 'The use of Scripture and the NG Kerk: a shift of paradigm or of values?' in J. W. Hofmeyr and W. S. Vorster (eds.), *New Faces of Africa* (Pretoria, 1984).

[8] Cf. D. Bax's essay, 'The Bible and apartheid 2' with that of Vorster, 'The Bible and apartheid 1' in De Gruchy and Villa–Vicencio, *Apartheid*, pp. 113f.

[9] See J. I. Mosala, 'African traditional beliefs and Christianity', *Journal of Theology for Southern Africa*, 43 (June 1983), p. 15f.

[10] See C. Villa–Vicencio, 'Race and Class in the English-speaking Churches', paper presented to the Conference on Economic and Racial Domination, University of the Western Cape, October 1984, p. 6f.

[11] See R. Elphick, 'Africans and the Christian campaign', in H. Lamar and L. Thompson (eds.), *The Frontier in History* (New Haven, 1982), p. 273f; G. M. Setiloane, *The Image of God among the Sotho–Tswana* (Rotterdam, 1976).

[12] Elphick, 'Africans', p. 277f.

[13] The opposition to Moravian missionary George Schmidt is an early example. See B. Kruger, *The Pear Tree Blossoms* (Genadendal, 1966), p. 31f.

[14] See A. J. Botha, 'Die Evolusie van 'n Volksteologie' (unpublished D.Th. thesis, University of the Western Cape, 1984).

[15] See A. Odendaal, *Vukani Bantu! The Beginnings of Black Protest Politics in South Africa to 1912* (Cape Town, 1984).

[16] See J. Guy, *The Heretic: A Study of the Life of John William Colenso, 1814–1883* (Johannesburg and Pietermaritzburg, 1983), pp. 69ff.

[17] See Cloete and Smit (eds.), *Moment of Truth*.

[18] On the relation between each of the three factors in the development of a *volks-teologie* see Botha, 'Evolusie van 'n Volksteologie'.

[19] See D. J. Bosch, A. Konig and W.D. Nicol (eds.), *Perspektief op die Ope Brief* (Cape Town, 1982).

[20] See A. A. Boesak, *Black and Reformed: Apartheid, Liberation and the Calvinist Tradi-*

tion (New York, 1984).

[21] See G. Thom, 'Calvinism in South Africa', in W. S. Reid (ed.), *John Calvin: His Influence in the Western World* (Grand Rapids, 1982), p. 349.

[22] See Villa–Vicencio, 'Race and Class'.

[23] See J. R. Cochrane, 'The Role of the English-speaking Churches in South Africa: A Critical Historical Analysis and Theological Evaluation with Special Reference to the Church of the Province and the Methodist Church, 1903–1930' (unpublished Ph.D. thesis, University of Cape Town, 1983).

[24] See J. W. de Gruchy, 'Catholics in a Calvinist country', in A. Prior (ed.), *Catholics in Apartheid Society* (Cape Town, 1982).

[25] See D. J. Bosch, 'In search of mission: reflections on "Melbourne" and "Pattaya"', *Missionalia*, 9, 1 (April 1981), p. 3ff.

[26] See J. W. de Gruchy, 'The great evangelical reversal: South African reflections', *Journal of Theology for Southern Africa*, 24 (September 1978).

[27] See 'Evangelicals at Vancouver: an open letter', *Journal of Theology for Southern Africa*, 45 (December 1983), p. 71f; E. Castro, 'Ecumenism and evangelicalism: where are we?', in P. Webb (ed.), *Faith and Faithfulness* (Geneva, 1984).

[28] See Boesak, *Black and Reformed*, p. 75.

[29] See D. J. Bosch, 'Currents and crosscurrents in South African black theology', in G. S. Wilmore and J. H. Cone (eds.), *Black Theology: A Documentary History, 1966–1979* (New York, 1979), pp. 220ff.

[30] See D. M. Tutu, 'Black theology/African theology – soul mates or antagonists?' in Wilmore and Cone, *Black Theology*, p. 483ff; G. Setiloane, 'Theological trends in Africa', *Missionalia*, 8, 2 (August 1980).

[31] L. J. Sebidi, 'A critical analysis of the dynamics of the black struggle in South Africa and its implications for black theology', unpublished paper, September 1984, p. 44.

[32] See especially the work of the Institute for Contextual Theology, Johannesburg: *ICT News*, September 1984, 2, 3, reports on the first Feminist Theological Conference held in South Africa.

[33] For a similar black American perspective see J. Cone, *For My People: Black Theology and the Black Church* (New York, 1984).

[34] See the discussion in *Missionalia*, 5, 2 (August 1977).

Frank Chikane: Doing theology in a situation of conflict

[1] L. J. Sebidi, 'Doing theology in a divided society', paper delivered at the EAATSA Conference, 18–20 May, 1983.

[2] Ibid.

[3] G. M. Setiloane, in K. Appiah–Kubi and S. Torres (eds.), *African Theology En Route* (Maryknoll, 1979), p. 62.

[4] J. M. Bonino, *Doing Theology in a Revolutionary Situation* (Philadelphia, 1976), p. 61.

[5] H. Assmann, *Oppression Liberacion: Desafiva los Crisianos* (Montevideo, 1972), p. 11.

[6] B. Goba, 'Doing Theology in South Africa: A Black Christian Perspective' (unpublished thesis, 1978), p. 15.

[7] A. Boesak, *Farewell to Innocence* (Johannesburg, 1977), p. 16.

[8] M. Bonino, *Doing Theology*, p. 91.

[9] Ibid.

[10] In T. O. Beidelman, *Colonial Evangelism* (Bloomington, 1980), p. 27.

[11] Ibid.

[12] *ICT News*, 1 and 2 September 1983, p. 1.

[13] A dialogue facilitated by EATWOT (Ecumenical Association of Third World Theologians) in 1983. Unpublished paper.

[14] Document published by MUCCOR, 1981.

[15] J. W. de Gruchy, *The Church Struggle in South Africa* (Cape Town, 1979), p. 224.

[16] Conference document, obtainable from EAATSA.

[17] Sebidi, 'Doing theology'

Itumeleng Mosala: African Independent churches: a study in socio-theological protest

[1] E. P. Thompson, *The Making of the English Working Class* (Harmondsworth, 1968), pp. 397ff.

[2] M. Dixon, *Things Which Are Done in Secret* (Montreal, 1976), pp. 108ff.

[3] C. West, in G. S. Wilmore and J. H. Cone (eds.), *Black Theology: A Documentary History, 1966–1979* (New York, 1979), pp. 553ff.

[4] N. K. Gottwald, *Tribes of Yahweh* (London, 1980), p. 625.

[5] Ibid.

[6] Ibid.

[7] Ibid., p. 630.

[8] Ibid.

[9] Dixon, *Things*, p. 35.

[10] K. Marx and F. Engels, *The German Ideology* (London, 1970), p. 42.

[11] S. Rostagno, 'The Bible: is an interclass reading legitimate?', *Radical Religion*, 2, 2 & 3 (1975), p. 19.

[12] D. R. Gandy, *Marx and History* (Austin, Texas, and London, 1979), pp. 118ff.

[13] Ibid., pp. 140ff.

[14] M. Mckale, 'Culture and human liberation', *Radical Religion*, 5, 2 (1980), p. 9.

[15] See especially M. West, *Bishops and Prophets in a Black City* (Cape Town, 1975) and B. Sundkler, *Bantu Prophets* (London, 1948).

[16] J. Clarke, 'Capital and culture: the post-war working class revisited', in *Working Class Culture* (London, 1979), p. 244.

Charles Villa–Vicencio: Theology in the service of the state: the Steyn and Eloff Commissions

[1] *Report of the Commission of Inquiry into the South African Council of Churches*, Chairman: C. F. Eloff (Pretoria Government Printer, RP 74/1983), p. 433 (hereafter referred to as the Eloff Commission).

[2] *Report of the Commission of Inquiry into the Mass Media*, Chairman: M. T. Steyn (Pretoria: Government Printer, RP 89/1981), p. 497 (hereafter referred to as Steyn Commission).

[3] See the essay in this volume by J. W. de Gruchy.

[4] Eloff Commission, p. 433.

[5] Ibid, p. 430.

[6] A. M. Greeley, *Unsecular Man* (New York: 1974), p. 14.

[7] V. M. Lidz, 'Secularization, ethical life and religion in modern societies', *Sociological Inquiry*, 49, 2 & 3 (1977), p. 195.

[8] J. de Gruchy and C. Villa–Vicencio (eds.), *Apartheid is a Heresy* (Cape Town, 1983), pp. 148–53.

[9] A. H. Luckhoff, *Cottesloe* (Cape Town 1978), p. 116, 119.

[10] See the essay in this volume by David Bosch.

[11] *Steyn Commission*, p. 1285.

[12] *Eloff Commission*, p. 145.

[13] Ibid., pp. 152, 443.

[14] *Ecunews*, 2, (March 1984), p. 20.

[15] *Eloff Commission*, pp. 427, 56f.

[16] *Steyn Commission*, pp. 77, 483f, 497f.

[17] Ibid, p. 77.

[18] Ibid., pp. 77–95, 483–686.

[19] Ibid., pp. 746–64, also 520f and 745f.

[20] Ibid., pp. 88–90.

[21] Ibid., pp. 652, 641.

[22] Ibid., p. 641.

[23] Ibid., p. 652.

[24] Ibid., p. 656.

[25] Ibid., pp. 497–8.

[26] *Eloff Commission*, pp. 140, 429.

[27] Ibid., p. 431.

[28] Ibid., p. 146.

[29] Ibid., pp. 146–7.

[30] Ibid., p. 148.

[31] See his submission to the Eloff Commission, February 1983.

[32] *Eloff Commission*, p. 145.

[33] Ibid., pp. 436–43.

[34] Submission to the Eloff Commission: *S.A. Raad Van Kerke: 'n Evaluasie deur die S. A. Polisie vir Voorlegging aan die Kommissie van Ondersoek na die SARK*, p. 10.

[35] Ibid., p. 109, also 120.

[36] Submission to the Eloff Commission: *Response to the Evaluation of the Activities of the SACC Division of Justice and Reconciliation in the Memorandum of the South African Police, submitted to the Eloff Commission*, pp. 7, 27f.

[37] Division of Justice and Reconciliation submission, p. 28.

[38] *Eloff Commission*, p. 146.

[39] Ibid., p. 439.

[40] Ibid., p. 430.

[41] R. J. Neuhaus, *The Naked Public Square* (Grand Rapids, 1984), pp. 42–3.

[42] *Eloff Commission*, p. 146.

[43] *Steyn Commission*, pp. 59–65, 70–76; *Eloff Commission*, pp. 430, 433.

[44] P. Lehmann, *The Transfiguration of Politics* (New York, 1975), p. 40.

[45] K. Barth, 'Church and state', in W. Herberg (ed.), *Community, State and Church* (Garden City, 1960), pp. 101–148.

[46] Ibid., p. 139.

[47] J. M. Bonino, *Towards a Christian Political Ethics* (Philadelphia, 1983).

[48] M. Horkheimer, *Die Sehnsucht nach dem ganz Anderen: Ein Interview mit Kommentaar von Helmut Gumnoir* (Hamburg, 1975), p. 60.

[49] Barth, 'Church and state', p. 118.

[50] G. Baum, 'Peter Berger's unfinished symphony', in G. Baum (ed.), *Sociology and Human Destiny* (New York, 1980), p. 119.

[51] *Eloff Commission*, p. 143.

[52] See the essay in this volume by Albert Nolan.

[53] Bonino, *Christian Political Ethics*, p. 43.

[54] Ibid., p. 90.

[55] Cf. R. Niebuhr, *An Interpretation of Christian Ethics* (New York 1935); K. Barth, *The Epistle to the Romans*, translated by E. C. Hoskyns (London, 1960). See translation by P. Lehmann, *Transfiguration*, p. 44.

[56] Barth, *Epistle to the Romans*, p. 493.

[57] K. Barth, *Church Dogmatics*, Vol.II, I (Edinburgh, 1957), p. 386.

Buti Tlhagale: Towards a black theology of labour

[1] D. Tutu, *Hope and Suffering* (Johannesburg, 1983), p. 128.

[2] See the critique of liberation theology by A. Fiero, *The Militant Gospel* (London, 1977), pp. 232–62.

[3] Ibid., p. 370.

[4] Quoted by D. O'Meara, *Volkskapitalisme* (Johannesburg, 1983), p. 10.

[5] Quoted from Karl Marx's *German Ideology* by N. Gottwald, *The Tribes of Yahweh. A Sociology of the Religion of Liberated Israel, 1250–1050 B.C.E.* (London, 1979), p. 631.

[6] J. Habermas, *Knowledge and Human Interest* (London, 1972), p. 26.

[7] G. Baum, *The Priority of Labour* (New York, 1981), p. 107.

[8] Ibid., p. 19.

[9] G. Piano, 'Human work: blessing and/or curse?', *Concilium* (December 1982), p. 6.

[10] C. Bundy, *The Rise and Fall of the South African Peasantry* (London, 1979), p. 112.

[11] T. R. H. Davenport and K. Hunt (eds.), *The Right to the Land* (Cape Town, 1974), p. 41.

[12] R. Davies, *Capital, State and White Labour in South Africa 1900–1960: A Historical Material Analysis of Class Relations* (Sussex, 1979), p. 56.

[13] Quoted in ibid., p. 67.

[14] Habermas, *Knowledge*, p. 29.

[15] B. Lonergan, *Insight: A Study of Human Understanding* (London, 1957), pp. 319–42.

[16] Baum, *Priority of Labour*, p. 73.

[17] E. Brunner quoted in P. Lehmann, *The Transfiguration of Politics* (London, 1979), p. 253.

[18] Habermas, *Knowledge*, p. 53.

[19] D. Mieth, 'Solidarity and the right to work', *Concilium* (December 1982), p. 58.

[20] Davies, *Capital*, p. 56.

[21] R. Dickinson, *Poor Yet Making Rich: The Poor as Agents of Creative Justice* (Geneva, 1983), p. 56.

[22] D. Hauk, *Black Trade Unions in South Africa* (Johannesburg, 1982).

Gabriel Setiloane: The ecumenical movement in Africa: from mission church to moratorium

[1] C. H. Hopkins, *John R. Mott, 1865–1955* (Grand Rapids, 1979).

[2] R. Rouse and S. C. Neill, *A History of the Ecumenical Movement, 1517–1948* (Geneva, 1952).

[3] *Drumbeats from Kampala*, Report of the First Assembly of the AACC (London, 1963), p. 5.

[4] Ibid., p. 6.

[5] Preamble to the constitution of the AACC. See ibid.

[6] AACYA message, In G. Setiloane, *What Is It to Us?* (Geneva, 1963).

[7] D. G. S. M'Timkulu, *Beyond Independence: The Face of New Africa* (New York, 1971), p. 18.

[8] *Drumbeats from Kampala*, p. 34.

[9] P. Ellingworth and K. Dickson (eds.), *Biblical Revelation and African Faiths* (London, 1969).

[10] See *African Theology En Route* (Accra, 1977).

[11] J. V. Taylor, *Christianity and Politics in Africa* (London, 1965).

[12] AACC Bulletin (June 1965).

[13] M'Timkulu, *Beyond Independence*.

[14] Ibid., p. 22.

Margaret Nash: Ecumenical vision and reality in South Africa

[1] Adapted from Christopher Fry, *The Boy with a Cart* (London, 1945), pp. 8, 23.

[2] Cf. P. Potter, 'Covenant', in H. Berkhof and P. Potter *Key Words of the Gospels* (London, 1964); and A. Yannoulatas 'Towards a "koinonia agapes"', in S. Samartha (ed.), *Towards World Community: the Colombo Papers* (Geneva, 1975).

[3] D Gill (ed.), *Gathered for Life: Report of 6th Assembly of World Council of Churches* (Vancouver, 1983; Geneva 1983).

[4] Ibid., p. 227.

[5] Ibid.

[6] Ibid., p. 89; and *Minutes of 36th Meeting of Central Committee* (Geneva, 1984), p. 49.

[7] Documents 2 and A4 of the WCC Central Committee, July 1984. (Emphasis added.)

[8] Ibid., Document 2, p. 11.
[9] Ibid., p. 14
[10] Potter, 'Covenant', p. 37.

Desmond Tutu: Spirituality: Christian and African
[1] E. W. Smith, *African Ideas of God* (London, 1961), p. 83.
[2] R. Smith, *The Religion of the Semites* (Oxford, 1927).
[3] M. Fortes and G. Dietern (eds), *African Systems of Thought* (Oxford, 1965).

Peter Randall: Spro-cas revisited: the Christian contribution to political debate
[1] K. Rahner, *The Shape of the Church to Come* (London, 1974), p. 79.
[2] See C. Villa–Vicencio, 'Ethics as a deabsolutising activity', *Journal of Theology for Southern Africa*, 31 (June 1980), pp. 16–17.
[3] R. Turner, *The Eye of the Needle* (Johannesburg, 1980), pp. 151–2.
[4] D. van Zyl, 'Five Biblical Principles', Spro-cas leaflet, September 1972. Reprinted in P. Randall (ed.) *A Taste of Power: The Final Spro-cas Report* (Johannesburg, 1973), p. 182.
[5] Randall (ed.), *Taste of Power*, pp. 82–3.
[6] Its work included a Church Leaders Programme, a Workers Project, a Resources Centre, and a publishing programme which issued *Black Review, Black Viewpoint,* and *Black Organisations Handbook* (these were intended as annual publications, but only one or two issues of each appeared as a result of bannings).
[7] Randall (ed.), *Taste of Power*, p. 6.
[8] S. C. Nolutshungu, *Changing South Africa* (Cape Town, 1983), p. 169.
[9] P. B. Rich, *White Power and the Liberal Conscience* (Johannesburg, 1984), pp. 131–2.
[10] P. Walshe, 'Mission in a repressive society: the Christian Institute of Southern Africa', in P. Randall (ed.), *Not Without Honour: Tribute to Beyers Naudé* (Johannesburg, 1982), p. 59. Walshe has also given a penetrating analysis of the interaction between the SACC, the CI and Spro-cas in *Church versus State in South Africa* (New York and London, 1983).
[11] Ibid., p. 61.
[12] Ibid., p. 66.
[13] C. Villa–Vicencio, 'A source of hope and despair', in Randall (ed.), *Not Without Honour*, p. 92.
[14] Ibid.
[15] C. Villa–Vicencio, 'An all-pervading heresy', in J. de Gruchy and C. Villa–Vicencio (eds.), *Apartheid is a Heresy* (Cape Town, 1983), p. 68.
[16] J. de Gruchy, 'Towards a confessing church', in De Gruchy and Villa–Vicencio, *Apartheid*, P. 76.
[17] Randall, *Taste of Power*, p. 9.
[18] Ibid., pp. 9–10.
[19] Villa–Vicencio, 'All-pervading heresy', p. 73.

James Cochrane: The churches and the trade unions
[1] Details of this brief account may be found in the author's doctoral dissertation, 'The Role of the English-speaking Churches in South Africa' (University of Cape Town, 1983) pp. 285ff.
[2] See the personal account by J. Leatt, 'A case study of the role of pressure groups in labour relations: the Fattis and Monis dispute', *Industrial Relations Journal of South Africa*, 1, 1 (1981).
[3] See *South African Labour Bulletin*, 6, 5 (1980), which contains an account of the whole affair by the Union of 'The Cape Town Meat Strike . . . '.

[4] Ibid., p. 69.

[5] For example see in T. Heffer, 'Trade Unions: Threat or Challenge?', University of Stellenbosch Business School Occasional Paper 7, 1984, pp. 41–9.

[6] For example Fr. De Fleuriot, who has written the one book on industrial mission in South Africa reflecting the perspective of the worker, *Church and Industry* (Greyville, 1979).

[7] On this process, see J. Maree, 'Independent Trade Unions in the 1970s', seminar paper given to the University of Witwatersrand African Studies Institute, 29 August 1983.

[8] E. Busch, *Karl Barth* (London, 1976), p. 69.

[9] K. Barth, 'Jesus Christ and the movement for social justice (1911)', in G. Hunsinger (ed.), *Karl Barth and Radical Politics* (Philadelphia, 1976).

[10] One may mention the significance of G. Taylor, G. Herron and W. Rauschenbusch to Tillich and P. Lehmann in North America, of Kingsley, Maurice, Ludlow and others to William Temple and COPEC in Britain, of J. Cardijn in France, Barth in Switzerland, Gollwitzer in Germany, and Verkuyl in Holland, of theologians of liberation, and of papal encyclicals from *Rerum Novarum* (1891) to *Redemptor Hominis* (1979).

[11] R. Turner, *The Eye of the Needle* (Johannesburg, 1972).

[12] *Worker Rights: A Statement of Christian Commitment* (Durban, 1983).

[13] Heffer, 'Trade Unions', p. 26.

[14] Quoted in *Diakonia News*, 8, 2 (May 1983).

[15] See M. A. Cullinan's address, 'How should the church help the worker struggles?', in *Diakonia News* (1981), 3.

[16] *Church and Work*, 3, 2 (1982), p. 4.

[17] Within the Church and Work Commission is a Department of Co-ordination of Movements, including YCW, Christian Social Action (CSA), the Movement of Christian Workers (MCW), Youth-on-the-move (YOM), and the Movement of All the Children (MATCH). The Commission also incorporates a chaplaincy to miners and migrant workers, as well as a publications and education section.

Albert Nolan: The option for the poor in South Africa

[1] D. Dorr, *Option for the Poor: A Hundred Years of Vatican Social Teaching* (Maryknoll, New York, 1983).

[2] Ibid., p. 243.

[3] For the latest account of the Latin American debate on the meaning of the option for the poor, see G. Gutierrez, *The Power of the Poor in History* (Maryknoll, New York, 1983).

[4] See A. Nolan, *Taking Sides* (London, 1983).

[5] Quoted in T. D. Hanks, *God So Loved the Third World* (Maryknoll, New York, 1983), p. 6.

[6] J. S. Croatto, *Exodus: A Hermeneutics of Freedom* (Maryknoll, New York, 1981), *passim*, and A. Fierro, *The Militant Gospel: A Critical Introduction to Political Theologies* (Maryknoll, New York, 1977), pp. 140–51.

[7] Hanks, *God So Loved*, and E. Tamez, *Bible of the Oppressed* (Maryknoll, New York, 1982).

[8] Fierro, *Militant Gospel*, pp. 140–2; Croatto, *Exodus*, p. 20.

[9] Tamez, *Bible of the Oppressed*, pp. 60–4.

[10] N. K. Gottwald, *The Tribes of Yahweh: A Sociology of the Religion of Liberated Israel, 1250–1050 B.C.E.* (Maryknoll, New York, 1979).

[11] J. Kegler, 'The prophetic discourse and political praxis of Jeremiah: observations on Jer. 26 and 36', in W. Schottrof and W. Stegemann (eds.), *God of the Lowly, Socio-Historical Interpretations of the Bible* (Maryknoll, New York, 1984), pp. 49–54.

[12] B. W. Anderson, *The Living World of the Old Testament*, 3rd ed. (Essex, England, 1978), pp. 399–400, 404–5, 418.

[13] The most comprehensive, although not the most critical, study of the spiritual

poverty of this period available in English is A. Gelin, *The Poor of Yahweh* (Collegeville, Minnesota, 1964).

[14] A. Nolan, *Jesus Before Christianity: The Gospel of Liberation* (London, 1977), pp. 92–100.

[15] Ibid., pp. 31–6, 41.

[16] Gutierrez, *Power of the Poor*, pp. 95, 116, 138, 140–2.

[17] Quoted in ibid., p. 207.

[18] See the interesting study on the meaning of words for poverty in the New Testament by W. Stegemann, *The Gospel and the Poor* (Philadelphia, 1984), pp. 13–21, 33–53.

[19] Hanks, *God So Loved*, p. 11; G. Gutierrez, *A Theology of Liberation* (Maryknoll, New York, 1973), pp. 290, 299–302.

[20] See the interesting approach of G. Theissen to the spirituality of the Jesus movement: *The First Followers of Jesus: A Sociological Analysis of the Earliest Christianity* (London, 1978), pp. 99–110.

[21] B. Tlhagale, 'Transracial communication', in *Missionalia*, 11, 3, pp. 113–23.

[22] See the spiritual journey in G. Gutierrez, *We Drink from Our Own Wells: The Spiritual Journey of a People* (Maryknoll, New York, 1984), *passim*.